Workbook for
PUBLIC
SPEAKING

Second Edition

Workbook for
PUBLIC SPEAKING

PATRICIA COMEAUX

University of North Carolina–Wilmington

Brown & Benchmark
PUBLISHERS

Madison   Dubuque, IA   Guilford, CT   Chicago   Toronto   London
Caracas   Mexico City   Buenos Aires   Madrid   Bogota   Sydney

Book Team

Executive Publisher *Edgar J. Laube*
Acquisitions Editor *Eric Ziegler*
Developmental Assistant *Kassi Radomski*
Publishing Services Coordinator *Peggy Selle*
Proofreading Coordinator *Carrie Barker*
Production Manager *Beth Kundert*
Production/Costing Manager *Sherry Padden*
Visuals/Design Freelance Specialist *Mary L. Christianson*
Marketing Manager *Katie Rose*
Copywriter *M. J. Kelly*

Basal Text *11.5/13 Times Roman*
Display Type *Helvetica*
Typesetting System *Mac/QuarkXPress*
Paper Stock *50# Solutions*
Production Services *Shepherd, Inc.*

President and Chief Executive Officer *Thomas E. Doran*
Vice President of Production and Business Development *Vickie Putman*
Vice President of Sales and Marketing *Bob McLaughlin*
Director of Marketing *John Finn*

A Times Mirror Company

Cover design by *Cathy Cook*

Copyedited by Shepherd, Inc.;Proofread by Francine Buda Banwarth

Printed in the United States of America by Times Mirror Higher Education Group, Inc.,
2460 Kerper Boulevard, Dubuque, IA 52001

10 9 8 7 6 5 4 3 2 1

CONTENTS

INTRODUCTION

Workbook for Public Speaking is written for college students enrolled in an introductory public speaking class and is intended as a supplementary or a sole text to assist students with the concrete application of the principles of rhetoric and public speaking found in most major texts. Each unit is self-contained and can be used with various other units to help students concentrate on areas in which they need to improve. Because different classes need help in different areas, I have produced this workbook customized to fit each situation. I hope that this tailormade approach is effective in helping students grasp various public speaking principles and improve their presentational skills.

The assignments and activities reflect the culmination of many years of effort not only to improve my teaching of public speaking but also to improve student performance in preparing and delivering speeches and in developing their communication skills. My enjoyment of teaching public speaking increased as I focused on helping students rely on their own abilities to analyze and develop their public speaking competencies. Therefore the materials and activities contained in this workbook take a learner-centered approach, challenging students to evaluate their abilities and to work systematically toward improving their knowledge and skills. In addition, the materials are based on classical and contemporary perspectives of rhetoric to help students develop and shape particular messages for particular audiences and situations.

The sample outlines and evaluative essays are the work of students enrolled in my public speaking and speech communication classes over the years at Illinois Wesleyan University, University of Southwestern Louisiana, Murray State University, and the University of North Carolina—Wilmington.

The revised edition has been expanded to include units on ethics, the first speech, and presentational aids. In addition, the previous unit on Analyzing Topics, Audiences, and Purposes has been expanded and divided into two units: Analyzing Audiences and Selecting Topics and Purposes. Finally, concepts and activities have been added in response to the excellent suggestions by the reviewers. In this revised edition, I have strived to make each unit compatible with a basic public speaking text or useful as a self-contained unit.

I would like to thank the following reviewers for their insightful comments and helpful suggestions at various stages in the development of the first edition manuscript: Leslie Klipper-Groll, San Diego Miramar College; James Knear, Trevecca Nazarene College; Loren McBain, University of Arizona; Rick Morat, California State University—San Bernardino; and David Ralph, Michigan State University. In addition, I would like to thank those reviewers who contributed to the development of the second edition: Tammala Bulger, University of North Carolina—Wilmington; Lynette Mullins, University of Minnesota—Crookston; and Myra Young, Johnson County Community College.

—Patricia Comeaux

Introduction to a Learner-Centered Approach and to Public Speaking

This unit outlines the objectives of this workbook and introductory public speaking courses. It is important to accept the perspective and focus of a learner-centered approach to developing your public speaking abilities. This approach encourages you to set your individual goals within the course structure, to analyze your abilities, and to work to improve those abilities. The workbook discussion questions and activities provide you with a way to analyze your public speaking abilities and set goals for self-improvement.

This unit provides a brief overview of the process of human communication. It is important to view public speaking as communication—a mutual exchange of messages between a speaker and an audience. The unit also provides you with an overview of the essential principles of public speaking. These principles will assist you in your speech preparation.

The components of UNIT 1 are:

Note to Students (includes course objectives)

Student Information Sheet

Assessing Your Public Speaking Abilities

Setting Goals for Self-Improvement

Achieving My Public Speaking Goals: A Student's Testimony

Public Speaking Anxieties: Pre-Questionnaire

Public Speaking Anxieties: Post-Questionnaire

The Process of Human Communication: Brief Notes

Describing Communication: A Discussion

Creating Communication Models

NOTE TO STUDENTS

Your success in an introductory public speaking course (and your success with the activities in this workbook) is highly dependent upon your interest and effort toward improving your ability to communicate effectively in public speaking situations. It is common knowledge that speaking in public is one of the strongest fears of most people and that public speaking courses are considered to be among the "dreaded but necessary" university courses. Most students recognize the need—sometime in the future—to be able to speak coherently and with confidence in public. Some students recognize the immediate need to develop these skills. Few students realize the relative ease with which these skills can be developed and improved.

To say that public speaking skills can be developed with ease does not diminish the effort necessary to accomplish the task. A credible and effective public speaker, like a dancer or an athlete, works diligently to develop and refine his or her skills. A speech that has substance and organization is the result of a conscious, systematic effort on the part of the speaker. The ability to speak confidently and coherently in public may possibly be one of the most valuable skills you can acquire. Whether you are giving an oral report in a history class or to your fraternity or sorority, or presenting your ideas on an effective selling strategy to the marketing department of your future employer, the concepts presented in this workbook will be applicable.

The focus in this workbook is on you, the student, as a learner. You will be challenged to set individual goals for performance achievement, to analyze your public speaking abilities, and to work diligently toward systematically improving your public speaking skills. A learner-centered approach to public speaking recognizes that students' abilities exist at different points on a continuum. Your goal is to analyze where you are on the continuum and to move forward. The instructor's goal is to facilitate that forward movement.

The following learning goals are designed for students enrolled in a public speaking course:

1. To demonstrate the ability to understand and respond to public speaking as a transactional process between speaker and audience.
2. To develop listening and observational skills by providing descriptive and evaluative feedback about speeches and speakers.
3. To demonstrate the ability to analyze and evaluate the competence of one's own public speaking and that of others.
4. To develop the ability to speak competently, confidently, and ethically in public settings.
5. To demonstrate the ability to collect, analyze, and use information to shape and adapt messages for various audiences, purposes, and settings.
6. To develop and adapt messages and message strategies to the needs and expectations of multiple audiences.
7. To organize ideas and supporting examples in a coherent and captivating message.
8. To speak in an extemporaneous, conversational style using language, voice, and bodily action effectively and appropriately for public settings.
9. To demonstrate the ability to apply public speaking competencies to multiple audiences and settings.

STUDENT INFORMATION SHEET

PRINT: Last name, First name_____

Campus or local address _____

Phone number (_____)_____

Circle one: Male   Female

Classification (circle one):   Freshman   Sophomore   Junior   Senior

Major: _____

Focus or interest in major:_____

High school graduated from:_____

Fraternity or Sorority: _____

Professional or service organizations:_____

Sports, hobbies, or interests: _____

List the names of any persons in this class that you know *well* (i.e., roommate, best friend, high school buddy, etc.):

ASSESSING YOUR PUBLIC SPEAKING ABILITIES

Please respond as accurately and as thoroughly as possible. (Use back if necessary.)

Name_____

        Last   First

1. What kinds of speaking experiences have you had in your classes, jobs, church, extracurricular activities, organizations, etc.? Please list and indicate size of audience, topic, etc.

2. When did you give your last speech? What was the topic?

3. What are your career plans? How will public speaking be important to your career?

4. What do you generally find easiest about making a presentation or a speech?

5. What do you generally find most difficult about making a presentation or a speech?

6. Do you have *severe* stage fright, stuttering, or anything else that might make it difficult for you to speak in public situations? Please indicate.

SETTING GOALS FOR SELF-IMPROVEMENT

Objectives

1. To understand the value of setting specific goals to improve your public speaking abilities.
2. To understand the importance of setting realistic goals for building confidence and success.

Explanation

Even though your public speaking instructor has specific course goals for all students to work toward, it is essential that each individual sets specific and realistic goals to accomplish during the semester. Effective public speaking is a learned skill, developed by understanding and applying principles of rhetoric and speech communication.

Students enrolled in an introductory course enter with different abilities and experiences in public speaking. You can learn from observing others; however, it is best to set your goals for improvement based on your *own* previous experiences in public speaking situations.

Instructions

After reading the following student essay entitled "Achieving My Public Speaking Goals," take some time to consider your particular strengths and weaknesses in public speaking. Then in the space below, list three specific goals that you would like to achieve by the end of your course in public speaking. Consider what you would like to learn or what skills you would like to improve.

Three goals I would like to achieve by the end of this course:

1.

2.

3.

ACHIEVING MY PUBLIC SPEAKING GOALS: A STUDENT'S TESTIMONY

Well, the semester is over, and I can honestly say that I really hate to see this class end. This class has given me more than I bargained for and has also allowed me to meet new people. I have learned a lot about the communication process by being part of the audience and through presenting informative speeches. My goals in taking this class were to learn how to prepare and give effective speeches and to overcome my nervousness and insecurity when asked to speak in public. I believe that I have achieved my goals.

My confidence as a speaker has at least doubled. Prior to taking this class I had done some public speaking but was usually so nervous that I would often forget what I wanted to say. I would trip over my words as I attempted to quote my speech verbatim from memory. My hands would shake, and my voice would quiver throughout the ordeal. I just knew everyone was watching me and waiting for me to make a mistake. I would present the speech without looking at the audience for feedback because my only concern was to state my speech and sit down. It always seemed that I would start out a little nervous and progressively become more nervous, especially if I knew that I had forgotten my lines exactly the way they were written, kind of like being in a play. I noticed during both of my speech presentations in class that this progressive nervousness did not occur. In fact, I found myself becoming calmer as time went on, actually looking members of the audience right in the eye! I now know that my inability to converse with the audience and my belief that I had to memorize a speech in order to present it effectively were two major contributors to my nervousness.

I think I have cured most of my nervousness by following the rules of preparing and presenting an extemporaneous speech. Just not trying to memorize my speech cured the majority of the jitters. By preparing a carefully planned, systematically structured outline of the thesis statement, the main ideas, and the key words and phrases, I was able to present my topic in a logical way to the audience. The extemporaneous method of presenting my speeches allowed me to relax and be more responsive to my audience and to receive feedback. By using an organized outline, I had flexibility and spontaneity, which I did not previously have with more rigid, memorized speeches. By communicating with my audience on a conversational level, I was able to focus on them, which helped me forget how nervous I was. Within one or two minutes my nerves had calmed, and I was actually enjoying being in front of an audience! I know that I can continue to overcome my nervousness by selecting a suitable topic for my audience about which I am knowledgeable, preparing a proper outline, and presenting my speech in an extemporaneous manner. I think this is definitely a winning combination for any speaker, nervous or not.

In my previous presentations, I felt comfortable with the topics, especially because I usually spoke to my fellow workers; however, I was not always comfortable with my ability to organize ideas. Therefore, one of my goals for this class was to learn to organize my presentations better. In this course I learned that the key to organization is preparing an outline with a clear thesis statement and main points. I organized my speeches so that the main points related back to my specific purpose and my thesis. This helped the speech to flow logically. I distinguished my main points from my minor points, letting the audience know exactly what I was talking about and where I was in the development of my ideas. I had never used this process before, and now know that it holds the key to the presentation of a logical speech.

I still have a number of areas in delivery that I need to work on. Even though I feel more comfortable, feedback from my classmates revealed that I do not appear to be comfortable. My facial expressions were noted as "tense" and "formal." In the future, I will try to appear less formal and relax my facial expression (perhaps a videotape would help). This is probably the main point that I will continue to work on, because it will be the hardest to overcome. I will also work on pacing my speech to allow time for pauses when necessary. My new-found confidence and knowledge of presenting an extemporaneous speech will not go to waste because I am occasionally requested to be on panels or to speak at a function as part of my job.

PUBLIC SPEAKING ANXIETIES: PRE-QUESTIONNAIRE

Objectives

1. To acknowledge your anxieties about public speaking by responding to the questionnaire below.
2. To score and compare your public speaking anxieties at the beginning of your course with others' scores of public speaking anxiety.

Instructions

This instrument is composed of thirty-four statements concerning feelings about communicating with other people in public speaking situations. Please indicate the degree to which each statement applies to you by marking whether you (1) strongly agree, (2) agree, (3) are undecided, (4) disagree, or (5) strongly disagree with each statement. Please just record your first impression. Again, the scale is:

1 = strongly agree   2 = agree   3 = undecided   4 = disagree   5 = strongly disagree

_____ 1. While preparing for giving a speech I feel tense and nervous.

_____ 2. I feel tense when I see the words "speech" and "public speech" on a course outline when studying.

_____ 3. My thoughts become confused and jumbled when I am giving a speech.

_____ 4. Right after giving a speech I feel that I have had a pleasant experience.

_____ 5. I get anxious when I think about a speech coming up.

_____ 6. I have no fear of giving a speech.

_____ 7. Although I am nervous just before starting a speech, I soon settle down after starting and feel calm and comfortable.

_____ 8. I look forward to giving a speech.

_____ 9. When the instructor announces a speaking assignment in class I can feel myself getting tense.

_____10. My hands tremble when I am giving a speech.

_____11. I feel relaxed while giving a speech.

_____12. I enjoy preparing for a speech.

_____13. I am in constant fear of forgetting what I prepared to say.

_____14. I get anxious if someone asks me something about my topic that I do not know.

_____15. I face the prospect of giving a speech with confidence.

_____16. I feel that I am in complete possession of myself while giving a speech.

_____17. My mind is clear when giving a speech.

_____18. I do not dread giving a speech.

_____19. I perspire just before starting a speech.

_____20. My heart beats very fast just as I start a speech.

_____21. I experience considerable anxiety while sitting in the room just before my speech starts.

_____22. Certain parts of my body feel very tense and rigid while giving a speech.

_____23. Realizing that only a little time remains in a speech makes me very tense and anxious.

_____24. While giving a speech I know I can control my feelings of tension and stress.

_____25. I breathe faster just before starting a speech.

_____26. I feel comfortable and relaxed in the hour or so just before giving a speech.

_____27. I do poorer on speeches because I am anxious.

_____28. I feel anxious when the teacher announces the date of a speaking assignment.

_____29. When I make a mistake while giving a speech, I find it hard to concentrate on the parts that follow.

_____30. During an important speech I experience a feeling of helplessness building up inside me.

_____31. I have trouble falling asleep the night before a speech.

_____32. My heart beats very fast while I present my speech.

_____33. I feel anxious while waiting to give my speech.

_____34. While giving a speech I get so nervous that I forget facts I really know.

To determine your score on the Personal Report of Public Speaking Abilities (PRPSA), complete the following steps:

1. Add the scores for items 1, 2, 3, 5, 9, 10, 13, 14, 19, 20, 21, 22, 23, 25, 27, 28, 29, 30, 31, 32, 33, and 34.
2. Add the scores for items 4, 6, 7, 8, 11, 12, 15, 16, 17, 18, 24, and 26.
3. Complete the following formula: PRPSA = 132 − (total from step 1) + (total from step 2).

Your score should range between 34 and 170. If your score is below 34 or above 170, you have made a mistake in computing the score. The higher scores indicate more anxiety; the lower scores, less anxiety.

This questionnaire and scoring formula are from _Communication: Apprehension, Avoidance, and Effectiveness,_ Third Edition, by Virginia P. Richmond and James C. McCroskey. Copyright © 1992 by Gorsuch Scarisbrick, Publishers (Scottsdale, Arizona). Reprinted with permission.

PUBLIC SPEAKING ANXIETIES: POST-QUESTIONNAIRE

pre-questionnaire number paper 1-20

2 Goals that I want to achieve before the end of the semester.

Objectives

1. To complete the same questionnaire about public speaking anxiety that you did at the beginning of the course.
2. To compare your scores on the pre- and post-questionnaire to determine if your public speaking anxiety has decreased, increased, or stayed the same.

Instructions

This instrument is composed of thirty-four statements concerning feelings about communicating with other people in public speaking situations. Please indicate the degree to which each statement applies to you by marking whether you (1) strongly agree, (2) agree, (3) are undecided, (4) disagree, or (5) strongly disagree with each statement. Please just record your first impression. Again, the scale is:

1 = strongly agree   2 = agree   3 = undecided   4 = disagree   5 = strongly disagree

1. _____ 1. While preparing for giving a speech I feel tense and nervous.

2. _____ 2. I feel tense when I see the words "speech" and "public speech" on a course outline when studying.

_____ 3. My thoughts become confused and jumbled when I am giving a speech.

3. _____ 4. Right after giving a speech I feel that I have had a pleasant experience.

4. _____ 5. I get anxious when I think about a speech coming up.

5. _____ 6. I have no fear of giving a speech.

6. _____ 7. Although I am nervous just before starting a speech, I soon settle down after starting and feel calm and comfortable.

7. _____ 8. I look forward to giving a speech.

8. _____ 9. When the instructor announces a speaking assignment in class I can feel myself getting tense.

_____ 10. My hands tremble when I am giving a speech.

9. _____ 11. I feel relaxed while giving a speech.

10. _____ 12. I enjoy preparing for a speech.

_____ 13. I am in constant fear of forgetting what I prepared to say.

11. _____ 14. I get anxious if someone asks me something about my topic that I do not know.

12. _____ 15. I face the prospect of giving a speech with confidence.

_____ 16. I feel that I am in complete possession of myself while giving a speech.

13. _____ 17. My mind is clear when giving a speech.

_____ 18. I do not dread giving a speech.

_____ 19. I perspire just before starting a speech.

14, _____ 20. My heart beats very fast just as I start a speech. 14

15. _____ 21. I experience considerable anxiety while sitting in the room just before my speech 15 starts.

_____ 22. Certain parts of my body feel very tense and rigid while giving a speech.

_____ 23. Realizing that only a little time remains in a speech makes me very tense and anxious.

_____ 24. While giving a speech I know I can control my feelings of tension and stress.

_____ 25. I breathe faster just before starting a speech.

16, _____ 26. I feel comfortable and relaxed in the hour or so just before giving a speech. 16

17. _____ 27. I do poorer on speeches because I am anxious.

17, _____ 28. I feel anxious when the teacher announces the date of a speaking assignment. 17

_____ 29. When I make a mistake while giving a speech, I find it hard to concentrate on the parts that follow.

_____ 30. During an important speech I experience a feeling of helplessness building up inside me.

18, _____ 31. I have trouble falling asleep the night before a speech.

19, _____ 32. My heart beats very fast while I present my speech.

20. _____ 33. I feel anxious while waiting to give my speech.

_____ 34. While giving a speech I get so nervous that I forget facts I really know.

To determine your score on the PRPSA, complete the following steps:

1. Add the scores for items 1, 2, 3, 5, 9, 10, 13, 14, 19, 20, 21, 22, 23, 25, 27, 28, 29, 30, 31, 32, 33, and 34.
2. Add the scores for items 4, 6, 7, 8, 11, 12, 15, 16, 17, 18, 24, and 26.
3. Complete the following formula: PRPSA = 132 – (total from step 1) + (total from step 2).

Your score should range between 34 and 170. If your score is below 34 or above 170, you have made a mistake in computing the score. The higher scores indicate more anxiety; the lower scores, less anxiety.

2 Goals I want to achieve in this class –

1.

2.

THE PROCESS OF HUMAN COMMUNICATION: BRIEF NOTES

I. It is important to know the types of communication and the value of studying them.
   A. Consider six types of communication:
      1. Intrapersonal—your knowledge of and communication with your self.
      2. Interpersonal—interaction between two people.
      3. Small group—face-to-face interaction among a small group; five to seven people is the ideal size.
      4. Public speaking—one-to-many situation in which a speaker presents a message to an audience.
      5. Organizational—a multidimensional exchange of messages in a particular organization.
      6. Mass communication—the transmission of messages through the medium of radio, television, and print.
   B. Consider three general purposes of communication:
      1. To inform or create understanding.
      2. To persuade or influence others.
      3. To establish relationships and fulfill human needs.
   C. Consider the reasons why we study communication:
      1. Communication is a learned skill, and everyone can improve their ability to communicate effectively.
      2. Effective communication means communicating clearly and concisely, with expressiveness and individuality.
      3. Effective communication is an art and a science.
         a. Familiarize yourself with artful public speaking models, such as:
            1) Ronald Reagan.
            2) Martin Luther King, Jr.
            3) Barbara Jordan.
            4) Franklin D. Roosevelt.
            5) John F. Kennedy.
         b. Learn the principles or rules of human communication and public speaking.
         c. Strive to improve your own individual style.
      4. The application of what you learn about effective communication can be applied to your benefit in college and throughout your professional career and your personal life.
II. It is important to understand communication as a dynamic process with interacting elements and possibilities of meaning.
   A. Consider the definition of communication: **Communication** is a *transaction* in which the participants (humans) are *mutually* engaged in the *process* of creating *meaning*.
      1. Connotations of the italicized words:
         a. Transaction—as opposed to exchange; suggests mutual satisfaction or understanding.
         b. Mutually—simultaneously, at the same time.
         c. Process—a way something occurs; a happening not a procedure; not sequential or linear.
         d. Meaning—understanding, not necessarily agreement.
      2. Communication, therefore, is a simultaneous exchange of messages.

B. Consider five elements of communication and their variables:
  1. People—the encoders and decoders or speakers and listeners (the *who*).
      a. Each person is always both a sender and a receiver.
      b. Roles and attitudes toward roles greatly influence meanings and perceptions.
      c. Individual factors that influence how you communicate and the interpretations you assign or perceptions you have include:
          1) Attitudes, knowledge, interests, occupational experience, emotional and physical state, physical appearance, gender, age, culture, and values.
          2) It is essential to consider these factors in both the planning and delivery of speeches.
  2. Messages—includes both the verbal and nonverbal exchange of messages (the *what*).
      a. Messages carry rather than contain potential meanings.
      b. Meanings are determined by people and not solely by words.
  3. Channels—the message system (the *how*).
      a. Language—the words.
      b. Gesture—includes paralanguage (pitch, rate, tone, emphasis) and space.
      c. Space—includes distance and movement.
  4. Context—the particular place or situation that frames the communication (the *where*).
      a. Classroom.
      b. Office.
      c. Home.
      d. Many other possibilities.
  5. Barriers—the internal and external noise and barriers to communication (the *why*).
      a. Barriers are always potentially present.
      b. Barriers exist within persons and systems.
III. It is important to understand how meaning is created in an exchange between people through mutual influence.
  A. Meaning may be described as understanding, common experiences, and shared interpretations.
  B. Effective communication is shared understanding.
      1. Example: If an instructor explains an assignment to you and you hear but do not understand, you have communicated but not effectively.
      2. The barriers that are operating in the above example may come from a variety of sources; the goal for effective communication is to get a common understanding.
  C. Effective communication does not require agreement on an issue.
      1. Example: If two people disagree on a value issue, they have communicated effectively if they understand that they disagree on that issue.
      2. To agree on the same value or goal may be important to two individuals but it is not a necessary condition for effective communication.
  D. The elements that affect meaning are:
      1. Context or situation that frames communication.
      2. Roles as well as attitudes toward the roles.
      3. Individual and cultural styles; use of language, gesture, and space.
      4. Barriers in the system and in people.

DESCRIBING COMMUNICATION: A DISCUSSION

Objectives

1. To explain your understanding of the process of communication.
2. To apply your understanding of the process of communication to particular situations.

Instructions

In small groups discuss your responses to the questions below. The goal for your discussion is to make sure each individual understands and agrees with the group's responses to the questions. As you discuss each set of questions, have one member of the group take brief notes on the group's answers. Each group will share their responses with the whole class, using the notes to prompt their presentation. Your discussion and your presentation should be centered around an explanation for each set of questions rather than just answers to individual questions.

Defining Communication and Its Elements

1. What is communication?

2. What happens during the process of communication?

3. Is there a beginning or an ending?

4. Is communication intentional or unintentional?

5. What elements are always present in communication?

6. What are the purposes of communication? Why do people communicate?

7. What is effective communication? What is the difference between communication and effective communication?

Accounting for Meaning in the Process of Communication

1. Is communication message-centered or meaning-centered? Explain.

2. Do words mean or do people mean?

3. How does meaning occur? What accounts for meaning?

4. What are some of the variables that affect meaning?

5. What are some of the common barriers to effective communication?

CREATING COMMUNICATION MODELS

Objectives

1. To demonstrate your understanding of the concepts about the process of communication.
2. To create your own model of the process of communication.

Instructions

Working in small groups, design a universal model that illustrates the process of communication between two people. Each group should construct a model and share it with the class. The class should agree whether the models meet the following criteria:

1. The model should illustrate the following definition of communication: Communication is a transaction in which humans are mutually engaged in the process of creating meaning.
2. The model should contain or account for the five elements of communication:
   a. People: differing interests, knowledge, age, etc. (who).
   b. Messages: potential meaning (what).
   c. Channels: language, gesture, space (how).
   d. Context: frame or situation (where).
   e. Barriers: potential interferences (why).
3. Most importantly, the model should illustrate the relationships among the elements; that is, how it is a process that involves a simultaneous exchange of messages.

Developing Listening Skills

This unit stresses the importance of listening in the communication process, especially in public speaking situations. The situations you are in and the reasons for listening greatly affect your attitudes and abilities as a listener. It is important to recognize effective listening and work toward developing and improving your listening skills. The exercises and questions for discussion in this unit will help you to do so.

The components of UNIT 2 are:

Listening Notes

Recognizing Barriers to Effective Listening

Listening: Observation and Analysis

Practicing Purposeful Listening

Practicing Active Listening

Giving Effective Feedback

Listening for Comprehension

Listening for Evaluation

Form for Listening for Evaluation

LISTENING NOTES

Listening as a Process Model

Listening can be categorized as a five-stage process:

1. **Hearing**—receiving or sensing sounds.
2. **Attending**—selective perception: selecting what message to tune in to; directing yourself to a particular message from your environment.
3. **Interpreting**—decoding and assigning meaning to messages.
4. **Responding**—giving feedback: sending messages through the use of language, gesture, or space.
5. **Evaluating**—making a value judgment of the effectiveness of the message or speaker.

Listening is an essential part of the communication process. As a public speaker you should consider your listeners from the very beginning as you develop your topic. In addition, as you present your speech to your audience you should become a listener by reading the audience's feedback. Looks of confusion from audience members can be acknowledged and responded to by a statement similar to the following: "I can see that this explanation is confusing to some of you. Let me put it this way. . . ." In that way, public speaking becomes a transactional process in which speaker and listeners simultaneously exchange messages. Listening as part of the communication process is greatly affected by the situation. As your listening situation changes—from a chat with a friend, to an interview, to a committee meeting, to being an audience member—your purpose and attitude toward the situation and the individual also changes. As you complete the activities in this unit, think of particular listening situations.

RECOGNIZING BARRIERS TO EFFECTIVE LISTENING

Objectives

1. To identify specific situations and factors that make listening difficult.
2. To share common barriers to listening with your classmates.

Explanation

Listening is a difficult process. We often do it passively and miss many of the messages that come our way. In addition, we tend to jump to conclusions by making superficial judgments before we have all the information necessary to arrive at an informed conclusion. A common example of this is when an audience may dismiss the speaker's message because of the way he or she dresses or sounds. Certainly, it is important as a speaker to be aware of this tendency of audiences to pay attention to how speakers sound and look. As a listener, however, it is your responsibility to go beyond the surface and listen with an open mind and attitude to better enable you to hear the message so that you can interpret it and evaluate it accurately and fairly.

Instructions

On a sheet of paper, list several reasons why you think listening is so difficult. Share your list with two or three of your classmates. After you have compared lists in your small group, list the most common reasons or barriers to effective listening.

LISTENING: OBSERVATION AND ANALYSIS

Objectives

1. To observe and describe listening behavior.
2. To learn to distinguish between description and judgment.
3. To learn to analyze listening effectiveness.

Instructions

In groups of three or four, students should select a topic that lends itself easily to discussion. Campus or community controversies provide excellent topics for discussion. Two students volunteer to participate in a conversation of the selected topic and the other student(s) volunteer(s) to unobtrusively observe the process. Observers should write down descriptions (nodding head, asking questions) rather than judgments or inferences (agreement, paying attention, good listening). After a three- to five-minute discussion of the topic, the observers should share their list of observed behaviors with the discussants. From that list the whole group should determine whether the listening behavior was generally effective or ineffective and discuss the reasons why. Use the questions below to stimulate your discussion.

Questions for Discussion

1. What makes effective listening difficult?

2. What are the barriers to effective listening?

3. Why is it important to distinguish between a description and a judgment of communication behavior?

4. How can you improve your listening behavior?

5. How does effective listening help the communication process as a whole?

6. How can a public speaker determine if the audience is listening?

7. What can a public speaker do to increase the chances that the audience will listen effectively?

PRACTICING PURPOSEFUL LISTENING

Objectives

1. To understand that the key to effective listening is knowing the reason or the motivation for listening.
2. To practice identifying the purpose for listening in different situations.

Explanation

Knowing the reason for listening is helpful in improving not only one's listening behavior but also one's ability to communicate effectively. For example, consider the times a friend has said to you, "I need to talk, I have a problem." Understanding your friend's particular needs (whether he or she wants you to just listen to the problem and sympathize or to go one step further and give advice) will make you a more effective listener in that situation. The often-asked classroom question "Will this information be on the exam?" is a question that asks, "In what manner should I listen: as a matter of interest, for an example, or for detailed information and retention?" Unfortunately, many teachers interpret this question to mean "Is what you are saying important?" As you can see, it is helpful to be able to identify the reason for listening in a particular situation.

Instructions

For each of the categories below, recall a particular person and situation and then write down what your purpose was for listening. After you have completed these, answer the questions at the end of this activity.

Listening to a friend:

Listening in a group:

Listening to an instructor:

Listening to a classroom speech:

Listening to a speech at a public event (at the university auditorium, in the community, etc.):

Questions for Discussion

1. Considering your preceding responses, how did you know or determine what the listening purpose was?

2. Does the other person usually state the reason why he or she wants you to listen? How might you find out what the purpose is?

3. How can a public speaker determine if the audience is listening?

4. What can a public speaker do to increase the chances that the audience will listen effectively?

PRACTICING ACTIVE LISTENING

Objectives

1. To develop more effective listening skills by checking for the accuracy of the meaning of the message.
2. To learn the value of paraphrasing the other's message as part of your response as a listener.

Explanation

Sometimes, in order to communicate more effectively, it is helpful to check the accuracy of what you hear to determine if your understanding is similar to the intended meaning of the speaker. This is a common practice (and an excellent one) when students ask a teacher for reassurance that they understood an assignment by repeating what they thought they heard. This process is known as *active listening*.

Instructions

Working in groups of three, students can take turns practicing active listening. Each individual must first repeat or paraphrase what was said before giving a response to it. The conversation can be about some event or topic both people know about. Two individuals can take part in a discussion or conversation while the other person unobtrusively observes and takes notes. After all three of you have had an opportunity to practice active listening, compare your notes and answer the questions below.

Follow-up Questions

1. What are some of the difficulties you experienced in practicing active listening?

2. In what situations should you practice active listening? What are the advantages? Disadvantages?

3. Based on your observations, formulate five guidelines for active listening.

GIVING EFFECTIVE FEEDBACK

Objectives

1. To learn the value of feedback as a description of behavior.
2. To practice giving effective feedback to speakers.

Explanation

Feedback is information provided to another about what you saw or heard. Effective feedback is descriptive and specific rather than evaluative and general. To tell someone that he or she gave an excellent speech might make that individual feel pleased, but it does not provide him or her with useful information. To provide individuals with useful information (effective feedback), it is essential to tell them exactly what they said or did that made you conclude that their speech was excellent.

Instructions

Practice providing effective feedback to speakers regarding their delivery or manner of presentation. After listening to a speech (live or videotaped), respond to the questions below.

Feedback Questions

1. Describe the speaker's use of eye contact and facial expressions.

2. Describe the speaker's use of voice, including tone of voice.

3. Describe the speaker's use of gestures and bodily action.

4. Describe the speaker's use of notes.

5. Considering the above descriptions, evaluate the effectiveness of the speaker's delivery style.

LISTENING FOR COMPREHENSION

Objectives

1. To understand the steps involved in listening for comprehension.
2. To practice listening for comprehension as an audience member.

Explanation

There are many situations where your listening goal or purpose is to listen for information and comprehension. Such situations include obtaining directions, taking notes in a lecture class, and responding to the content of a speech. When you are listening to a speech it is important to (1) know *why* you are listening, (2) identify the major ideas, (3) identify the structure of the speech, (4) examine the supporting materials, and (5) relate the speaker's major ideas to your ideas, values, and attitudes.

Instructions

After listening to an informative classroom speech (videotaped or live), respond to the questions below.

Comprehension Questions

1. What was the speaker's main purpose or thesis?

2. What were the major ideas in the speech?

3. What examples and supporting materials stood out as helpful in your understanding of the major ideas?

4. Describe the structure of the speech.

5. How do the main ideas relate to your ideas, values, and attitudes?

LISTENING FOR EVALUATION

Objectives

1. To understand the steps involved in listening for evaluation.
2. To practice listening to a speech for evaluative purposes.

Explanation

When you listen to a speech for the purpose of evaluating it, you go a step further than listening for comprehension. In other words, in order to evaluate the speech and the speaker fairly, you must first understand the speech and be able to describe the behavior (delivery style) of the speaker. In addition, you need to know the criteria for effectiveness that you will use to evaluate the speech. For example, effective speakers use direct and inclusive eye contact and speak in a tone of voice that sounds enthusiastic about or interested in the topic.

Instructions

After listening to an informative classroom speech, evaluate it using the form and the criteria specified in each question on the following page.

FORM FOR LISTENING FOR EVALUATION

Speaker_____   Respondent_____

Content and Organization

1. Did the speaker know and understand his or her topic well? Explain.

2. Was the thesis of the speech clear? Why or why not?

3. Were the main points clear and easy to follow? Why or why not?

4. Were the examples and the explanations of the main points clear and helpful in aiding understanding? Why or why not?

Delivery

1. Did the speaker use direct and inclusive eye contact?

2. Did the speaker sound enthusiastic and interested in the topic? If not, how did he or she sound?

3. Did the speaker use his or her notes effectively? Why or why not?

4. Did the speaker appear confident and well prepared? Why or why not?

Managing Anxiety and Developing Confidence

This unit describes communication behaviors that can help bolster your confidence when speaking in public situations. Clearly, confidence is more than a matter of delivery. Your knowledge of your speech topic and your careful adaptation of your topic to your audience influence how confident you look and feel. Once you feel more comfortable about the prospect of standing before an audience, then you can concentrate on the essentials of audience analysis, topic development, and organization.

Although the actual delivery of your speech is the last step you should consider, we will consider it first in this introductory course because it is probably foremost in your mind. The fear of public speaking is widely known and experienced not only by students but also by professors, business executives, and actors. It is important to identify your specific fears about public speaking and develop strategies to manage those fears. In addition, it is valuable to describe and practice effective confident delivery skills. Although you may not *feel* confident, you can *look* confident. The activities in this unit will help you manage your public speaking anxiety and develop confidence in your speaking abilities as you present your speeches.

The components of UNIT 3 are:

Recognizing Fears about Public Speaking

Analyzing Public Speaking Anxieties

Students' Suggestions for Managing Public Speaking Anxiety

Student Essay 1

Student Essay 2

Ways of Controlling Speaker Apprehension

Describing a Confident Public Speaker

Behaviors and Attitudes That Make You Look Confident

A Public Speaking Model: The Elements of Success

RECOGNIZING FEARS ABOUT PUBLIC SPEAKING

Objectives

1. To learn to recognize and accept nervousness while speaking in public situations.
2. To share common fears and concerns about speaking in public with your classmates.

Explanation

Public speaking has often been cited as the number one fear of many individuals. Public speaking apprehension is experienced not only by students but also by actors, business executives, bank presidents, and many others who have limited experience in speaking in public. Even experienced public speakers get very apprehensive in particular situations. The major advantage that experienced speakers have over novice speakers is that experience has taught them to recognize their fears and develop strategies to deal with them. Overcoming your fear of public speaking and developing confidence are achievable goals. You can accomplish these goals through the systematic process described in this unit.

Instructions: Step 1

Think about the speeches you will have to deliver in this class or think about the speeches you have given in the past. In the space below write down two to three of your worst fears about speaking in public. In effect you will be completing the sentence: "I am afraid that. . . ."

Worst Fears about Public Speaking:

1.

2.

3.

Instructions: Step 2

Working in groups of three to five people, share your list of "Worst Fears about Public Speaking." Discuss the fears, make a composite list for your group of the three most common fears of your group, and list them on the next page. List any other fears your group feels are noteworthy under the heading of "Other Fears." The groups will share their lists with the whole class.

Common Fears about Public Speaking:

1.

2.

3.

Other Fears about Public Speaking:

1.

?

3.

ANALYZING PUBLIC SPEAKING ANXIETIES

Objectives

1. To learn to deal rationally with your fears about public speaking.
2. To develop strategies for managing public speaking anxiety.

Explanation

All speakers want to feel confident, yet we know from research and experience that speakers look confident more often than they feel confident. Your long-term goal should be to feel confident and to even enjoy speaking in public. In the meantime, a more realistic and achievable goal is to adopt the behaviors that will make you look confident while speaking in public. Confidence, like energy, is contagious. The more confident you appear the more confidence your audience will have in you, sending you nonverbal messages that can encourage and help sustain your confidence. Therefore, your goal is to develop specific strategies (things you do and say in preparation and delivery) that will help you appear confident.

Instructions

Using your group's list of the "Worst Fears about Public Speaking," develop a list of specific things you can do to alleviate these fears or to be assured that they will not occur. Using the following page, first list the specific fears under the left-hand column and then develop the strategies to manage each particular fear, listing it in the corresponding right-hand column.

Strategies for Managing Public Speaking Anxiety

Fears	Strategies

STUDENTS' SUGGESTIONS FOR MANAGING PUBLIC SPEAKING ANXIETY

Objectives

1. To realize that public speaking anxiety is common among all college students.
2. To gain ideas on how to identify public speaking fears and on ways to lessen those fears.

Instructions

Read the following two essays written by college students enrolled in an introductory public speaking course. As you read, note how the students specifically identified their fears and how they explained the ways their nervousness manifested itself during their speeches. Also note the specific things they did to manage their anxiety.

After you read the essays, answer the questions below.

Questions for Discussion

1. Describe the "worst" fears articulated in Essay 1 and Essay 2.

2. What specifically did these speakers do to lessen their main fears?

3. What other things did these speakers do before and during their speeches to manage their fears?

4. What were these speakers' attitudes about speaking in public *before* the course and *after* the course? Why did they change their attitudes?

5. What did these speakers learn about public speaking to help them manage their anxiety and develop confidence?

STUDENT ESSAY 1

"Practice makes perfect!" Although I am not yet perfect in my speaking capabilities, this class has certainly given me a lot of practice.

I have found that public speaking is not learned in a day, a week, or even a year. It is rather like building a card house. First, one must have the formal rules as a foundation. As life progresses with experiences, card after card is raised to form walls, rooms, and finally a roof. This class has helped me finish my foundation and start working on the walls of my card house.

The audience, that faceless sea of eyes that made me so apprehensive, was furthest from my thoughts as I gave my former speeches. I thought of the audience as a bull thinks of the rider: the sooner they were off my back, the sooner I could get away. Because of this, I was able to shorten five pages of notes to five seconds of the most exercise my mouth had ever had. I now realize that the audience is yearning for attention and that I must create an understanding of my topic in them.

I was afraid to ask myself just a few questions. Did this mean that I must prolong my time in front of their speculating gazes from five seconds to perhaps sixty or even more? That I must speak clearly and concisely, even stopping for pauses to let my words sink in? Did catering to the audience mean that I would have to lift my eyes from the security blanket of notes and endeavor to look into their eyes? Did it mean to define the mass as not a mass at all, but as many individuals? Yes, it did! As I learned what was expected of me, I began to feel the weight of responsibility sitting squarely on my shoulders.

Even though I have slowed the spewing of words considerably, in my weaker moments they rush out at a tremendous speed, disrupting my thoughts and leaving me in an embarrassed state as I "ah" and "uhm" my way back to my outline. And that's all fear's fault. *I* doubt that I will be able to get rid of the anxiety I have when it comes to speaking in public. This course makes my legs quiver like they are made of Jell-O and my stomach believe it has been besieged by huge moths. My hands, seeming to take on a life of their own, will not be stilled until they are clenched white. This posture makes the important appearance of gestures practically impossible.

Yes, gestures were invented to relax the audience by giving the speaker a flowing movement. The friendly smile, the relaxed posture and flowing movement of the hands as they make their point, all work to help the audience feel relaxed and open to your knowledge.

Unfortunately, using these gestures is easier said than done. If my hands are in a clutched grip, they cannot move. If I move my feet, I am sure I will fall flat on my face. I need to work on using gestures!

Some things I did to lessen my nervousness were practicing at home in front of my family, being well acquainted with the material, and remembering that I had better not mess up or I would be in *big* trouble!

I have heard it said that no matter how many times a person has spoken in public, he or she will still feel some anxiety. To tell the truth, I hope I always will. The anxiety I feel helps me be more in tune with my speech and the audience. For example, if I did not feel any anxiety and was real relaxed, I might put in a lot of "you knows" and "likes" and get off the subject. The tension I feel makes me extra careful about what I say and how I say it. It also makes me more aware of the feedback. If I felt I was just "shootin' the breeze," I would most likely be more interested in what I had to say rather than being aware of how it affected my listeners. I think I can compare the importance of anxiety or tension in a speech through a lesson I learned on the swim team.

Before a swim meet I would feel the same sort of tension, the gnawing at the stomach and the ceaseless trembling of my limbs. But being so anxious always made me swim faster and gave my strokes more concentration. One day I decided I was sick of being so anxious, so I willed myself to totally relax. Not only did I get the worst time ever, I came in last place. After that I never said anything bad about a little tension. I think the trick is not to let others know you are feeling it.

The way I compensate for my nervousness is to smile a lot—too much, I think. I like to make people laugh, but I think I need to work more on being serious and believable. I have a lot of improving to do and, as I said once before, the only way to get better is to have more experience.

This course has already helped me in my Sunday school teaching and my role as a Young Adult representative for my church. The practice and the experience I have gained gives me a confidence I never had—I no longer feel as if my audience is laughing at me. I think I am finally getting my message across.

THANK YOU!

STUDENT ESSAY 2

Throughout the public speaking portion of this course, I have survived giving two speeches: one on heartworm disease in dogs and one on the importance of rape prevention advocates in the community. I feel that my abilities have greatly improved and that I have learned enough to keep on improving them. I will address both my confidence as a speaker and my strengths and weaknesses as a speaker in this essay.

First, my confidence as a speaker has greatly improved. I was originally terrified of speaking to an audience of my peers. I feared stuttering, losing my place, and blacking out. I learned to overcome these fears by reminding myself of two very important points: the risks involved were not nearly as great as I imagined, and a speech is nothing more than a form of communication. I realized that I would not die from stuttering or stumbling over a word or two. My audience would not laugh and point if I lost my place and had to backtrack. And the chances of totally blacking out were extremely slim. Also, by viewing the speech as a transaction of communication, I become more comfortable and at ease. I saw myself talking to my friends, not speaking to an audience. This was an extremely useful way of controlling my nervousness. Now I feel much more confident and I am convinced that I can successfully speak in public.

Second, I will address my strengths and weaknesses as a speaker. The sole reason for taking this course was to build some strengths in public speaking. I had intended to gain skill and confidence. As a potential educator, I need to appear knowledgeable and confident about the subject that I am teaching. I felt that this course would help achieve these abilities. Originally, my only strength was showing an interest in my topic. My weaknesses included constantly speaking softly and hiding behind the podium. But now I feel I have overcome these weaknesses and have gained new strengths.

I feel that the greatest of these strengths is my ability to speak in an extemporaneous, conversational manner. As stated before, I have learned to view the speech as a transaction of communication. Although the audience cannot verbally respond to my words, I have learned to read their nonverbal messages. For example, when I was using a visual aid during my first speech, I noticed that several audience members were straining to see my poster. I then held my poster up high so all could see and spoke from there. Also, the ability to speak solely from notes, not from a written speech or memorization, is a key strength for a speaker. I feel that I have somewhat achieved this skill. Although I spoke in phrases during my second speech, I did not appear as a robot simply spewing out facts to an audience. I knew what I wanted to say, and I said it. This enabled me to have excellent eye contact with my audience as well. Since I was not tied to a strictly formatted speech, I could clarify points that seemed confusing to the audience. For example, I was able to do this when a few audience members still seemed confused after my definition of a secondary victim. After a second try, they seemed to understand the definition.

One of my main weaknesses concerns giving the introduction to the speech. With both speeches, I started talking real low and soft. Considering that these first sentences were to be my attention-getting statements, I really needed to speak loud and clear. Another problem that I had with my introduction was during my first speech. I had tried to give too much background on the transmission of heartworms. I should have incorporated this information into the body of the speech and provided an overall preview of my speech before I moved into the details.

Another weakness of mine is not making the main points clear. During both speeches I only included signposts at the conclusions, instead of throughout the speech; my mind was trying to speak faster than my mouth could. Another way that I failed in making my main points clear to the audience was by including too much technical information; my diction was inappropriate. The first speech was loaded with medical terminology that should have been translated into lay terms.

By recognizing these weaknesses, I believe that I have already started improving. I know what I am doing wrong, and through practice I believe I can overcome my difficulties. I also believe that spending more time organizing my speech will help me avoid problems with the introduction's structure.

Overall, I feel that my speaking abilities have greatly improved. Although I will still be nervous when speaking before a large audience, I feel that I have gained the skills necessary to do so effectively. I have also learned how to control my nervousness by viewing the speech as a transaction of communication.

WAYS OF CONTROLLING SPEAKER APPREHENSION

1. Recognize that speaker apprehension—fear of public speaking—is normal and widespread.
2. Recognize that apprehension is not necessarily detrimental; it can energize you. Realize that no one can see the way you feel at the start of your speech. You need not be nervous about being nervous. Just control yourself sufficiently to appear before your audience and your tensions can be dissipated after you start to speak.
3. Plan an introduction that will relax you as well as your listeners. Have your first sentence down cold but *don't* memorize your speech.
4. Remember the main ideas and realize that if you are focusing on creating understanding with your audience, you will find the exact wording when you are actually speaking. This will allow you to speak in a conversational style.
5. Just before coming up to speak, take three or four deep breaths and clench your fists firmly.
6. Pause for two to five seconds before speaking. Look at your audience in a responsive manner and wait for all of them to give you their attention. Your responsiveness invites reciprocation.
7. Concentrate on communicating your meaning and engaging in a dialogue *with* the audience.
8. Use body, gesture, facial expression, and purposeful movement. Realize that purposeful physical movement helps ease nervousness.
9. Speak to individuals in the audience that are receptive to your message. Pick out one person on the right side, then in the middle, and then one on the left side and speak to that one person only. Look for new faces in your audience but talk only to one person at a time. Their nods, smiles, frowns, and so on will help you to get the feedback you need to adapt your message to them and to reinforce a sincere desire to communicate.
10. Have your conclusion "down cold." This way you can always be sure to have a strong and emphatic ending. Do not end with "Thank you" or "That's all."
11. Pause and stand in place two to five seconds after you have finished speaking. This shows the audience that you have enjoyed the exchange and feel poised and confident enough to not have to run back to your seat.
12. Know that with practice you develop the courage and ability to speak in public; it gets better and easier over time and with experience.

DESCRIBING A CONFIDENT PUBLIC SPEAKER

Objectives

1. To articulate an image of a confident, persuasive speaker.
2. To learn to use concrete, descriptive language.
3. To learn to observe and describe human behavior.

Instructions

Picture in your mind a confident public speaker. This image might be of a real person or a combination of several people. Working alone or in groups, describe how this speaker acts, thinks, and feels. The questions below might prove useful in stimulating your image. Make sure you use language that is concrete and specific. To say someone is confident or enthusiastic is not enough. What does confidence look like? Sound like? How does enthusiasm manifest itself in human behavior? Descriptive language provides useful information to guide speakers and listeners.

After discussing the confident, persuasive public speaker with your group members, record a composite list on a sheet of paper. Turn in that list to your instructor. Use words or phrases to record the way your confident speaker acts, talks, moves, gestures, and looks.

Questions for Guidance*

The questions below can be useful in creating a concrete description of a confident, persuasive public speaker.

- How does the speaker utilize space? Is this speaker tied to a spot behind the lectern or does this speaker use the space comfortably, easily, and with purpose?
- How does the speaker gesture? Are the gestures stiff, sparse, or repetitive? Or are they natural, well timed, and expressive? Do they seem to flow from the speaker's personality comfortably and easily?
- How does the speaker's voice sound? Is it dull, monotonous, and without any variation? Or lively, crisp, and articulate?
- How about the speaker's diction (i.e., choice of words)? Is it colorless and vague, or does the speaker paint vivid, colorful images with his or her words?
- How does the speaker organize his or her material? Is the introduction "ho-hum," or does it get attention and provoke thought? Is the argument difficult to follow, or do the main points stand out clearly?
- How does your ideal speaker use charts? Graphs? Diagrams? Pictures? Objects? In other words, are the visual materials available used as if they were an afterthought? Or are they an integral, relevant part of the performance and displayed appropriately?
- How does the speaker choose topics, examples, statistics, and so forth? Are they chosen without regard to the needs, wants, desires of the audience, or are they specifically tailored to match a target audience?
- How does the audience respond? Do they pay polite attention and give the obligatory applause at the end? Or, does the audience "sparkle" with interest?

---

*The above questions are adapted from a workshop presentation by Carol Thompson, "A Streamlined No-Lecture Speech Course," Southern Speech Communication Association Conference, April 7, 1988, Memphis, TN.

BEHAVIORS AND ATTITUDES THAT MAKE YOU LOOK CONFIDENT

Explanation

The following speech outline specifies particular behaviors and attitudes that will help you look confident in public speaking situations. Feeling confident comes with experience. Read the outline and practice these behaviors and attitudes in the impromptu and introductory speaking assignments in this unit.

Introduction

I. How much do you fear public speaking?
   A. Next to cancer, public speaking is most feared by Americans.
   B. Public speaking anxiety is very common and can be overcome or controlled.
II. As a public speaker and teacher of public speaking for 15 years, I conceive of public speaking as:
   A. Essentially similar to interpersonal communication.
   B. Polished, refined dialogue with an audience.
III. Thesis: Public speaking becomes an art when you make it a dialogue or conversation with the audience.
   A. Use behaviors that make you look and feel confident.
   B. Adopt an attitude of concern for the audience's understanding.

Transition: How do you make that happen? Focus on behaviors.

Body

I. Demonstrate behaviors that make you look and feel confident.
   A. Use direct and frequent eye contact.
   B. Use relaxed facial expressions and gestures that do not distract from the meaning.
      1. It is essential to be natural.
      2. Focus on meaning and understanding.
   C. Your voice should respond to meaning by means of:
      1. Emphasis.
      2. Pace.
      3. Pause.
   D. Demonstrate purposeful use of space and movement:
      1. Stand near or next to speaker stand.
      2. Use movement as transition between ideas.
   E. Use extemporaneous delivery:
      1. Not written out.
      2. Not memorized.
II. Portray an attitude of concern for the audience's understanding.
   A. Portray a sincere desire to communicate with the audience.
      1. Read audience feedback.
      2. Show enthusiasm and interest.
      3. Focus on the audience's understanding of your message.

    B.   Think of your speech as a dialogue or conversation with your audience.
        1.   Use nervous energy to engage audience in a dialogue—talk with, not *at* them.
        2.   This can help you feel comfortable and build your confidence.

Conclusion

  I.   Successful public speaking requires appropriate behaviors and attitudes:
    A.   Behavior that makes you feel confident.
    B.   An attitude of concern for the audience's understanding.
 II.   Public speaking is at its best when it becomes art—a dialogue with your audience.

Preparing and Presenting Your First Speech

This unit provides you with a basic overview of the speechmaking process. The essential steps involved in planning and preparing your speeches are outlined in this unit. In addition, it contains several speech assignments for your first speech. These assignments provide you with suggestions for topics, ways to organize your ideas, and criteria for effective delivery for your first speech.

The components of UNIT 4 are:

Preparing to Speak in Public: An Overview

The Process of Preparing a Speech

Group Introductory Speech

Introductory Values/Belief Speech

Personal Experience Speech

Practice Speeches

PREPARING TO SPEAK IN PUBLIC: AN OVERVIEW

The most important quality of an effective speaker is the ability to engage the audience in a dialogue, in a process of communication. Communication essentially involves a simultaneous exchange and shaping of messages between people who are attempting to achieve a common meaning. It is a transaction between people—senders and receivers—who simultaneously share these roles. You are a sender as you listen to your instructor in lecture and send nonverbal messages of confusion, interest, agreement, or boredom. When it is your turn to speak before an audience, it is essential to respond to the nonverbal messages you receive from your audience.

You engage an audience in a dialogue by earnestly and sincerely attempting to communicate with them. Reach out directly and involve your audience in your message by using examples that they can relate to and by speaking with (not at) them. In other words, adjust your message to your audience. For example, you might reexplain a concept in response to puzzled expressions in your audience. When you concentrate on attempting to communicate the meaning of your message to your audience and when you think of them as *individuals* engaged in a dialogue with you, you take the attention, focus, and fear of failure away from yourself.

Public speaking involves speakers, messages, and audiences:

Speakers who need to know:
   Why am I speaking? What is my purpose?
   What does my audience expect/know?
   How can I match my purpose and audience expectations?

Messages that consist of:
   Content
   Organization
   Style

Audiences who have:
   Universal or common characteristics
   Particular knowledge and expectations
   Particular interests and attitudes

The key to effective public speaking is the ability to make appropriate choices before and during your presentation. Making appropriate choices involves a consideration of knowing who your audience is, why they have gathered, what they know, and what the best plan of action is to achieve your purpose and meet audience expectations. To effectively make these choices and design a plan of action, you need a knowledge of the concepts of public speaking and the willingness and ability to make choices before your speech (in the planning stages) and during your speech (adjusting to needs of audience and occasion).

Below is a procedure to help you prepare to speak in public:

1. Clarify your purposes for speaking.
2. Consider your audience from beginning to end.
3. Consider possible ways of achieving your purpose and meeting audience needs.
4. Select the best methods or ways to match purpose and needs—make rhetorical choices.
5. Plan how to present messages in a cohesive and interesting manner; organize ideas.
6. Feel confident through use of direct eye contact and maintenance of interest in your topic and audience during delivery.
7. Concentrate on creating meaning and engaging your audience in a dialogue.

THE PROCESS OF PREPARING A SPEECH

The process of preparing a speech is essentially the same for all types of speeches. While many beginning speakers are initially concerned with delivery (or the act of standing before an audience), it is the selection of topic and its adaptation to an audience that are perhaps the most challenging.

The key to a successful presentation is a systematic plan of action that is delineated in the outline below. The first major step in planning your speech is to consider topic, purpose, and audience. The second major step is to organize your ideas and supporting materials into a coherent message. The final major step is to practice your delivery skills.

I. Planning the speech requires a simultaneous consideration of topic, purposes, and audience.
   A. Select and narrow your topic.
      1. Knowledge and interest of speaker.
      2. Interesting and significant to audience.
      3. Limited in scope and purpose.
         a. For time limit.
         b. For audience understanding and expectations.
   B. Determine your general and specific purposes.
      1. General: answers why speaking.
      2. Specific: concrete goals to achieve.
   C. Analyze your audience, occasion, and setting.
      1. Effective public speaking—audience centered.
         a. Audience knowledge about topic.
         b. Audience interests or attitudes toward topic.
      2. Particulars about occasion and setting.
II. Organizing materials and ideas requires a sequential consideration from rough draft, to research, to final copy.
   A. Write a rough draft of thesis, main ideas, and subpoints.
      1. Thesis: direct, declarative statement expressing main point of speech.
      2. Main ideas explain or elaborate thesis.
   B. Research and gather supporting materials relevant to audience.
      1. Examples.
      2. Statistics.
      3. Testimony.
   C. Compose final outline complete with examples, introduction, and conclusion.
      1. Functions of introduction and conclusion.
      2. Abbreviated speaking outline.
III. Practicing presentational skills is the final consideration when preparing a speech.
   A. Practice aloud for clarity and fluency.
   B. Practice aloud in conversational style.

GROUP INTRODUCTORY SPEECH

Objectives

1. To become acquainted with the members of your class.
2. To practice effective delivery skills.

Task

As a group, introduce yourselves to the class in a *creative, interesting,* and *memorable* way.

Instructions

Discuss the similarities and differences among group members. Use that discussion to develop a two- to four-minute group introductory speech. All members should participate in the planning and delivery of the speech.

Suggestions

Remember that you are a group composed of individuals. We want to remember you as a group and also know your individual names. Discover and present what is unique about your group. What do you have in common? Your group's introduction should be creative, interesting, and memorable. You might think of this as a commercial to get in the spirit of this assignment.

Summary Discussion

1. Which group(s) accomplished the task most effectively?

2. How did they accomplish it? In other words, what did they do or say to make their introduction creative, interesting, and memorable?

INTRODUCTORY VALUES/BELIEF SPEECH

Objectives

1. To practice conversational, extemporaneous speaking.
2. To practice using voice, gesture, and bodily action to convey meaning.

Instructions

Select an excerpt from a poem, an essay, or a speech that reflects your values, beliefs, or philosophy of life. Use that excerpt to guide you in preparing your introductory speech.

Requirements and Expectations

Content (ingredients)

1. Give a brief summary on author's thesis of the poem, essay, or speech.
2. Explain your connections to it, that is, *why* it is important to you or why you value the idea or hold the same belief.
3. Read an excerpt.

Organization

The three ingredients will be organized in the way you deem most appropriate or effective. For example, you may begin by reading an excerpt (manuscript mode) and then summarizing the author's ideas and explaining your connections to the values or ideas in the excerpt (extemporaneous mode) and conclude by reading another portion of the excerpt (manuscript mode).

Style

The purpose of the speech is to practice effective delivery. Your grade will be based on the effectiveness of your delivery style and your use of the following:

1. Sincere desire to communicate, establishing a dialogue with audience.
2. Direct and inclusive eye contact.
3. Voice, gestures, bodily action used to convey meaning of message, rather than nervousness.
4. Extemporaneous delivery (brief reference to notes; reading allowed for quotes only and must be done in a "speaking" voice).
5. Clear evidence of preparation and organization (including time limit).

PERSONAL EXPERIENCE SPEECH

Objectives

1. To develop coherent and captivating messages.
2. To develop effective delivery skills.

Task

Prepare and present a personal experience speech to your group or to the class. Your goal is to use vocal and bodily expressions and to present a coherent and captivating message.

Suggestions for Preparation

1. Select a personal experience that had a significant impact on you. Possibilities might include:

   Your most embarrassing moment
   Your most exciting moment
   Your greatest accomplishment
   A car wreck
   Climbing a mountain
   An exquisite sunset
   The most delicious food you have ever tasted
   Your favorite vacation
   The most gorgeous man/woman you have ever seen
   Whatever you feel very strongly about or have vivid memories of

2. Develop and organize your speech by addressing these three questions: What? How? Why?

   a. If you are using an event or an experience, address:
      1. What happened or what you did.
      2. How you felt about it.
      3. Why you felt that way or why it was significant.
   b. If you are using a food, a place, or a person, address:
      1. What it/they look(s) like.
      2. How the food tastes; how that place or person makes you feel.
      3. Why you find it/them delicious or beautiful or wonderful.

3. Outline your speech in the most effective and logical order, addressing the three issues above. Use only key words or phrases.
4. Practice your speech aloud, concentrating on reliving the experience. Do not merely list things, use words to paint a picture of what happened or what you are describing. For example, if your speech is about the time you saved a drowning person, do not merely state, "I jumped in and pulled him out." Tell what he was doing; describe his struggles; tell how deep the water was; tell how far he was from shore; recount your fears and other feelings as you pulled him toward shore; explain how the current almost took you under; demonstrate the way you held him by the hair; emphasize such items as your fatigue and exhaustion as you fought to stay afloat. Be descriptive and detailed in your accounts so your audience can relive the experience too.
5. Prepare a brief introduction and conclusion.

Suggestions for Delivery

1. Do not use note cards or stand behind a podium. Be open and free to use gestures to relive the experience.
2. It may be appropriate to sit on a stool or lean on the end of a desk to create an intimate or relaxed atmosphere.
3. As you tell your story, concentrate on recreating the experience for yourself and your listeners. Your attitude should be one that demonstrates a sincere and extreme desire to have the audience understand and share your experience.

Suggestions for Listeners

1. Allow yourself to partake in the experience created through the speaker's words.
2. Make note of particularly vivid words the speaker uses.
3. Find a way to unobtrusively record the vivid descriptive words and phrases the speakers in your group use. You might take turns sitting off to the side and writing down words and phrases that are particularly vivid or descriptive.
4. Turn in the list of words to your instructor and/or share the list of words aloud with the rest of the class.
5. Select one member to tell his or her story to the rest of the class.

PRACTICE SPEECHES

Objectives

1. To develop coherent and substantive messages.
2. To develop effective delivery skills.

Instructions: Step 1

Select one of the topics and methods of organization below and prepare a two- to three-minute speech using a brief, keyword outline that can be limited to a 5" by 8" index card (front and back can be used). Do not write out your whole speech—just write the key words for the main ideas.

Topics

The death penalty
The value of joining a Greek organization
Legalized abortion
Abolishing the grading system
Pollution of the environment
The changing roles of males and females in relationships/in the workplace
Topic of your choice: something you feel strongly enough about to take a stance on

Methods of Organization

Organize the introduction of your speech in the following way:

1. Open with a question or statement that will gain the attention of your audience and help them focus on the topic.
2. Say why you chose that topic or why it is important to you.
3. State your position about the topic. For example, "The death penalty should be abolished."

Organize the body of your speech in one of the following ways:

1. State two reasons why you believe in your position.
2. State two reasons why your audience should accept the claim or position you stated.
3. State two advantages for accepting your position.
4. State the problem suggested by the topic; then state a solution.

You should be prepared to elaborate on the two main points in the body of your speech by providing examples and explanations.

Organize the conclusion of your speech in the following way:

1. Restate your two main points in the body of your speech.
2. Provide a closing appeal to the audience to accept your position.

Instructions: Step 2

After you have written your brief outline on one 5" by 8" index card, practice your speech aloud using the specific suggestions from the outline entitled "Using Voice and Body for Effective Delivery" in Unit 13. Practice a second time in front of friends or family members and ask for feedback on your behaviors.

Understanding Ethical Public Speaking

This unit challenges you to delve into the complex issue of ethics in human communication. The activities in this unit are designed to help you (1) appreciate the value of ethical practices in public speaking; (2) recognize ethical practices; and (3) develop guidelines to implement ethical practices in your speeches.

The components of UNIT 5 are:

The Value and Understanding of Ethics

Analyzing Ethical Concerns: A Situation

Analyzing Ethics: A Student Outline

Discovering Ethical Standards: What is Plagiarism?

Outline 1 for Analysis of Plagiarism

Outline 2 for Analysis of Plagiarism

Determining Appropriate Ethical Speech Topics

Analyzing Appropriate and Ethical Topic Choice and Development

THE VALUE AND UNDERSTANDING OF ETHICS

Ethics deals with issues of morality, fairness, justice, and honesty. These are complex issues that are intricately linked to one's individual value system and cultural background. It is important for people to discuss ethical standards and guidelines for living together in a community, for working together in an organization, and for governing themselves.

In recent years there has been a growing interest and desire to study ethics in such academic subjects as medicine, business, advertising, journalism, and public speaking. Perhaps this desire is a response to the growing concerns of unethical practices in advertising, political campaigns, and business practices. Americans seem to be inundated with ethical dilemmas.

Ethical Public Speakers are:

1. Responsible.
2. Fully prepared.
3. Honest.

ANALYZING ETHICAL CONCERNS: A SITUATION

Objectives

1. To discuss ethical considerations for public speaking situations.
2. To analyze particular speaking situations for their ethical standards.

Explanation

As you discovered earlier in this unit, the context or the situation greatly influences the meaning in any communication situation. A message that might be appropriate between two friends in a social setting may be very inappropriate and even unethical in a public situation. You should strive for responsible, ethical public speaking. In other words, it is important to know the expectations of your audience and of the situation. In addition, you have a responsibility to be well informed about your topic and to be well prepared in your presentation. In your topic selection, in development of ideas and supporting materials, and in presentation of your speech, you should treat your audience in a manner that you would wish to be treated. As a public speaker you have an obligation to be honest with your audience and honest in the information, ideas, and arguments you select and present. Such practices help you to establish credibility and "goodwill" as a public speaker.

Instructions: Step 1

Working with a small group of students, discuss the issue of ethics and honesty and then come up with a list of ethical and unethical practices. Compare your list with those of other groups to make a composite list of ethical and unethical public speaking practices.

Instructions: Step 2

Using the lists created above or your own standards of ethics, analyze the following two speaking situations by responding to the questions that follow.

Situation for Analysis

Jane was preparing her persuasive speech on the increasing occurrence of suicide among college students. She had pulled together a substantial amount of research and felt like she would have a solid base of evidence to support her persuasive arguments. She felt her speech had logical appeal and was well organized; what was missing, however, was emotional appeal. To truly capture the audience's attention at the beginning of her speech so that they would listen carefully and consider her arguments, she felt that she needed a really emotion-packed, moving story about a real suicide. Jane did not really know anyone personally who had committed suicide, so she made up a story about a fictitious friend and patterned it after a couple of the emotionally moving stories she had read in her research. In her speech, she presented the story as a true story about her best friend in high school. When asked after her speech for more information about her friend, she told her audience that she had made the story up to help focus their attention on the tragedy, knowing that such tragedies had happened to other people.

Questions for Discussion

1. Since Jane's major motive in making up that story was to focus her audience's attention on the real problem of suicide, was what she did unethical? Why or why not?

2. If you were a member of Jane's audience, how would you feel if you discovered after her speech that she did not have a friend who committed suicide as she had claimed earlier?

3. What if Jane would have continued presenting her story as true after her speech was over? Would that change how you responded to Question 1?

4. In sum, were Jane's choices and actions ethical or unethical? Why or why not?

ANALYZING ETHICS: A STUDENT OUTLINE

Objectives

1. To discuss ethical considerations for public speaking situations.
2. To analyze a student speech outline for its ethical standards.

Instructions

Using the lists created in the previous exercise or your own standards of ethics, determine whether you would consider the following outline ethical. After you consider your responses to the questions below, share them with two or three of your classmates.

Student Outline for Analysis

The following is a copy of a student outline for a four- to six-minute informative speech in an introductory public speaking course in a midwestern university.

Topic: Boredom in dorms.
General Purpose: To inform.
Specific Purpose: To inform my audience of ways to alleviate boredom in dorms.

Introduction

I. Attention-getting statement: Do you ever find yourself sitting in your dorm room feeling like you're on the verge of bouncing off the wall? Or wanting to scream your head off? This is commonly known as boredom.
II. Need for listening: As students, most of us live on campus. And being in this small town, we are subject to boredom.
III. Thesis: Fortunately there are some imaginative ways to alleviate boredom in the dorm rooms.

Body

I. One of the oldest ways to alleviate boredom is by engaging in phone pranks, whether your victim is someone you know or a total stranger.
   A. Phone tags.
   B. Call—then hang up.
   C. Obscene phone calls.
   D. Commercial phone pranks.
II. Another way to alleviate boredom is by harmlessly defacing property.
   A. Toilet paper.
   B. Streamers and balloons.
   C. Signs.
   D. Tape.
III. My final way to alleviate boredom is by engaging in imaginative recreational activities. These are by far the most enjoyable and sometimes the most challenging because they're done in the halls.
   A. Catch.
   B. Fluffball.
   C. Golf.

D. Bowling.
E. Frisbee.
F. Volleyball.

Conclusion

I. These are just a few of the creative ways you might alleviate boredom in the dorms.
II. If you know of any others, let me know and I will add them to my list.

Questions for Discussion

1. Is the topic development ethical? Why or why not?

2. What parts of the speech would you consider ethical? What parts unethical?

3. How could this topic development be changed to make the speech ethical and appropriate?

DISCOVERING ETHICAL STANDARDS: WHAT IS PLAGIARISM?

Objectives

1. To determine what constitutes plagiarism in the development of topics for classroom speeches.
2. To analyze student's speech outlines to determine if a case of plagiarism is warranted.

Explanation

Plagiarism is considered any act that involves the "obtaining, by any means, of another person's work and the unacknowledged submission or incorporation of it in one's own work."* This would include word-for-word copying as well as interspersing a few words of one's own here and there while basically copying the work of another.

Instructions

On the following pages you will find two very similar outlines on the same topic, "Fire Prevention." After reading the following situation based on an actual occurrence, compare the two outlines based on the questions for discussion. The first outline was a sample student outline included in a public speaking workbook as a good example of a persuasive structure on a fairly common topic. This workbook was required for students enrolled in an introductory public speaking course at a university in the Midwest. One hundred sixty students were enrolled in that course. The students met once a week in a large lecture and then divided up into smaller lab sections of twenty students. Although this outline was not required reading, it was available to all students as an example of a good persuasive structure.

---

*This definition of plagiarism is taken from *Student Handbook & Code of Student Life,* The University of North Carolina at Wilmington, 1991–92.

OUTLINE 1 FOR ANALYSIS OF PLAGIARISM

Note: The outline below is reprinted exactly as it appeared in the public speaking workbook required for the course in which John Doe (outline 2) was enrolled.

Fire Prevention

General Purpose: To convince my audience.

Specific Purpose: To convince my audience of the utility and importance of learning the many areas of fire prevention.

Attention

I. If this building caught on fire right now, what would you do?
II. We as students, parents, sisters, brothers, etc., face the problem of not knowing enough about fire prevention.
   A. Example of my sister.
   B. I wish I had known more.
III. People are not aware that knowledge of fire prevention is needed daily in every place they go and everything they do.

Need

I. We face the problem of being apathetic toward the subject of fire prevention.
II. To further examine this problem, we can look at the effects that it has had in the United States.
   A. We face the problem of property loss and property damage.
      1. The National Fire Prevention Association estimated a total of $6,707,000,000 worth of properties lost because of fires in 1984.
      2. The National Fire Prevention Association also estimated a total of $631,000,000 worth of properties damaged by fire in 1984.
      3. We do not know enough about how to prevent property loss and property damage.
   B. We face the problem of injuries as a result of our lack of knowledge in fire prevention.
      1. According to the *Fire Journal,* an estimated 23,125 people were injured in fires in 1984.
      2. On December 9, 1971, eight other girls, our instructor, and myself were involved in a fire.
         a. Two girls suffered from third degree burns.
         b. Five girls suffered from cuts and scratches.
         c. One girl was lucky and was not injured.
   C. We also face the problem of death due to fires.
      1. In 1984 there were an estimated 5,240 deaths due to fires.
      2. On December 9, 1971, the other girl, my sister, and the instructor were killed in the fire.
   D. Chief Olivier of the Central Fire Department says, "If people were more knowledgeable in the area of fire prevention, these statistics would drop tremendously."

Satisfaction

I. An increase in lives and property being saved can be achieved by learning more about fire prevention and fire safety.

II. Fire prevention can be accomplished through the use of alarms and other devices, safety tips, and the basic fire-preventing steps.

   A. There are many types of devices that detect fires and aid in putting them out.
1. Smoke detectors aid in preventing fires.
2. Sprinklers also aid in putting out and preventing fires.
3. Alarms also warn us that there is a possible fire.
4. Fire extinguishers help to put out fires.

   B. Safety tips are very important in fire prevention.
1. If the room fills with smoke, get on the ground and crawl because smoke rises.
2. If someone is on fire, put something over that person and roll him or her on the ground.
3. Never open a hot door; stop the fire from spreading and avoid fumes.

   C. Home fire prevention is essential to know.
1. Inspect your home for fire hazards and correct them.
2. Have heating equipment checked.
3. Check up after people who may smoke.

   D. Know your escape route.
1. If you suspect fire, get everyone out and then call the fire department.
2. Develop and practice a home fire escape plan.

Visualization

I. Fire prevention is a tool of survival.

II. Fire prevention gives us the chance to not only help ourselves, but also to help others.

Action

I. We have a responsibility to ourselves and to others.

II. If protecting our loved ones and living safely is an important priority, then we owe it to ourselves to learn more about fire prevention.

References

"Fire Loss in the United States." *Fire Journal,* September 1985, pp. 1–7.

McKinnon, P. Gordon. *Fire Protection Handbook,* 15th edition, September 1981.

OUTLINE 2 FOR ANALYSIS OF PLAGIARISM

Note: This outline has been reproduced exactly as the student wrote it—only the student's name was changed to ensure confidentiality.

Fire Prevention

by John Doe

General Purpose: To convince my audience.

Specific Purpose: To convince my classmates how important it is to learn the different areas of fire prevention.

Attention

    I.   If this building caught fire right now, what would you do?

    II.   We as humans don't know enough about fire prevention.

    III.   The ignorance of fire prevention is knowledge that we can use in everyday life.

Need

    I.   We have a problem of not caring about fire prevention until it happens and when it does, we forget about it a couple of months later.

    II.   To examine this problem further, we can look at the effects of it on the United States.

        A.   We face the problem of property loss and property damage.

            1.   The National Fire Prevention Association estimated approximately five billion dollars worth of property loss in 1985 because of fire.

            2.   The National Fire Prevention Association estimated approximately five hundred million dollars worth in property damage in 1985 because of fire.

            3.   We don't know enough about property loss and property damage.

        B.   We face the problem of injuries as a result of our lack of knowledge on fire prevention.

            1.   According to a newspaper article we average approximately 21,000 injuries a year due to fire.

            2.   Incident in Franklin Hall.

        C.   We also face the problem of death due to fires.

            1.   According to a newspaper article we average approximately 6,000 deaths a year.

            2.   Incident of my next-door neighbor.

Satisfaction

    I.   There can be an increase in lives and property saved by learning more about fire prevention and safety.

    II.   There are many different areas to fire prevention such as alarms, safety tips, and basic fire prevention.

        A.   Alarms.

            1.   Smoke detectors.

            2.   Sprinklers.

3. Fire alarms.
4. Fire extinguishers.
B. Safety tips.
1. If there is smoke in a room get onto the ground and crawl because smoke rises.
2. If someone catches fire, have him or her drop to the ground and roll.
3. Never open a hot door, because most likely there is fire on the other side and second to keep it from spreading.
C. Inspect your home for possible fire hazards.
1. Check your fireplace and chimney.
2. Check your water heater.
3. Have ashtrays.
D. Know all escape routes from your house.
1. Develop and practice a fire escape plan.
2. If you suspect a fire, get everyone out and call 911.

Visualization

I. Fire prevention is a key to our survival.
II. Fire prevention gives us a chance to help ourselves and others before the crisis happens.

Action

I. So it is our responsibility to learn more about fire prevention to protect ourselves and others from casualties of fire.

References

Life Safety Codes Handbook, National Fire Protection Association, 1985.
Planner, Robert G. *Fire Loss Control*, 1986.
Courier Journal Newspaper, April 22, 1990

Questions for Discussion

1. Given its very close similarity with the first outline on fire prevention, is the second outline a case of plagiarism? Why or why not?

2. If John Doe genuinely had no idea that he was "cheating" because he changed some of the words, could he be justifiably accused of plagiarism?

3. What constitutes plagiarism? How much of a role do intentions play in the issue of plagiarism?

4. Whose responsibility is it to be informed about the issues of plagiarism: the professor, the graduate students, or the students in the course?

5. If a classmate of John Doe's recognized that speech as very similar to the one in the workbook, would he or she have an obligation to report that information?

DETERMINING APPROPRIATE ETHICAL SPEECH TOPICS

Objective

1. To determine what kinds of topics and topic developments would be considered appropriate or ethical for classroom public speaking assignments.

Explanation

In most cases when you are asked to give a presentation to a particular group, the topic is already selected. In other words, you will be asked to speak because of your knowledge about a particular topic. In the classroom situation, topic selection becomes a bit more complex. You are asked to speak on a topic that you have some knowledge of and interest in, and you must develop your topic in a manner that will be of interest and significance to your audience. An important consideration is the fact that your audience is a "captive" audience; that is, they are not at your presentation by choice. This can be considered a disadvantage; however, this same audience can be very empathetic. They know they will face the same challenge you do—to select an appropriate topic and develop it in an interesting, informative, or persuasive manner.

Instructions

On a sheet of paper, list the topics or kinds of topics that you would consider inappropriate or unethical for a classroom speaking assignment. Compare your list with those of two or three of your classmates. From this comparison, generate five rules or guidelines to account for ethics and appropriateness in topic selection and development.

Guidelines for Determining Appropriate and Ethical Topics

1.

2.

3.

4.

5.

ANALYZING APPROPRIATE AND ETHICAL TOPIC CHOICE AND DEVELOPMENT

Objective

1. To analyze a student's topic and development in terms of its ethics and appropriateness.

Instructions

Using the guidelines established in the previous exercise and the questions below, analyze the following student outline to determine the ethics or the appropriateness of the topic and the development.

The following student outline has been reproduced from the original without any corrections or changes.

Method of organization: Statement-of-reasons method for persuasive speaking.

General purpose: To convince my audience about an issue.

Specific purpose: To persuade my audience that Mr. Gattis' has the best pizza in town.

Introduction

I. How many people have eaten pizza in the last week? Almost everyone in this room enjoys eating pizza, although most of the time we end up paying too much for a bad product.
II. I know that your tastes and preferences vary but I plan to prove beyond a shadow of a doubt to you that Mr. Gattis' has the best overall product in what is known today as the "Pizza Industry."
III. Anyone who enjoys eating pizza should try Mr. Gattis' pizza.
  A. It is the freshest product.
  B. It is the most reasonably priced.
  C. Mr. Gattis' has the best overall process.
  D. We also have the most satisfying service.

Body

I. First, Mr. Gattis' has the freshest product of any pizza restaurant.
  A. The dough is made fresh daily.
    1. It is prepared at the store.
    2. We have the only dough that is allowed to rise twice.
  B. The produce is shipped fresh and prepared in store daily.
  C. The sauce is prepared and mixed in store with fresh ingredients.
II. Second, Mr. Gattis' has the best overall process.
  A. The sauce is completely covered by cheese.
    1. Covering keeps sauce from burning.
    2. This process creates a better taste.
  B. The cheese is put under the toppings.
    1. This allows the pizza to cook faster.
    2. Also keeps cheese from burning.

C. The toppings are placed on the pizza in a certain order to allow it to cook correctly.

III. Third, Mr. Gattis' has the most reasonably priced product on the market.
   A. It is the best pizza for the money.
      1. You will usually pay more anywhere else.
      2. The product isn't as good.
   B. Mr. Gattis' offers a buffet daily.
      1. It satisfies a big appetite with minimal cost.
      2. It gives a variety of pizza for one set price.
   C. Weekly coupons and specials are offered.

IV. Last, Mr. Gattis' offers the most satisfying service.
   A. The pizza is prepared and cooked very fast.
      1. Preparation time takes approximately two to three minutes.
      2. Cooking time takes approximately five to six minutes.
   B. We offer delivery usually within thirty minutes of your order.
   C. If the order isn't to your satisfaction we will make it right.
      1. We give discounts.
      2. We make the order over.

Conclusion

I. As you can see, Mr. Gattis' is far superior to their competition in that they have a fresher product, the best process, the most reasonable prices, and the most satisfying service.

II. Now you will all have the opportunity to sample, firsthand, the best pizza in town!

References

1. Interview, Buddy Stevenson, November 1988.
2. Interview, Mathew Appleton, November 1988.
3. Work experience: four years.

Questions for Analysis

1. Is the specific purpose appropriate for a classroom speech? Why or why not?

2. In what ways does the issue of a "captive audience" affect this choice of specific purpose?

3. The wording of the specific purpose and main ideas are very similar to advertising messages. Is that inappropriate for a classroom speech? Why or why not? Is that unethical? Why or why not?

Analyzing Audiences

This unit provides you with an overview of the essential principles and concepts of public speaking. These concepts will assist you in the initial stages of your speech preparation. To prepare an effective presentation, you need to thoroughly analyze your audience. The concepts and activities presented in the following pages will help you accomplish your preparation in a systematic and thorough manner.

The components of UNIT 6 are:

Understanding Communication Is Essential for Audience Analysis

Effective Public Speaking Is Audience Centered

Audience Analysis Exercise

Adapting Topics and Messages to Audiences: A Process of Identification

Adapting Topics to Audiences and Situations: An Exercise

Sample Speech Outline: Speech Purpose Adapted for Audience

Sample Audience Analysis: Aerobic Exercise Speech

Informative Outline Developed from Audience Analysis: Aerobic Exercise

UNDERSTANDING COMMUNICATION IS ESSENTIAL FOR AUDIENCE ANALYSIS

Communication is the process of creating meaning between people who are simultaneously engaged in the process of exchanging messages.

The *sincere desire to communicate* is the most valuable quality of a clear, effective, and honest speaker, and it follows that speakers possessing that quality will:

- Have interesting and well-supported ideas (*content*) with examples adapted to their audience.
- Express them in a coherent manner (*organization*).
- Express them in an appropriate style (*delivery*) that includes direct and inclusive eye contact, expressive voice and body, and confidence and interest in both topic and audience.

Remember, all speech communication is contextual. Its success depends upon the transaction among the elements of communication:

Speakers who have particular purposes.
Audiences who have certain expectations.
Messages that have content, organization, and style.
Channels such as language, gesture, body movement, and use of voice.
Barriers such as differences in language and meanings, interruptions, and so on that are always present.

All of these elements interact to create meaning in a particular context or situation. So, as a speaker, ask yourself:

Why am I speaking? (what's my purpose?)
What does my audience expect/know?
How can I best accomplish it? (match purpose and audience)

Your goal as a public speaker is to make the choices and evaluate them, based on the principles of speech communication within the context of your audience and the situation. Therefore, analyze your audience according to age, gender, culture, ethnic background, values, and beliefs. Then analyze your audience specifically for interest in and knowledge of your topic.

EFFECTIVE PUBLIC SPEAKING IS AUDIENCE CENTERED

The most important quality of an effective speaker is the ability to engage the audience in a dialogue, in a process of communication. Communication essentially involves a simultaneous exchange and shaping of messages among people. You engage an audience in a dialogue by earnestly and sincerely attempting to communicate with them. Reach out directly and involve your audience in your message by using examples that they can relate to and by speaking with (not at) them. In other words, adjust your message to your audience. For example, you might reexplain a concept in response to puzzled expressions in your audience. When you concentrate on attempting to communicate the meaning of your message to your audience and think of them as *individuals* engaged in a dialogue with you, you take the attention, focus, and fear of failure away from yourself.

Public speaking involves speakers, messages, and audiences:

Speakers who need to know:
Why am I speaking? What is my purpose?
What does my audience expect/know?
How can I match purpose and expectations?

Messages that consist of:
Content
Organization
Style

Audiences who have:
Universal or common characteristics
Particular knowledge and expectations
Particular interests and attitudes

The key to effective public speaking is the ability to make appropriate choices before and during your presentation. Making appropriate choices involves a consideration of knowing who your audience is, why they have gathered, what they know, and what the best plan of action is to achieve your purpose and meet audience expectations. To effectively make these choices and design a plan of action, you need a knowledge of the concepts of public speaking and the willingness and ability to make choices before your speech (in the planning stages) and during your speech (adjusting to needs of audience and occasion).

Below is a procedure to help you prepare to speak in public:

1. Clarify your purposes for speaking.
2. Consider your audience from beginning to end.
3. Consider possible ways of achieving your purpose and meeting audience needs.
4. Select the best methods or ways to match purpose and needs—make rhetorical choices.
5. Plan how to present messages in a cohesive and interesting manner; organize ideas.
6. Feel confident through use of direct eye contact and maintenance of interest in your topic and audience during delivery.
7. Concentrate on creating meaning and engaging your audience in a dialogue.

ADAPTING TOPICS AND MESSAGES TO AUDIENCES: A PROCESS OF IDENTIFICATION

One of the most useful strategies for adapting your topic and message to your audience is to use the process of identification. What do you and your audience have in common? And conversely, how are you different? What ideas or examples in your speech can your audience identify with?

It is essential to select a topic that you know well, that you feel comfortable with, or that you have a strong interest in. Once that step is completed, you need to consider the audience as you develop and shape your topic. It is essential to present your message (speech) from the audience's point of view. For example, a nursing major in a public speaking class wanted to give a demonstration speech on the proper way to insert an IV (intravenous needle). Since her audience was a more general audience (a mixture of majors) rather than a specialized audience (nursing students), they had little potential use for the information presented from the point of view of the "nurse." So the student used her expertise and knowledge to shift the point of view to the audience. She changed her message from how to insert an IV to how to relax while *receiving* an IV; therefore, she made the same message more useful to her audience. Her intention was to help them feel less fearful or apprehensive about an IV.

Consider the following questions in adapting your topics and messages to a particular audience:

What do you and your audience have in common? How are you different?

What ideas or examples in your speech might your audience identify with?

How can your topic or the information benefit your audience? How can they use it? What will it enhance?

What is your audience's interest in or attitude toward your topic? How will you address that or compensate for it?

What does your audience know about your topic? What might they want or need to know more about?

ADAPTING TOPICS TO AUDIENCES AND SITUATIONS: AN EXERCISE

Objectives

1. To apply the principles of audience analysis to a particular situation.
2. To adapt a topic for a particular audience and situation.
3. To use audience analysis and topic adaptation to formulate a specific purpose for a speech.

Instructions

Select one of the situations below and analyze how you will develop your topic to meet the needs and interests of the audience and the situation. Use the questions below to help you analyze the audience, topic, and situation. After you answer the questions, discuss your response with several of your classmates.

Topic Situation 1:

General Topic: Your academic major.

General Purpose: To create understanding.

Situation: You have been asked to speak to a group of twenty-five students who will attend Freshman Orientation at your university and have expressed an interest in your major and its future potential. You were asked to speak to this group by a friend of yours who is aware of the uncertainty felt and information needed by this particular group of students. You have been asked to keep your remarks to fifteen minutes and to speak from your own experience in providing this group some initial, important thoughts and information.

Topic Situation 2:

General Topic: College.

General Purpose: To create understanding.

Situation: One of your friends, teachers, or the principal has asked you to speak to the senior class of your high school for fifteen minutes about college. The occasion is a special day called "Careers and Choices in Life." You were told that you could speak about anything of your choice related to that topic and the occasion.

Questions for Discussion

1. What are the needs and interests of your audience? Describe them specifically and in detail.

2. What will your specific purpose be? In other words, what will you want your audience to know, understand, or appreciate as a result of your speech?

3. How will you adapt your topic to your audience and to the situation?

SAMPLE SPEECH OUTLINE: SPEECH PURPOSE ADAPTED FOR AUDIENCE

Objectives

1. To understand the importance of adapting your speech topic for a particular audience.
2. To analyze a speech outline for an appropriate purpose.

Instructions

The following outline is provided as an example of a college student's speech that was adapted for a particular audience. Read the situation and the outline below and discuss, with several of your classmates, the process of adapting speech topics and purposes to particular audiences.

Situation

This student was enrolled in a general education communication class. She was a senior marketing major; her classmates ranged from freshman to senior with a variety of majors. Originally she wanted to present the seven steps of selling. But she realized that her audience members were not marketing majors and, furthermore, were probably not interested in learning how to sell products. However, she thought her audience would (or should) be interested in the selling process from a buyer's point of view. So after analyzing her audience and considering that her assignment was to develop a topic for a particular audience, she prepared the following speech outline.

Speech Outline

Informative Speech Outline

General Purpose: To inform/to create understanding.

Specific Purpose: After listening to my speech, my audience will better understand (from a consumer standpoint) the selling process and the precautions to be taken into consideration during the buying process.

Introduction

I. Attention-getting statement: Have you ever walked into a store just to look around, been greeted by a friendly salesperson, and ended up leaving the store with something you never intended to buy?
II. Need for listening: During the past two summers I have participated in a marketing internship program that involved door-to-door sales. It was very enjoyable for me. I also discovered that many people are not even aware that there is a sales process. Many people buy a product without ever realizing exactly why they bought it. I feel it will be helpful to you as consumers to recognize that there are strategic steps that salespeople take to help you reach a buying decision, and there are also precautions you can take to avoid being taken advantage of.
III. Thesis: Consumers can benefit from the ability to understand the selling/buying process.
   A. Selling/Buying process.
   B. Precautions.

Body

I. People buy because they are led through a buying process.
   A. Salespeople are specifically trained.
      1. Find consumers.
      2. Fill the need.
      3. Customer commitment.
      4. Cement the sale.
   B. Stores are specially designed.
      1. Displays.
      2. Accessories.

Transition: As a consumer, it is important to realize that there are steps you can take to ensure a satisfying purchase.

II. There are precautions to help you in your buying process.
   A. Precautions.
      1. Bait and switch.
      2. Benefits vs cost.
      3. Trial period.
      4. Buying on credit.
   B. Alternatives.
      1. Return.
      2. Exchange.
      3. Refund.

Conclusion

I. It is important as a consumer to make satisfying buying decisions and to realize the precautions and alternatives you can take if the product does not fulfill your expected needs.
II. Remember: Spend your hard-earned money the way *you* want to spend it.

SAMPLE AUDIENCE ANALYSIS:
AEROBIC EXERCISE SPEECH*

Note: This is an example of a detailed audience analysis; such detail is not always necessary.

Topic: Aerobic exercise—positive long-term effects on the body and the mind.

Audience: Sigma Sigma Sigma social sorority of USL.

General Purpose: To create understanding.

Specific Purpose: To create understanding about aerobic exercise and the positive effects it can have on one's health and well-being—stressing the importance of this in relation to being college students.

Analysis of Occasion:

A. Nature: Weekly meeting held on Tuesdays at 6:00 P.M. in which all areas of business at hand are addressed, discussed, or reviewed.

B. Prevailing Rules: A time limit of about five minutes and additional time for questions, with speech beginning directly at 6:00 P.M.

C. Precedents and Consequences: Speech to be given directly at 6:00, at beginning of the meeting so that the members' minds are fresh and clear to solely focus or concentrate on the importance of my subject.

D. Physical Environment: The speech is to be held at the sorority lodge in the main meeting room with rows of chairs set up for the audience. Tables where the officers usually sit are to be set up in front of the chairs. (I spoke in front of these tables—sitting on one in the middle.)

Analysis of Audience:

A. Composition:
1. About forty-five old and new members, plus the seven officers and the three alumnae.
2. Age: The forty-five old and new members and officers range from ages 18–22, and the alumnae range in ages 28–35.
3. Sex: All females.
4. Occupation: Majority are college students with many interests. Occupations of alumnae: nurse, housewife/mother, small-business owner.
5. Education: Majority are pursuing degrees in Sciences and Arts. The alumnae all have bachelor's degrees only (in nursing, management, and marketing).
6. Membership in groups: Some members of the sorority are involved in many clubs at school and participate in intramurals, like softball, basketball, flag football, volleyball, etc. Also, some are members of health clubs or take aerobics at school or use the weight room.
7. Cultural/Ethnic Background: All members are Anglo-Americans, except for one member who is from Venezuela and two who are Mexican, but were raised in America (this is really of no concern).

B. Knowledge of Subject:
1. Most members have general knowledge of the importance of eating right and exercising.
2. Some of the members have specialized knowledge in aerobics itself and the benefits that come from it.

*This analysis is based on a sample analysis from Ehninger, D., et al. *Principles and Types of Speech Communication:* 9th ed.; Glenview, Illinois: Scott, Foresman Publishers, 1982, pp. 95–98.

3. Most members have probable knowledge of the importance and positive aspects of being in an aerobics program—to stay fit mentally and physically. In other words, it's the year of the "fitness craze," and almost everybody is aware of this.

C. Beliefs, Attitudes, and Values:

   1. Some members value their body and mental attitude and believe they should take care of it (preventing diseases and being able to sleep better, think better, and have more self-confidence). Other members don't care about the way they look or feel (many mixed values and beliefs).

   2. Some members have the attitude that there are no benefits from aerobic exercise because maybe they haven't witnessed or experienced them, whereas others have the attitude that it is *the* form of exercise in which you get the most benefits mentally and physically. (There are a lot of mixed attitudes, values, and beliefs.)

D. Disposition Toward the Speaker: Members probably see me as a credible representative of the subject because I am involved in an aerobics program and always come to the meeting after aerobics class in my aerobics attire. Almost all the members know I'm an "aerobics freak."

E. Disposition Toward Subject: Interest in the importance of aerobics is mixed. Just being around some members and hearing them talk, I can gather that some of them don't care about aerobic exercise (mostly by their attitude and how they look). On the other hand, I can gather that other members are interested in or concerned about the importance of aerobics because many of them ask me questions all the time about aerobics in general. They tell me that they want to start doing aerobics because they've heard it was fun or that they've heard about the benefits of it.

F. Disposition Toward Speech Purpose and Occasion: Most sorority members are aware of and interested in hearing about the importance of aerobic exercise because of the positive effects it has on one's health and well-being, but others are probably not aware or don't care for exercising at all. Although a speech of this nature is not common at the sorority meetings, several members I spoke with said they would be interested and would be there on time.

Proposed Adaptation to Audience and Occasion:

A. Introduce speech and make a brief connection with subject and the value of it in relation to being a college student.

B. Bring up the fact that most college students gain at least ten pounds within the first year because of lack of exercise; hence, they need to be informed about the importance of aerobic exercise.

C. Stress my values, attitudes, and beliefs about aerobic exercise and show them my knowledge about the subject and how important I think exercise is.

D. Keep language simple, straightforward, serious, positive, clear throughout the speech—especially when explaining the studies that were done.

E. Be prepared to answer general or specific questions about my topic.

Thesis Statement: Aerobic exercise can have a long-term positive effect on the functions of the body and the mind.

INFORMATIVE OUTLINE DEVELOPED FROM AUDIENCE ANALYSIS: AEROBIC EXERCISE

Note: Inclusion of transition statements.

General Purpose: To create understanding.

Specific Purpose: To create understanding about aerobic exercise and the positive effects it has on one's health and well-being.

Thesis: Aerobic exercise can have a long-term positive effect on the functions of the body and the mind.

Introduction

I. Did you know that aerobic exercise can be the number one answer to all your health and mental needs?

II. These days everyone seems to be taking better care of themselves. Also, I'm in an aerobics program, so I can speak from experience.

III. Aerobic exercise can have a long-term positive effect on the functions of the body and mind.

    A. Effects of aerobics on the functions of the body.

    B. Effects of aerobics on the functions of the mind.

Transition: First let's consider the effect of aerobics on the body.

Body

I. Aerobic exercise can make the body function better.

    A. Your sleeping habits are affected.

        1. Sleep comes much easier and you are able to sleep more soundly.

        2. The active person who sleeps less than most is usually more wide awake all day, compared to the inactive person who can stay in bed ten hours and still feel listless the next day.

    B. Aerobic exercise can also help to prevent or aid in the care of certain diseases.

        1. Lung diseases such as asthma, bronchitis, and emphysema all seem to be more common among the inactive.

        2. Heart disease, even though hereditary, can be controlled through aerobic exercise.

Transition: If aerobic exercise benefits the body, it can do wonders for the mind.

II. Aerobic exercise can help the mind function better.

    A. Improved endurance and performance through exercise makes the body less susceptible to fatigue and consequently less prone to commit mental or physical errors.

        1. Performance on test—able to recall more and think more clearly.

        2. Performance of your job can be sustained longer without necessity for frequent breaks—therefore, you have a more productive day.

    B. Aerobic exercise can improve your self-image.

        1. Seem to gain an overwhelming amount of confidence in yourself.

        2. Have a better outlook on your problems and everything that is going on around you. (Review of study done.)

Conclusion

I. So, as you can tell, an aerobics program can be essential to a longer and happier life because of its effects on these functions of the body and mind.

II. Remember that just as the mind can psychosomatically impose ailments (like ulcers) on the body, the body can also impose ailments on the mind—aerobic exercise can be a valve for relieving both.

Selecting Topics and Purposes

This unit provides you with the essential information necessary to select and develop a topic that will match your purpose and your audience's expectations. In addition, this unit helps you understand the similarities and differences between specific purpose and thesis statements. The ability to compose clear and specific purpose and thesis statements is essential to achieving coherence in your messages. The exercises in this unit will help you in the initial planning stages of your speech as you select and develop your topics.

The components of UNIT 7 are:

Selecting Topics and Purposes: Notes

Self-Analysis for Speech Topics

Narrowing Speech Topics

**Understanding the Similarities and Differences Between
Specific Purpose and Thesis Statements**

Specific Purposes and Thesis Statements: An Exercise

Writing Thesis Statements

Topic Justification Exercise: Informative

Topic Justification Exercise: Persuasive

SELECTING TOPICS AND PURPOSES: NOTES

One of your most important tasks in the public speaking course is selecting a topic and developing it for a particular purpose (usually assigned by the instructor) and for your particular audience. Technically this task consists of four separate components: (1) selecting a topic, (2) determining your purpose, (3) analyzing your audience, and (4) developing your topic to match your purpose and audience expectations. When you consider their connections, however, it works best to approach these tasks simultaneously. In other words, how you select and develop your topic is, in part, determined by the purpose and occasion for speaking as well as your particular audience. Unit 6 provides you with exercises to help you analyze your audience while this unit provides you with exercises to help you select and develop your topic and purposes for speaking.

Your knowledge of and interest in a topic should be the primary consideration when selecting topics for your classroom speeches. In situations outside the classroom, individuals are invited to speak because of their expertise and experience in a particular area. In a classroom situation this is not the case. Nevertheless, you should approach your speaking engagement in the classroom in a similar manner. That is, select a topic based on your knowledge, experience, and interest in that topic.

The second criteria for selecting and developing a topic should be its interest and significance to the audience. Although you may be an "expert" on a particular topic, that topic may not be suited for your audience or for the situation, or it may be a topic that has been overused. For example, wearing seat belts and drinking while driving are two topics that are frequent choices for classroom speeches. Unless you can develop those topics with fresh approaches, you might want to select another topic to fulfill the second criteria of interest and significance to your audience.

The final consideration in selecting and developing a topic is that it must be limited in scope and purpose. You need to consider the time limitations for delivering your speech as well as the general purpose for speaking. The general purpose must address *why* you are speaking. The three general purposes for speaking in public are:

1. To entertain or to generate enjoyment.
2. To inform or to create understanding.
3. To persuade or to gain acceptance of an idea or to motivate the audience to act.

SELF-ANALYSIS FOR SPEECH TOPICS

Objectives

1. To use a brainstorming process to generate topics for classroom speeches.
2. To use one's own knowledge and interest to select topics for classroom speeches.

Explanation

The basic premise for effective speech preparation is simple: The more you know about a subject, the more comfortable and confident you will feel. If you are strongly interested in a particular topic, that interest will carry through in preparation and in delivery. Interest, like energy or excitement, is contagious. Look to your own knowledge and interest for topics. Consider the things you do and know well. For example, one student gave a very informative and interesting speech on how to pot and nourish houseplants. What made the speech interesting is that she could (through her own knowledge and experience) go beyond the ordinary and the mundane. She knew the effect of water and sunlight on particular plants. She understood and explained particular kinds of soil composition. What she presented was not merely read in a book and presented in an organized fashion. It was a speech on a subject that she knew well and about an activity that she enjoyed.

Instructions

Using a brainstorming technique of freethinking and uncensored response, complete the following activity to help you select your speech topic from your own knowledge and interest. Select a place where you feel comfortable and can relax and concentrate. Allow enough time to really get into the spirit of this exercise. This initial self-analysis can prove an invaluable reference aid throughout the course.

Take a blank sheet of paper for each category. Write the general topic plus the three columns of *what, areas,* and *interest* at the top of the page. Using concentration and association, jot down whatever comes to your mind. Use the questions in each category to stimulate your thinking. See the example below.

Example: Hobby or Leisure Activities

What	Areas	Interest
Sailing	Racing	Peaceful
	How to sail	Relaxing
	Wind directions	Social activity
	Types of boats	Types of people
		Challenging

Hobby or Leisure Activities

1. What are your hobbies? What do you like to do in your spare time?

2. What particular aspects of these hobbies or activities are you knowledgeable in or interested in?

3. Why are you interested in them? Why do you enjoy them?

Major/Minor Areas of Study

1. What are they? What are you considering?

2. What aspects interest you?

3. Why?

Career Goals

1. What kind of career/job do you want?

2. What particular areas of interest do you have in that kind of job? What in particular do you know or want to know about that career?

3. Why do you want that kind of job or career?

Major Events/Problems at Your University or Local Community

1. What are they? What aspects of the event/problem affect you?

2. What are your particular concerns or areas of interest?

3. Why are you concerned? How are you affected?

The following questions can also generate topics reflecting your knowledge and interest:

1. Who is/was the most influential person or character in your life? Why?

2. What is your favorite book/film? Why?

3. What was the most interesting vacation? Where? Why?

NARROWING SPEECH TOPICS

Objectives

1. To narrow a general topic to a specific one.
2. To analyze and adapt your topic to purpose, audience, and time limit.

Explanation

One of the most common problems in classroom speeches is that students try to cover too much territory in too little time. In effect, they attempt to tell all they know about a given topic instead of creating understanding about one aspect of that topic. In merely giving information about a topic, speakers usually fail to relate or adapt the message to their audience.

Instructions

Analyze the following topics, audiences, and general purposes and use them to write a specific topic and a specific purpose for a five- to seven-minute speech.

Topic: College education.
Audience: Seniors in your high school.
General Purpose: To influence or to convince.
Specific Topic:

Specific Purpose:

Topic: College education.
Audience: Your classmates in public speaking.
General Purpose: To influence or to convince.
Specific Topic:

Specific Purpose:

Topic: College education.
Audience: Your classmates in public speaking.
General Purpose: To inform or to create understanding.
Specific Topic:

Specific Purpose:

UNDERSTANDING THE SIMILARITIES AND DIFFERENCES BETWEEN SPECIFIC PURPOSE AND THESIS STATEMENTS

The ability to compose a clear, specific purpose is essential in the development of your topic. A specific purpose for an informative speech is exactly what you want the audience to understand about your topic. In a persuasive speech, the specific purpose states what you want your audience to think, to believe, or to do. In planning the specific purpose for your speech, make sure that the specific purpose:

1. Will fulfill the general purpose for the speech.

2. Can be accomplished in the time limit.

3. Is clear and specific rather than vague and broad.

4. Is relevant and significant to your audience.

The thesis (or central idea) is a direct, declarative statement expressing the main point of your informative speech. It is an assertive statement that expresses your observation or conclusion about your topic. The thesis is similar to the specific purpose in content but it is different in form. The thesis is a declarative sentence while the specific purpose is a full infinitive phrase. The following example illustrates the similarity and the difference:

General Purpose: To inform or create understanding.

Specific Purpose: To describe the mental and physical benefits of aerobics.

Thesis: Aerobic exercise has a positive effect on the mind as well as the body.

It is important to have a strong, assertive thesis and not just a topic sentence. For example, "Today I want to talk about the value of aerobics" is merely a topic sentence and is ineffective as a thesis because it is vague.

In a persuasive speech, the specific purpose states what you want your audience to think, to believe, or to do. The proposition, similar to the thesis, is the statement in your speech that asserts what you want your audience to do, to think, or to believe. Again it is similar to the specific purpose in content but different in form. Consider the following example:

General Purpose: To persuade.

Specific Purpose: To convince my audience that they should preserve the wilderness because of its cultural and heritage values.

Proposition: We must preserve our wilderness areas because they are part of our culture and our heritage.

SPECIFIC PURPOSES AND THESIS STATEMENTS: AN EXERCISE

Name_____ Date_____

Objectives

    1. To understand the difference between a specific purpose and a thesis statement.
    2. To develop specific purposes and thesis statements from topics.

Instructions

From the list of topics below, write a specific purpose and a thesis statement for a six- to eight-minute informative speech.

Topic: My favorite cartoon character or hero.
Specific Purpose:

Thesis:

Topic: My favorite recreation.
Specific Purpose:

Thesis:

WRITING THESIS STATEMENTS

Name_____ Date_____

Objective

1. To write thesis statements that are simple and direct (to the point), declarative, and assertive (making a point or asserting an idea).

Instructions

Rewrite the following vague or inappropriate thesis statements so that they adhere to the characteristics of a good thesis statement.

1. How to execute a football play.

2. The tradition of Christmas tree trimming.

3. I would like to tell you about some useful occupations.

4. People make many wrong decisions in their lives.

5. The trauma of dorm life.

TOPIC JUSTIFICATION EXERCISE: PERSUASIVE

Name_____ Date_____

1. What is the specific purpose of your speech? In other words, what do you want your audience to believe or to do as a result of your speech?

2. Describe your knowledge, experience, and interest in your topic or specific purpose. (*Convince* your instructor that you feel strongly about your specific purpose.)

3. After interviewing members of your audience, what are their predispositions (attitudes) toward your topic or specific purpose? In addition, describe your audience's knowledge of your topic.

4. What are the causes for your audience's predispositions? In other words, why do you think they feel the way they do?

5. How will you address your audience's predispositions to your topic? In other words, what organizational strategies and appeals will you use to accomplish your specific purpose?

Developing and Supporting Ideas

A thorough understanding of your audience's needs and expectations, with a knowledge of the specific speaking purpose and situation will go a long way in helping you develop your speech. This unit challenges you to develop ideas and supporting materials for several different topics for your classroom speeches. In addition, you are asked to analyze outlines that are poorly developed and unsupported as well as outlines that are well developed and supported. An excellent speech must first of all be one that has substance—ideas that are well developed and supported and are relevant to the audience and the speech purpose.

The components of UNIT 8 are:

Types of Supporting Materials

Developing Main Ideas from a Thesis or a Specific Purpose

Prepare Speeches, Not Reports: An Exercise

Problematic Development of Ideas and Supporting Materials

Discovering and Improving Supporting Materials

"Air Bags" Speech for Analysis of Supporting Materials

"Drunk Driving" Speech for Analysis of Supporting Materials

Documenting and Using Credible Sources

"Endangered Birds" Speech

TYPES OF SUPPORTING MATERIALS

Supporting materials make the difference between a dull, mundane speech and an interesting, vivid speech. They also make the difference between a speech that lacks logic, credibility, and believability and a speech that is logical, valid, and convincing.

Supporting materials are those pieces of information you use to explain, to illustrate, and to quantify your ideas in order to enhance understanding and to strengthen your speech purpose. The particular kinds of supporting materials you select to develop your ideas will depend on your speech purpose and your audience.

Types of Supporting Materials

1. Examples: factual or hypothetical instances.
2. Illustrations: factual or hypothetical narratives.
3. Testimony: opinions from expert, famous, or peer individuals.
4. Analogy: use of comparison and contrast.
5. Statistics: numbers that explain, make predictions, or show trends.

Criteria for Using Supporting Material

1. Does it relate to the speech purpose?
2. Is it appropriate for audience and situation?
3. Is it accurate?
4. Is it relevant?
5. Is it a reliable and unbiased source?
6. Does it enhance understanding?
7. Does it support your idea or point?

DEVELOPING MAIN IDEAS FROM A THESIS OR A SPECIFIC PURPOSE

Objectives

1. To practice developing a speech, working from a thesis to main ideas.
2. To practice developing main ideas with supporting materials.

Instructions

Develop two main ideas for the thesis and two main ideas for the specific purpose below. After you develop the main ideas, discuss what kinds of supporting materials you would use to develop the main points. Make sure that the ideas and their development meet the needs of the situation and audience.

Situation 1

Situation: One of your friends, teachers, or the principal has asked you to speak to the senior class of your former high school about college. The occasion is a special day called "Careers and Choices in Life." You have been asked to keep your remarks to about ten minutes.

Thesis: Choose a college, based on the quality of the academic major and the quality of the social life.

Situation 2

Situation: You have been asked to speak to a group of twenty-five students who will attend Freshman Orientation at your university and have expressed an interest in your major. You were asked to speak to this group by a friend of yours who is aware of the uncertainty felt and information needed by this particular group of students. You have been asked to keep your remarks to ten minutes.

Specific purpose: To explain to this group of freshmen the kinds of courses and requirements needed for your major and the learning experiences it can offer.

PREPARE SPEECHES, NOT REPORTS: AN EXERCISE

Objectives

1. To understand the difference between a speech and a mere report of information.
2. To develop a speech from information.

Explanation

The speech outline below is an example of a student classroom informative speech. As is obvious when you read it, the student merely reports information based on E. T. Hall's concept of distance. The student fails to develop the information for the audience and fails to use any of his or her own ideas.

Instructions

Working in small groups, discuss how you could use the information in the outline below to develop an informative speech for your classmates. Consider why and how this information would be useful to your audience. Develop a specific purpose, a thesis, and the main ideas of your own composition. In addition, discuss how and where in your speech you would use Hall's ideas as supporting materials.

Speech Outline

General Purpose: To inform.
Specific Purpose: To inform my audience about Edward T. Hall's four distances.

Introduction

 I. Attention-getting statement: Those of you in the front are probably distressed that I am attempting to give my speech standing so close to you, just as others of you might feel when a stranger sits down in the seat beside you in an uncrowded movie theater.
 II. Need for listening: Edward T. Hall researched why humans feel uncomfortable in situations like these and determined that the reason was an invasion of personal space.
 III. Thesis: There are four distances described by Hall that dictate how we will react in certain situations when approached by other humans.
   A. Intimate distance.
   B. Personal distance.
   C. Social distance.
   D. Public distance.

Body

 I. Intimate distance.
   A. Measures distance from actual touching to eighteen inches.
     1. Presence of other person is unmistakable.
     2. Sensory inputs are increased.

B.   Distance of lovemaking, wrestling, comforting, and protecting.
    1. Muscle and skin communicate messages.
    2. Hands are used most.
C.   Other situations.
    1. Crowded subways and buses.
    2. Usually involuntarily.

II. Personal distance.
    A.   Measures from one and one-half feet to four feet.
       1. Can grasp someone if arms are extended.
       2. No visual distortion.
    B.   Subjects of personal involvement and interest are discussed at this distance.
    C.   Distance used with friends and close associates.

III. Social distance.
    A.   Measures from four feet to twelve feet.
       1. Nobody expects to touch or to be touched.
       2. Gaze will shift to take in entire face.
    B.   Impersonal business occurs at this distance.
    C.   Common distance for social gatherings.
    D.   This is the distance of interviews, and it is important to maintain eye contact in order to encourage conversation flow.

IV. Public distance.
    A.   Measures from twelve to twenty-five feet.
       1. Gives the individual a feeling of protection.
       2. Fine details of skin and face are not visible.
    B.   Distance used by public speakers, actors, and performers.
    C.   A distance of thirty feet is automatically set around public figures.
    D.   The nonverbal part of communication shifts to gesture and stance.

Conclusion

I. Edward T. Hall's four distances are important in our everyday living and explain why people are offended when their space has been violated.

References

Hall, E. T. *The Hidden Dimension,* New York: Doubleday, 1966.

Hall, E. T. *The Silent Language,* New York: Anchor Books, 1959.

Sommer, R. *Personal Space: The Behavioral Basis of Design,* New Jersey: Prentice-Hall, 1969.

PROBLEMATIC DEVELOPMENT OF IDEAS AND SUPPORTING MATERIALS

Objectives

1. To analyze a poorly developed speech outline that has inconsistencies in ideas and purposes.
2. To analyze a speech outline that has inaccurate and confusing supporting materials.

Explanation

Unfortunately, some students do not do their homework and end up presenting a speech that has inaccurate and poorly developed supporting materials. The following speech outline is such an example. It appears that this individual obtained his or her information about "Cajuns" from a superficial, very uninformed source. Even if you do not know much about the Cajun culture, you can discover the inconsistencies and inaccuracies in this outline.

Instructions

Working with a small group, identify the problems with the development of ideas and the supporting materials in the outline below. In addition, discuss why this speech might be offensive or inappropriate considering its development and some of the statements made.

Speech Outline

Introduction

I.   When I say "Cajun," what type of person do you visualize? Do you visualize a person who wears overalls, a straw hat, and no shoes? a person who talks funny? or a person who has no education?

II. How would you feel if someone were prejudiced toward you for these reasons?

III. I think it is important for people to understand more about the Cajun lifestyle and language because television commercials and books have created a great deal of misconceptions about Cajuns.

IV. Thesis: Some people discriminate against Cajuns because they don't know where the Cajuns originated and why Cajuns live and talk differently.
   A.   Background.
   B.   Lifestyle.
   C.   Language.

Transition: First, I'll tell you about their background.

Body

I.   Cajun people have originated from several places and races.
   A.   They are descendants of French-Canadians.
   B.   They were originally located in Acadia (now Nova Scotia) where they were forced from. They wouldn't swear allegiance to the British Crown.

C. They relocated in the Gulf region of southern Louisiana.
D. Their ancestry is Indian, White, and Black.

Transition: Now we'll look at how they live.

II. Their lifestyle is definitely different from ours.
A. They live in self-contained communities.
B. They do a lot of farming.
C. They believe in making home crafts.
D. They do all their own spinning and weaving.

Transition: Finally, I will explain their language and why you can't understand Cajuns.

III. Their language is a distinctive dialect.
A. Most of their language is from archaic French.
B. It also has influences from Spanish, English, German, Black, and Indian.

Conclusion

I. Even though a Cajun's background, lifestyle, and language are different from yours, they are still people with feelings. This is true for any person of a different race or nationality.
II. So the next time you think someone who is Cajun talks funny, or someone who is Black looks weird, or someone who is Chinese dresses funny, think about what that person might think about you.

DISCOVERING AND IMPROVING SUPPORTING MATERIALS

Objectives

1. To identify the proper use of supporting materials in a speech outline.
2. To evaluate the use of supporting materials in a speech outline.

Instructions

On the following pages you will find two fully developed speech outlines. Identify the kinds of supporting materials used in each speech by specifying the name in the margin. For example, the first speech on "Air Bags" starts out with a hypothetical illustration. After you identify the kinds of supporting materials in the margins, evaluate the use of the supporting materials in each speech. Use the questions below as a guide in your evaluation. In addition, make suggestions as to ways the speeches could be improved through the use of different supporting materials or through the improved use of the supporting materials in the speeches.

Criteria for Evaluating Supporting Material

1. Does it relate to the speech purpose?
2. Is it appropriate for audience and situation?
3. Is it accurate?
4. Is it relevant?
5. Is it a reliable and unbiased source?
6. Does it enhance understanding?
7. Does it support your idea or point?

"AIR BAGS" SPEECH FOR ANALYSIS
OF SUPPORTING MATERIALS

General Purpose: To convince the audience.

Specific Purpose: To convince the audience (my class) that air bags should be required as standard safety equipment in all cars.

Attention

I. It's late at night. You're driving home on a small, unfamiliar country road after having visited friends that evening. You're thinking about what a great time you had or maybe about a term paper you need to write for a class. Suddenly, you come upon a sharp curve in the road. You're only going 15 mph, but you still can't make the curve. You lose control of the car. The car leaves the road and slams head-on into a tree.

II. In less than one-tenth of a second your body travels the two and one-half feet distance from the seat to the windshield. Your face hits with a force equal to that which you would experience if you had jumped off a six-story building. Chances are that you will not survive.

III. According to the Allstate Insurance Group, head-on and frontal collisions are the deadliest of all.

    A. Yet, when I surveyed the class, 80 percent of you are either unfamiliar with or skeptical toward one of the best devices for preventing serious injury or death in such collisions.

    B. That device is an air bag.

Need

I. Air bags could prevent many deaths and injuries each year.

    A. About 21,000 people are killed in cars each year.

        1. Many more are severely injured.

        2. More than half occur in frontal collisions.

    B. The Allstate Insurance Group has done extensive testing of methods to prevent injury and death in such collisions.

        1. Air bags are much more effective than seat belts at speeds in excess of 30 mph.

        2. They are certainly better protection than nothing for people who do not wear their seat belts.

II. But there is a problem.

    A. Air bags are not widely available.

        1. Optional on a small number of cars.

        2. Standard on even fewer.

    B. When available, the cost is high ($800) because they are not mass produced.

    C. The Secretary of Transportation has declared that if states representing two-thirds of the national population adopt seat belt laws, then air bags will not be mandatory.

        1. This either/or approach will not help save lives.

        2. We need both.

Satisfaction

I. Air bags should be required as standard safety features on all automobiles sold in the United States.
  A. Allstate's study reports that if air bags were in all cars, 10,000 deaths could be prevented each year.
  B. Allstate's study reports that if air bags were in all cars, 100,000 serious injuries could be prevented each year.
II. Air bags are safe and reliable.
  A. They work very efficiently.
    1. Inflate in less than 1/25 of a second upon sufficient collision.
    2. Provide soft cushion for your body.
    3. Deflate quickly after crash to allow breathing and exit.
  B. Extensive testing at Dynamic Science Laboratories resulted in no accidental inflations.
    1. Do not deploy in "fender-benders," panic stops, road bumps, or potholes.
    2. Always worked as expected.
  C. In fact, air bags are the most tested and proven auto safety system in history.
III. The use of air bags is endorsed by many important organizations.
  A. National Safety Council.
  B. American Medical Association.
  C. Insurance Institute for Highway Safety.

Visualization

I. Now let's go back to that same evening we envisioned earlier.
  A. It's late at night, and you're driving down that unfamiliar country road.
    1. Suddenly a sharp curve in the road appears.
    2. You lose control.
    3. The car leaves the road and hits a tree.
  B. But this time the sensors detect the crash, and immediately the air bag comes out of the steering wheel.
    1. A soft cushion is provided between you and the windshield.
    2. You walk away with minor cuts.
II. If air bags were standard equipment, it would save money.
  A. The cost of air bags would go down to about $200.
  B. According to Richard Hayen, President of Allstate Insurance Group, auto, health, and life insurance costs would decrease.

Action

I. To those of you who were unfamiliar or undecided about air bags, I hope you now see and believe how important they are.
II. To those of you who were skeptical about their reliability, I hope I have dispelled your doubts and fears.
III. What can you do to help get air bags in all cars?
  A. When buying your next car, search for one with an air bag.
  B. Write to representatives in Congress and urge them to pass laws requiring air bags in all new vehicles.

IV. Air bags can save lives, maybe even yours or someone's you love, but only if they are made more available.

References

"The Airtight Case for Air Bags," *The Saturday Evening Post,* November 1986, pp. 36–40.

"DRUNK DRIVING" SPEECH FOR ANALYSIS OF SUPPORTING MATERIALS

General Purpose: To convince my audience.

Specific Purpose: To convince my audience not to drive if they have been drinking.

Introduction

I. As most of you know, there are several traffic accidents caused by drunk drivers every day. But did you know that the number of traffic accidents involving drunk drivers last year is almost twice what it was two years ago?

II. Because several of my friends and I have gotten DUIs and several of my friends have been seriously injured or killed, I know what can result from drinking and driving. My audience survey revealed that about half of you drink and drive, so I would like to tell you what the likely consequences of drinking and driving will be.

III. We should refrain from drinking and driving because:

    A. It could save your life and/or the lives of other innocent drivers.

    B. If you are caught with a DUI, it will cost you a lot of money.

    C. If you are caught with a DUI, it could cause serious problems with your present or future employment.

Body

I. First, you should refrain from drinking and driving because you could seriously injure or kill yourself or others.

    A. The *Statistical Abstracts of the United States* reports that there are many fatalities that result from drunk drivers every year.

        1. There were 61,434 deaths in motor vehicles last year.

        2. Of these deaths, 20,384 of them resulted from drunk drivers.

        3. So, 33 percent of these deaths were caused by drunk drivers.

    B. I know from firsthand experience how such injuries or deaths can occur.

        1. A friend of mine was killed two months ago.

        2. Another friend of mine was seriously injured and almost died two years ago.

        3. I also have a former employer who is serving eighteen years in the penitentiary.

II. Second, you should refrain from drinking and driving because if you are caught, it could cost you a lot of money.

    A. The consequences for being convicted for DUI in Kentucky are severe.

        1. For the first offense:

            a. Five hundred dollar fine.

            b. A night in jail.

            c. Thirty-day suspension of license.

            d. Drunk drivers' school.

            e. Retake written test and eye test.

        2. For the second offense:

            a. Five hundred fifty dollar fine.

            b. Thirty days in jail or an alcohol treatment center.

            c. One-year loss of license.

            d. Retake written and eye test.

B. The consequences for being convicted is even more severe in other states, such as Florida.
    1. For the first offense:
        a. Automatic seven days in jail.
        b. One thousand dollar fine.
        c. One-year loss of license.
        d. Drunk drivers' school.
    2. For second offense:
        a. Thirty days in jail.
        b. Two thousand dollar fine.
        c. Five-year loss of license.
        d. Retake written test and eye test.
C. DUI can also affect your car insurance.
    1. First offense: rate usually doubles or triples.
        a. A friend's went from $2,100 to $6,300.
    2. The company could also cancel your policy.
D. Even if you are not caught, driving drunk increases the chances for costly damages to your car.
    1. Cost a friend of mine $9,000.
    2. Cost me $4,000 three years ago.

III. Last, you should refrain from drinking and driving because it could cause serious problems in holding your present job or getting a future job.
    A. My stepbrother lost his job because of a drunk driving conviction.
    B. Job applications and interviews require a response to any convictions.
    C. Some businesses won't hire you because of high insurance rates.

Conclusion

I. We should all refrain from drinking and driving because it could help save your life or those of others; it can save you a lot of money; and it can help prevent employment problems.

II. The effort it takes to find safe transportation when you drink will be well worth it in the long run.

References

"Fatal Traffic Accidents," *Statistical Abstracts of the United States,* 1989, p. 610. Judge Royce Smith, District Court, Jennings, KY. November 17, 1989.

DOCUMENTING AND USING CREDIBLE SOURCES

Objectives

1. To understand the importance of documentation and credible sources.
2. To analyze a speech for its use of documentation and sources.

Instructions

Read the following speech, "Endangered Birds," presented by a university student enrolled in a public speaking class. Respond to the questions below and discuss your responses with your classmates.

Questions for Discussion

1. Did the speaker sufficiently document his or her sources? Explain.

2. Did the speaker effectively incorporate source references in the speech? Explain.

3. Are the sources reliable and unbiased? Why or why not?

4. Are the sources relevant and appropriate for the topic and the audience? Why or why not?

5. Evaluate the speech for its use of documentation and sources.

"ENDANGERED BIRDS" SPEECH

Introduction

   I.   There are 8,700 species of birds worldwide.
- A.   In 1985, the Convention on International Trade in Endangered Species (CITES) found forty-seven species that would not make it to the turn of the century.
- B.   In 1990, CITES found nearly one thousand species that would not make it to the turn of the century.

  II.   A great deal of this destruction could be avoided if the United States would pass legislation against the collection of birds for the U.S. pet trade.

 III.   Today, I would like to illustrate the extent of the devastation of endangered species.
- A.   I would like to propose a simple plan to alleviate some of the problems.
- B.   I will show several plans that are already in effect.
- C.   I would like to urge you to do your part in the preservation of both the pet bird industry and the wild bird population.

Body

   I.   We can no longer ignore the cries of our fellow earth species.
- A.   Ed Castles, President of the International Union for Conservation of Nature and Natural Resources (IUCN), states that twenty million birds are trapped each year for the U.S. pet industry.
- B.   Only eight million will survive the travel, the rest die.
- C.   The Environmental Investigation Agency (EIA) investigated the current system for bringing imported birds to the U.S. pet trade.
  - 1.   Birds are trapped by waterholes, using a lure.
  - 2.   Packed into huge crates, overcrowded, little ventilation.
  - 3.   Travel in these boxes in stifling heat for hundreds of miles to a distribution center.
  - 4.   Air shipped to U.S. quarantine stations for sixty days.
- D.   The current system blocks importation of certain species that are "very" endangered.
- E.   Poaching is widespread: 100,000 birds were smuggled in through Texas last year.
  - 1.   After being trapped or robbed from the nest, the birds are drugged and bound.
  - 2.   Then the birds are smuggled in spare tires or behind body panels of cars into the United States.
- F.   Smuggled birds offer a substantial health risk to U.S. citizens.
  - 1.   Wild birds are carriers of chlamydia.
  - 2.   In 1970, twelve million dollars worth of chickens, turkeys, and waterfowl were killed by Newcastle disease—directly related to smuggling activities.

Satisfaction

   I.   A nationwide, complete ban of the importation of exotic birds for the pet trade would greatly increase the chances of survival for the birds.
- A.   Support from the public by not purchasing any products from any stores that continue to sell importation-stricken pets.

1. Resist smugglers trying to offer a deal that sounds too good to be true.
2. Establish a nationwide marking system to distinguish between imported and domestic birds.

Visualization

I. A full ban has been enacted in the state of New York since 1984.
   A. The pet shops have not suffered.
   B. The customers have not suffered.
   C. The only problems have been with neighboring states.
   D. There will be a full ban throughout the western European countries effective in 1993.

Conclusion

I. In conclusion, this is not a matter of finances, lifestyles, or even international protocol. These animals are being butchered in the wild to support our desire for luxury.
   A. I have illustrated the extent of the destruction. I have proposed a simple plan to alleviate some of the problems. I have shown two plans that are helping.
   B. Now, I urge all of you to do what you can to help the populations in the wild recover.
      1. Do not support any stores that sell imported birds.
      2. Do not purchase any birds from known poachers or smugglers.
      3. Support any legislation that may help the ban on imported birds in the U.S. pet trade.
   C. The time is now for action, not rhetoric. Unfortunately, action moves slowly in our country, but extinction moves swiftly and is forever.

References

Ambramson, Joanen. "The Large Macaws," *American Cage Bird,* October 1991, pp. 28–32.
Clark, William D. "Hyacinths of the Pantanal," *Bird Talk,* February 1991, pp. 27–35.
Currey, Dane. "Will Europe Ban Wild Bird Imports?" *Defenders,* November/December 1990, pp. 21–25.
Samuelson, Phillip. "Voice Your Concern," *Bird Talk,* November 1991, p. 5.
Simon, Laura. "New York's Crusade for Exotic Birds," *Defenders,* November/December 1990, pp. 26–38.

Using Logical and Emotional Appeals

In preparing persuasive speeches you need to provide logical as well as emotional reasons why your audience should accept your proposition—what you want them to think, believe, or do. You want your audience to see the argument that you present in the same way that you do. This unit will help you understand logical and emotional appeals and how to use them effectively in your persuasive speeches.

The components of UNIT 9 are:

Logical Appeals and Sound Reasoning

Emotional Appeals and Motivational Needs

Questions of Fact: An Exercise

A Proposition of Fact for Analysis

Questions of Value: An Exercise

A Proposition of Value for Analysis

Questions of Policy: An Exercise

A Proposition of Policy for Analysis

Analyzing Persuasion: An Exercise

The Value of the Western Movie: An Outline

Join the Military: An Outline

LOGICAL APPEALS AND SOUND REASONING

Persuasive speeches must contain logical appeals or sound reasons why the audience should accept the speaker's proposition or claim. An effective persuasive speech uses logical, well-reasoned arguments supported with evidence or proof that is cogent and believable.

Types of Reasoning for Logical Appeals

1. **Inductive reasoning** is the process of reasoning from specific examples to a general conclusion. Using this process, you reach a conclusion (or a claim) that is based on specific examples, testimonies, facts, and statistics. For example, a speaker might assert the following:

   My brother, John, said the logic course he took was difficult.
   Mary, who is an honor student, barely made a "C" in another logic course.
   I saw one of the texts, and it looks quite complicated.
   Therefore, logic courses are difficult.

   For the audience to accept the conclusion, they would need to be convinced that the examples are representative and valid.

2. **Deductive reasoning** is the process of reasoning from a general premise to a specific conclusion. Using this process, you can organize your arguments in the form of a syllogism that has a major premise, a minor premise, and a conclusion. To make a logical and valid argument, you must substantiate your major and minor premises. For example, in speaking to a group of high school seniors, the speaker might claim the following:

   A college degree is required for higher-paying, white collar jobs.
   Most of you desire white collar jobs.
   Therefore, you need to get a college degree.

   For the audience to accept the conclusion (the need for a college degree), the speaker would have to provide evidence (proof) that a college degree is indeed required for high-paying jobs. In addition, the speaker would have to convince the audience that they should value white collar jobs.

3. **Causal reasoning** is the process of establishing a relationship between causes and effects. For example, a speaker might argue that when the highway speed limit was increased to 65 mph, highway fatalities increased. Therefore, the speaker would be suggesting that the higher speeds are causing the increase in fatalities. A common error in causal reasoning is assuming that events have only one cause. Acknowledging multiple causes for any event is important, as well as realizing that not all the causes are equally important; some may have more impact than others.

4. **Analogical reasoning** is the process of reasoning by comparing two similar cases and inferring that what is true for one case must be true for the other. Reasoning by comparison or contrast is frequently used for questions of policy in which the speaker asks the audience to accept a new policy. In this case, the speaker would describe how the present policy is inadequate and how the proposed policy would be more effective by comparison.

The Value of Evidence

Whatever type of reasoning you use, you must prove your arguments with evidence from credible sources. Evidence consists of facts, examples, statistics, and expert opinions. These supporting materials as well as the credibility of the sources are discussed in Unit 8, "Developing and Supporting Ideas."

EMOTIONAL APPEALS AND MOTIVATIONAL NEEDS

Individuals are not motivated solely by logic. Our values, beliefs, and desires are the emotional appeals that govern our thoughts and actions. Therefore, in preparing your persuasive speeches it is important to understand the basic motivating needs of human beings. Human motivations are governed by an individual's needs, wants, or desires. A motivational need, therefore, is an impulse to think and act in response to a psychological want or a biological urge.

Abraham Maslow* classified the fundamental human needs into five categories, beginning with the most basic needs.

1. *Physiological Needs:* the basic bodily requirements of food, drink, air, sleep, sex.
2. *Safety Needs:* security, stability, protection from harm or injury; need for structure, order, law, predictability; freedom from fear and chaos.
3. *Acceptance and Love Needs:* love and affection with spouse, children, parents, friends; need to belong and be a part of social groups; need for approval.
4. *Esteem Needs:* self-esteem based on achievement, competence, confidence, freedom, independence; need for recognition by others; prestige, status.
5. *Self-Actualization:* self-fulfillment, to realize your potential, to actualize your capabilities.

In analyzing your audience and preparing your persuasive speech, consider the power of motivational needs to impel human action and direct human thought. Use these needs to appeal to your audience for reasons why they should listen or how they might benefit from your speech. Many successful public speakers use the basic human wants, needs, and desires to persuade their audience.

---

*Abridged selection from *Motivation and Personality,* Third Edition by Abraham H. Maslow; revised by Robert Frager et al. Copyright 1954, 1987 by Harper & Row, Publishers, Inc.; Copyright ©1970 by Abraham H. Maslow.

QUESTIONS OF FACT: AN EXERCISE

Objectives

1. To understand how to use logical arguments to develop a proposition of fact.
2. To analyze a speech for its use of logical appeals.

Explanation

Persuasive speeches that center on questions of fact must establish the truth of the proposition or claim. In such cases, the speaker structures an argument using facts, statistics, examples, or expert opinions to gain audience belief or acceptance of the proposition.

Instructions

Read both the speech situation below and the speech on the following pages and then respond to the questions for analysis. Share your responses with your classmates.

Speech Situation

This speech, "The Dimensions of the Oppression of Women," was delivered by Phyllis Jones Springen in December 1970 at the Danforth Foundation's Annual Conference. The foundation has encouraged people to empathize with humane values through its concern for liberal education and equal education opportunities for the disadvantaged. One of the foundation programs provides graduate fellowships for women. Ms. Springen, a teacher and adult educator, spoke to an audience probably sympathetic to her message.

Questions for Analysis and Evaluation

1. What evidence does the speaker offer in support of the proposition that "there exists a tremendous amount of legal and economic discrimination against the American woman"?

2. Does the speaker provide sufficient evidence to support her proposition? Why or why not?

3. Do you agree that her proposition was accurate back in 1970? Could you agree with her proposition today? Why or why not?

4. What emotional appeals does the speaker use?

5. Evaluate the effectiveness of this speech based on its use of logical appeals and evidence.

A PROPOSITION OF FACT FOR ANALYSIS

The Dimensions of the Oppression of Women*

by Phyllis Jones Springen

1. When I was asked to speak on "The Dimensions of the Oppression of Women," I laughed. "Oppression" is such an ugly word. Our chairman must have been thinking of those Arab countries where women can't vote and where a woman can be forced to marry any man her father selects, but in the United States women are hardly "oppressed." But as I began to do my research, I quit laughing. There exists a tremendous amount of legal and economic discrimination against the American woman. Much of it is subtle and, therefore, hard to recognize.

2. You would think that we had all the legislation for women we need, but we don't. Two especially important pieces of legislation concerning women have been in Congress in the past six years. The first was Title VII of the Civil Rights Act of 1964, which prohibits discrimination in employment on the basis of race, color, religion, national origin, or sex. What most people don't know is that the word "sex," was proposed by eighty-one-year-old congressman Howard Smith of Virginia. We all remember Howard Smith, Chairman of the Rules Committee. He was no promoter of civil rights and certainly no feminist. His "little amendment," as he called it, was designed to defeat the bill. The bill passed, and although the provision for no discrimination on the basis of sex is not stringently enforced, it did lay the foundation for women's fight for equal employment.

3. The second piece of legislation, which did not pass in the last session of Congress, was the proposed Equal Rights Amendment to the United States Constitution. It read: "Equality of rights under the law shall not be denied or abridged by the United States or any state on account of sex." The amendment failed to pass, possibly because most people are unaware of the tangle of laws all across the United States which discriminate against women.

4. There are no clear-cut divisions, but we might divide these discriminatory laws into three categories. First, there are laws which are still on the books in many states which resemble archaic remnants of the feudal coverture law in which a married woman's legal responsibilities were covered by her husband. She had none. Texas recently repealed a law which held that a married woman could not be held responsible for a debt which she had incurred (her husband had to pay it).

5. When my husband and I moved to North Carolina eleven years ago, we were surprised to learn that if he had died without children and with a will, our property would have gone to his family. Fortunately, that law has been changed, but it's disturbing to realize that an archaic law like that was still in effect only eleven years ago. Many of these archaic coverture laws are still on the books.

6. Many states still restrict a married woman's right to sign a contract. Several states severely restrict her right to engage in a separate business. In Florida, for example, the law requires a married woman—no matter how well-educated—to petition and set forth her name, age, character, habits, education, and mental capacity for business, and reasons why such disabilities to engage in her own business should be removed. She must get her husband's consent or serve him with a copy of the petition. Only after the judge is satisfied, will he decree that she is able to control her own business.

7. Let's go to the second category. We find laws which are a sort of "back-handed compliment" to women. She is supposed to be of a higher order of virtue than the male. For example, many states require that a woman convicted of a crime be sentenced differently and generally more severely than a man. Right here in Pennsylvania in the Daniels case a woman was convicted of robbery and sentenced a maximum of four years. Then someone discovered a state law requiring different sentences for women, and she was given ten years instead of four. The conviction was finally

*From *Vital Speeches of the Day,* Vol. 37, February 15, 1971, pp. 265–267. Reprinted with permission.

overturned by the Supreme Court, but laws are still on the books in other states which require the different sentences.

8. This same assumption of a woman's higher virtue shows up in the double sex standard. In Oakland two prostitutes are appealing. They were convicted, but their clients were released. In Kentucky a husband can divorce a wife for a single act of adultery, but she cannot obtain a divorce on the same basis. Perhaps the most notorious injustice is the "Unwritten Law Defense" in New Mexico, Texas, and Utah in which a husband can be excused for murdering his wife's lover, but if the wife murders her husband's mistress, she is tried for murder.

9. A third group of discriminatory laws are those which were designed to protect women as fragile creatures but actually hurt them economically. Many state laws prohibit women from working at night—which in effect prevents them from getting overtime. The legislators forgot about protecting the cleaning women who clean the offices at 2:00 a.m. There are laws forbidding women to be bartenders but not bar maids who happen to receive less pay. And there are state laws which prohibit women from jobs in which certain weight restrictions are imposed. A woman is prevented from lifting a thirty-five pound sack at work but not a thirty-five pound child at home.

10. A final insult in the area of law is that only twenty-eight states permit women to serve on juries on the same basis as men. Let me give you an example of what has been happening in New York. A woman could be excused from jury duty by merely saying, "I am a woman." Up until last year if a female teacher decided to serve on a jury, she did not receive her pay because she could have been excused. A male teacher received his pay.

11. It was laws such as these: first, the coverture laws, which deny a woman legal responsibilities; second, the "back-handed compliment" laws, which assume a higher order of virtue for the woman; and third, the overprotective laws, which hurt her economically—it was these laws that the Equal Rights Amendment wanted to overturn. It will take years to overturn these laws one by one when a single amendment could have done it.

12. We have looked briefly at the legislation which discriminates against women. Let's look at the economic discrimination in detail. We find it appalling. Let me give you some figures from the most recent Department of Labor Fact Sheet on the Earnings Gap and from the April 1970 Report on the President's Task Force on Women's Rights and Responsibilities. The median wage or salary income of a woman who worked full-time in 1968 was only 58.2 percent of the male's. The gap has widened 5.7 percent since 1955. There is far more economic discrimination by sex than by race. The median earnings of white men employed full-time is $7,366, of Negro men $4,777, of white women $4,279, of Negro women $3,194. Women with some college education—both white and Negro—earn less than Negro men with eight years of education. Let me repeat that last statement. Women with some college education—both white and Negro—earn less than Negro men with eight years of education. These are full-time workers.

13. Many people are not bothered by these statistics. They assume that the man is the breadwinner and the woman is working either for a nebulous self-fulfillment or to put aside some extra money for the children's college education. Many of the women who work, work for harsh economic reasons. Many are widowed or divorced. Women head 1,723,000 impoverished families. Three-quarters of all the families at the poverty level are headed by women; one fourth of these are white. Only seven percent of those headed by white males are in poverty.

14. There are nearly a million "latch-key" children at this level. No one is watching them, and they wear an apartment key around their necks while their mothers work for menial wages. When those radical Women's Liberation females march December 12 in New York City and demand child-care centers, these are the children they are talking about.

15. Look at the other end of the economic scale. The earnings gap widens still further at the upper brackets. Women scientists and engineers are paid $2,500 to $3,000 a year less than men.

16. An infuriating example of unequal pay for equal work concerned a New Jersey manufacturer. Their chief financial officer was a woman paid $9,000 a year. When she left, they had to pay

a man $20,000 a year to do her job. When he left, they hired another woman at $9,000. When she left, they hired a man at $18,000. According to the recruiter, they were all good at the job.

17. The September 1970 AAUP Bulletin has an article on women in academe. Generally, girls have to have better academic records than boys even to enter graduate school. For those women who finally get Ph.D.'s the picture is still bleak. Columbia gives more doctorates to women than any other university and hopefully would have liberal hiring and promotional policies. A recent study was done of 195 males and 25 females on their faculty who had received their Ph.D.'s in the 1960s. Over fifty percent of the 195 males had received tenure at the rank of associate professor or above. None of the 25 females had. One had received tenure at the rank of assistant professor.

18. In 1969–70 thirty percent at the instructor level at Stanford were women; 1.6 percent of the full professors were. At the University of Michigan forty percent at the instructor level were women; 4.3 percent of the full professors were.

19. The Department of Labor Fact Sheet on the Earnings Gap showed that in 1966 the median annual salary for women who had finally made full professor was over $1,000 less than the men's. Clearly, even in academe *where reason and logic prevail,* women are still at the bottom.

20. I have tried to show how unfair laws are damaging to women, and I have tried to show briefly the extent of the economic discrimination against them. A third area, which I don't have time to develop, I'll mention briefly. It might be called psychological damage.

21. Gunnar Myrdal added an appendix to his *American Dilemma* entitled, "A Parallel to the Negro Problem." He traced the emancipation of both the slave and the woman with the economic changes of the Industrial Revolution. He went on to say that as in the Negro problem, most men had accepted as self-evident the doctrine that women had inferior endowments in most of those respects which carry prestige and power in society. (About the only thing not said about women is that they all have rhythm.)

22. Myrdal continued that as the Negro had his "place," so there was a "woman's place." The myth of the contented woman who did not want suffrage or civil rights had the same social function as the myth of the "contented Negro."

23. Her education was first neglected, then changed to a special type to fit her for her "place." He went on to say that the most important disabilities affecting a woman's status were those barring her attempt to earn a living and attain promotion in her work.

24. The same cycle Myrdal described is still present in 1970. A woman is not expected to earn a living. Laws still on the books treat her as an inferior creature. And the woman who does work— no matter how well qualified—often works for far less than the male—even the Negro male who is known to be the victim of discrimination.

25. I'd like to tell you what Shirley Chisholm, a Negro and a woman, had to say, and I'll use this as my conclusion. She was running for a congressional seat in Brooklyn in 1968 against James Farmer, who many of you remember was our speaker here at the Danforth Conference three years ago. His campaign staff was out in the streets telling the people that what they needed was a *strong male* leader. Mrs. Chisholm, who incidentally won, replied that just because a minority group wanted to get ahead, it did not follow that women had to take a step backward. I feel the same way.

QUESTIONS OF VALUE: AN EXERCISE

Objectives

1. To understand how to use emotional arguments to develop a proposition of value.
2. To analyze a speech for its use of emotional appeals.

Explanation

Persuasive speeches that center on questions of value must mesh the value judgments presented with those of the audience. In such cases, it is important for the speaker to establish credibility with his or her audience.

Instructions

Read both the speech situation below and the speech on the following pages and then respond to the questions for analysis. Share your responses with your classmates.

Speech Situation

This speech by Diane Klemme, "The Age of Gerontion," won first place in the Women's Division of the Interstate Oratorical Association contest. The speech was delivered by Ms. Klemme in Montana in May 1970.

Questions for Analysis

1. The speaker uses causal reasoning to present her case for the elderly. According to the speaker, what has our society done to cause problems for the elderly?

2. The speaker argues that we, as a society, do not value the elderly. What emotional appeals does she use to make these claims?

3. Do you agree with the speaker's claim that we, as a society, do not value the elderly? Why or why not?

4. What does the speaker say we need to do to learn to value the elderly?

5. Do you agree with the speaker's suggestions for dealing with the problems of the elderly? Why or why not?

6. Evaluate the effectiveness of this speech for its use of emotional appeals and evidence.

A PROPOSITION OF VALUE FOR ANALYSIS

The Age of Gerontion*

by Diane Klemme

1. She turned seventy-five last December. A year ago her husband suffered a cerebral hemorrhage which crippled and killed him before my grandmother's shocked eyes. Now she lives alone in the house she shared with grandfather for half a century, economically independent, proud that she can provide for herself in these her later years. Yet her independence cannot compensate for the limited mobility which isolates her from family and friends. Her pride cannot quell the fear she experiences daily: fear of assault and robbery by someone tempted by her slow steps and faltering cane.

2. Perhaps the problems of the independent elderly could be eased if they resided in a rest home or in the home of a relative. But in a home the aging often exchange problems of fear and isolation for problems of dehumanization and dependency. The twenty-three thousand rest homes in America servicing patients between the ages of sixty and eighty years for a period of five to ten years reduce the aging from human beings to statistics. Moreover in the home of a relative the aging member frequently assumes the position of a dependent child: a sixty-four-year-old mother who has enjoyed the domain of her own kitchen for forty years is pushed from the pots and simmering casseroles by an ever watchful, overzealous daughter determined to have her mother "relax" after years of housework; a fifty-seven-year-old widower so accustomed to juggling finances to educate three sons at college is not consulted when financial questions arise. Although the aging American may choose residency which guarantees economic well-being, he all too often sacrifices human dignity.

3. Either independent but fearful and immobile, or secure physically and socially but reduced to dependency—these are the circumstances in which the aging and aged find themselves, a limbo described by T. S. Eliot in "Gerontion":

> Here I am, an old man in a dry month,
> Being read to by a boy, waiting for rain. . . .
> I have lost my sight, smell, hearing, taste and touch,
> How should I use them for your closer contact?

4. Closer human contact between the aging American and succeeding generations has been prevented by a cycle of perceptions which defines a role for the elderly. Although the perceptions interact, the cycle can be sifted, and each perception analyzed: first, societal perception of the aging; second, familial perception; finally, the perception of the aging individual himself.

5. How do we as a society perceive the aging? In a culture that measures a man's worth on the basis of his productivity, those who age, who deteriorate physically and mentally are considered nonproductive. Sociologist Ruth Cavan indicates that ninety percent of the male heads of households find full-time employment before their sixty-fifth birthday; yet after they reach sixty-five, only thirty-four percent can hope for even part-time employment. And the "magical number" of sixty-five is being lowered. Industries like Ford Motor Company, feeling the pinch of inflation, have trimmed costs by trimming departments; those first considered for "Special Early Retirement" are fifty-five-year-olds deemed less productive than their younger colleagues. Society, therefore, perceives the aging as less productive, better suited to hobbies or to charity work.

6. Turning from the society that disclaims his usefulness, the aging American seeks understanding from his family, but even within the family, perceptions have changed; close human contact is denied. The children that he once fed, clothed, and educated, whose stories he patiently

*From *Winning Orations,* 1970. Reprinted by permission of Larry Schnoor, Executive Secretary, Interstate Oratorical Association.

listened to at the dinner table—these children have grown, married, and raised children of their own; the son and daughter of the widower ignored in financial decisions and the mother hustled from the kitchen no longer perceive themselves as dependent children owing allegiance to a self-sufficient parent; rather, the parents have become dependent, obligations, even burdens. The daughter might explain, "Mother has her own room which Tommy had to give up; we make no demands on her. She doesn't even have to come to the dinner table. What more can she want?" Or the son might rationalize, "Dad doesn't support himself on his own income like my wife and I do. He's no different in this case than our ten-year-old son. Why should he have any more to say about how we spend our money than our son does?" The supporting children may also attempt to alter the lifestyle of the parent, simply to spare themselves problems of adjustment. In the book *You and Your Aging Parents,* Doctors Stern and Ross report a case in which a daughter discarded her father's old golden oak desk; for her the desk was an eyesore, which she quickly removed, but to her father the desk had been a catch-all of memories, a place where he had studied late into the night to gain a degree and a better position, a place where his children had run for help with their homework.

7. Ostracized from society and deposed from independence by families—these are the circumstances of aging Americans. It is not surprising, then, that they perceive the role designed for them as less than a full life, an existence within the confines of the decisions of others. But the elderly only gradually assume that role. A man's children leave his house to begin families of their own; he retires and putters about the garden. The neighborhood shifts and changes around him; he no longer knows the names of his neighbors across the street; he only knows that their rowdy children trample the lawn he trims with ever increasing difficulty. He finds himself reading the obituary columns of the newspaper to learn of the deaths of friends, former employers. One day the woman with whom he has spent a lifetime dies; to him her death is a betrayal, for by her death he becomes completely isolated from human contact. And so he lives in memories, but these too are stripped from him as easily as a daughter removes an old golden oak desk. Finally he becomes like the widow in *Dandelion Wine,* convinced by the neighborhood children that she has never been young:

"How old are you, Mrs. Bentley?"
"Seventy-two."
"How old were you fifty years ago?"
"Seventy-two."
"You weren't ever young?"
"Never."
"Never in a million trillion years?"
"Never in a million trillion years."

8. The cycle is complete: perceptions of society, family, and individual carve an existence for the aging. And underlying the cycle there roots rejection of age, fear of dying. Our culture denies age by emphasizing youth. The media claims that to be over thirty is to be old. "The Jackie Gleason Show" will be canceled because it appeals to viewers who purchase less than their younger counterparts. A NASA scientist observed that a younger man's Ph.D. commands more options on the academic market. The tempo and fashions of our culture further the myth. Soft drinks like Pepsi are "for those who think young." Hair stylists tout coiffures which conceal balding spots of sensitive customers. *Bazaar* magazine runs an ad displaying a bare midriff as the female face of the future—a face both young and beautiful. We celebrate Aquarius.

9. We celebrate youth because we fear dying. As historian Arnold Toynbee explains:

Death is un-American. If the fact of death were once admitted to be a reality even in the United States, then it would also have to be admitted that the United States is not (an) earthly paradise.

Denial of age and fear of death underlie the cycle which dictates the role of the aging. The Age of Aquarius refuses to acknowledge the Age of Gerontion.

10. How can the cycle be broken so that the aging may fulfill dignifying roles? First, realize that the decades past fifty constitute a significant portion of human existence. Recently, an ad in *Newsweek* magazine announced: "If you were born in 1919, then you shouldn't be reading this ad. You're supposed to be dead." Life expectancy is no longer fifty years, but more than seventy years; a man remains dependent for twenty years, becomes independent for thirty-five years, then lives another twenty years in retirement—almost one-third of his life.

11. In that latter third of life, the aging must realize that as past options end, new options arise for creating an existence which does not merely "use up" the years remaining. Rather than allowing others to define the Age of Gerontion for what it is not, the aging themselves can redefine later life for what it is and can be. It is a season for intellectual betterment dictated not by professional demands but by personal goals, as a sixty-seven-year-old student of Oakland University demonstrates; having sold his pickle factory to the Vlasic Company, Mr. Schucart seeks a bachelor's degree in philosophy, attending every term except the winter semester. Aging is also a season for assisting a family with advice and counsel without the burden of maintaining that family. It is a season for preservation of lifestyles not simply materialistic, as the father of a young professor at my university has discovered; a restauranteur for four decades, he has an old world finesse which enhances the atmosphere of the modern restaurant in which he serves. Younger men may serve fifteen tables while he caters to ten, yet who would judge his charming but slower style less productive?

12. But those of us who have yet to age and those who approach the reflective season of our lives must also begin now to alter the cycle, to ensure options for ourselves as we grow older. With political action we can ensure that rest homes are made less impersonal by skilled, compassionate employees; we can enact legislation making it profitable for industry to use merit, not age, as criterion for retirement. With community resources, we can provide the aging options for travel; one Michigan Community offered reduced rates to senior citizens touring Europe last year. Individually, we must acknowledge that each of us will see the dry month; we must take time now to plan activities, to provide our own options for the latter third of our lives.

13. In a society which seeks to perpetuate longevity, we can no longer afford to celebrate youth and deny age. Both young and aging alike must work to overcome the cycle which deems age unproductive and burdensome. Only then can we answer Eliot's questioning "Gerontion." The answer Justice Oliver Wendell Holmes provided on his ninetieth birthday:

> The race is over, but the work never is done while the power to work remains. . . . For to live is to function. . . . And so I end with a line from [the] Latin poet: 'Death plucks my ear and says, Live—I am coming.'

QUESTIONS OF POLICY: AN EXERCISE

Objectives

    1. To understand how to use logical and emotional appeals to develop a proposition of policy.
    2. To analyze a speech for its use of logical and emotional appeals.

Explanation

Persuasive speeches that center on questions of policy argue that some action must be taken; these speeches are characterized by the word "should," with the speaker advocating that we should adopt a particular policy or plan of action. These speeches are also characterized by analogical reasoning, by which the speaker must show why the present system or policy is not working and why what is advocated will work.

Instructions

Read both the speech situation below and the speech on the following pages and then respond to the questions for analysis. Share your responses with your classmates.

Speech Situation

This speech by Kenda Creasy, "A Time for Peace," won first place at the Interstate Oratorical Association contest. The speech was delivered in Denver, Colorado, in May 1980.

Questions for Analysis

    1. The speaker compares the traditional American approach to terminal illness with the hospice approach. What does she claim are the problems with the traditional approach?

    2. What logical and emotional appeals does the speaker use to assert that the traditional approach is not working?

    3. According to the speaker, in what ways will the hospice approach be more advantageous and meet the needs of the terminally ill?

    4. What logical and emotional appeals does the speaker use to advocate the hospice approach?

5. Do you agree with the speaker's position? Why or why not?

6. Evaluate the effectiveness of the speech for its use of logical and emotional appeals and use of evidence.

A PROPOSITION OF POLICY FOR ANALYSIS

A Time for Peace*
by Kenda Creasy

1. "To all things there is a season; a time to every purpose under heaven—a time to be born, and a time to die. . . ."

2. Except today. Today modern medicine is better prepared to prolong life in all seasons. But for millions of Americans this year, it won't be enough. They will be diagnosed as terminally ill—and once labeled terminal, our medical know-how no longer applies. According to the Department of Health, Education and Welfare, you and I stand a one in four chance of suddenly assuming unexpected responsibilities because someone in our family has been diagnosed as terminally ill. But we could have help—with hospices.

3. A hospice is an alternative method of terminal care comprised of a team of doctors, psychologists, clergy, and volunteers who, basically, make house calls. A hospice's aim is to help people die with as little discomfort and as much serenity as possible, involving family and friends along the way, and usually taking place in the person's home. Hospices do not cure; instead, they make medical, psychological, and spiritual help available to both the patient AND his family, before and after the funeral. As one health analyst put it, "A hospice is really more of an idea than a place." Unfortunately, even though the hospice movement is supported by the American Medical Association and HEW, hospices in the United States are too unknown to have the impact they could have. So what can we do? Well, first we must compare hospices with our present ailing approach to terminal illness, and then see what we can do to remedy the problem. At least then we can stop sacrificing a quality of life for a quantity of days.

4. The traditional American approach to terminal illness ignores three basic facts of life: the limits of curative medicine, the isolation of institutions, and the psychological impact death has on both the patient and his family. The first problem is the inherent limits of a medical system designed to cure. Hospitals *maintain* life: everything from visiting hours to progress reports are designed for the temporary stay. But the terminal patient's stay is *not* temporary; he will not get well. *Time* magazine pointed out in June, 1978, "Imbued as the medical establishment is with the idea of fighting at all costs to prolong life, it is naturally geared to the hope of success rather than to the fact of failure." But as *Changing Times* explained in April, 1979, "When care designed to cure and rehabilitate is applied to a person who knows he has a terminal illness, it creates a feeling of isolation and despair, especially if he senses the staff is just going through the motions."

5. Hospices make no such false promises. Dr. James Cimino explains, "For the hospice patient, it is too late for cures. The operations, radiation, and chemotherapy have been tried elsewhere. They've been declared incurable and inoperable. The patient is entirely aware of his situation." Hospices provide two choices: either the person can go to the hospice, or, more likely, the hospice will come to him, 24 hours a day, if necessary, with a team of doctors, psychologists, clergy, good neighbors, and volunteers. Treatment is palliative—that is, designed to ease pain and manage symptoms, such as nausea, but no heroic effort is made to cure the disease. The results? The person is comfortable, and his mind is clear.

6. Unfortunately, there is more to dying than just futile treatment of an illness. The second problem is institutionalization, which is more often easy than essential. Nearly 70% of terminally ill Americans spend their final year in a hospital or a nursing home—but at the moment, there is not much choice. For one thing, says John Abbott of Hospice, Inc., families doubt their own ability to care for a dying member and find institutions more convenient. But in a hospice, he says, "When

---

*From *Winning Orations,* 1980, pp. 81–83. Reprinted by permission of Larry Schnoor, Executive Secretary, Interstate Oratorical Association.

families ask, 'Can we care for our loved one?' we say, 'Yes you can—and we'll help you.'" The problem is, first you've got to find the hospice.

7. This summer, a family friend's grandmother spent the last six weeks of her life in the hospital begging to go home. The family was unable to find someone willing to provide round-the-clock painkillers to a ninety-three-year-old woman dying at home, and they called me to see if I knew of anyone. "The physical pain," they said, "doesn't hurt her half as much as not being home." Well, I didn't know of anyone—and two weeks later she died; in the hospital, by herself. To all things there is a season.

8. Had I known at that time that a hospice was located in central Ohio, that expensive and futile hospitalization could have been avoided. And more importantly, a person who desperately wanted to be at home when she died could have been spared the trauma of an institution. Hospices in New Haven, Connecticut, allow 50% of terminally ill patients in that area to live at home—at a cost, incidentally, of about $25 a day, as opposed to $200 a day in a hospital. In those hospices which do provide residential facilities, rules are avoided, visiting hours are round-the-clock, and pets and personal effects are encouraged. Hospices allow that choice. Institutions do not.

9. But the third problem of terminal illness comes *after* the funeral, for in which psychologists call our "death-denying culture," we ignore the family and deny them the catharsis of knowing they have done everything that they can. The Comptroller General's Report to Congress found that, as a result of a dying person's illness, family suicides jumped significantly. Three sociologists' study of widows found that 24% developed reactive depression. Twelve percent became emotionally unstable, and 4% turned to alcohol within the first year of their husbands' deaths. Two separate studies show that parents stand a 70% chance of divorce within two years of the death of a child.

10. Susan Silver, of the National Hospice Organization, explains: "When a family is intimately involved with a dying member, there is much less guilt afterward. They witness the natural dying process, they give of themselves, and their grief is not so prolonged." Hospice personnel do everything from drafting wills to feeding pets to providing family counseling—including a follow-up after the funeral. Volunteers either help out within the households or are trained by the hospice professionals. One woman, after a hospice team had helped her cope with her mother's death, said, "When she died it was a victory for all of us. None of us felt any guilt."

11. Today we appreciate life more—and go to greater lengths to preserve it—than any society in human history. But the fact is, for some of us, modern medical miracles will fail. Terminal illness is not discriminating: heart disease has no season, sickle cell anemia has no cure. There is a cancer death every 80 seconds—and one out of every four people you've met this weekend will eventually have cancer. What if, when you call home tonight, you find out it has hit there as well? It does happen.

12. The hospice movement in the United States needs our support, and with three simple steps we can provide it. First, encourage federal, state, and local government efforts to enhance the hospice movement. For example, as some states have already done, Medicare and Medicaid must be expanded to include hospice care for the aged and the poor.

13. Second, protect yourself. Buy insurance that covers hospices as well as hospitalization. Blue Cross and Blue Shield already do that; but with incentive, other companies would follow suit.

14. And most importantly, you and I have got to provide the personal concern that sets hospice care apart in the first place. Tell your parents about hospices; if they become ill tomorrow, wouldn't you want them to know? Or what if they did know, but there was no hospice that was near enough to help? Many hospices begin through local churches or community organizations, with grants available from HEW; consider them for yours. And above all, when someone *you* care for is diagnosed as terminally ill—and it will happen—don't simply say, "Well, if there's anything I can do. . . ." Call him up, walk the dog, provide cassettes for last notes, help tie up school or business ends. The important thing to remember is that hospices are not places, they're people. But without the support of family and friends, hospice becomes just another empty room.

15. When Joseph Califano visited the New Haven hospice, he said: "I visited with the idea that hospice was about dying. I came away realizing it's about living." We can't give a dying person more time—for to all things there is a season. But with little effort and much compassion, we can give him back the time he has. . . . A time to cry, and a time to laugh; a time for love, and a time for peace.

ANALYZING PERSUASION: AN EXERCISE

Objectives

1. To recognize fallacies in reasoning.
2. To analyze two speech outlines for their use of logical and emotional appeals.

Instructions

Read both the speech situation below and the two speeches on the value of the western movie and the military, respectively. With a group of your classmates, analyze the effectiveness of each speech using the questions below as a guide in your analysis and discussion.

Speech Situation

These speeches were delivered in 1989 by two university students enrolled in a public speaking class. Their assignment was to present a persuasive speech using logical and emotional appeals supported with evidence. Their outline was to contain their main arguments, evidence, and references.

Questions to Guide Analysis and Discussion

1. What reasons did the speaker give for accepting the value of the western movie? Of the military?

2. What inferences about their audiences did these speakers make? What should they have done differently to make stronger arguments?

3. Did the speakers adequately mesh their values with those of the audience? Why or why not?

4. What logical and emotional appeals did each speaker use to gain acceptance of the proposition? Were they effective? Why or why not?

5. Evaluate the use of evidence and the credibility of the sources for each of the speeches.

6. Are these persuasive speeches? Why or why not? What could be done to develop these as persuasive speeches?

THE VALUE OF THE WESTERN MOVIE: AN OUTLINE

Introduction

I. Does certain dialogue remind you of types of movies?

II. The western film was one of the most popular types of movies of all time, but not anymore.
   A. Every major studio made dozens of westerns every year.
   B. Early television was saturated with westerns.
   C. So many westerns were made that there was nothing new left to say or do, so they stopped making them.

III. The western movie has a very real value for the modern audience just as it did for the audience of old.

IV. Western films are not only entertaining but also perform a real function in today's society.
   A. They are a great way of looking fondly at our past.
   B. They provide a great means of escape.
   C. They actually teach moral values.

Body

I. Westerns provide a nostalgic look at our historical past.
   A. Westerns look back to a simpler time.
      1. According to the magazine *Film Comment,* "The West was a blank, natural slate where everyone's born free."
      2. There were no taxes, no crooked politicians, no drug problems, and certainly no problems with smog.
      3. "The West is a blank space into which rides the cowboy, a natural man unburdened by policies."
   B. Real historical characters were often portrayed, although often glamorized beyond the actual facts.

II. Western films are a great form of escape in which the audience assumes the role of the hero in their own minds for the duration of the film.
   A. The western hero was someone we all want to be.
      1. They were strong, independent, quick-witted, physically agile, and usually very handsome.
      2. According to *Esquire* magazine of June 1986, they were "unfettered by employment, men of the gun, free to be avengers, defenders, and fighters for right and justice."
         a. They never really had jobs or were really cowboys.
         b. The same article said, "Heroes weren't really cowboys, even John Wayne followed some other line of work than punching cows."

III. The most important value of the western film is that it teaches moral values.
   A. According to an article entitled "Rise and Fall of the Western" in *National Review* magazine of December 1989, the values of the western are those of all Americans.
      1. "Naturally enough, the morals and policies of the western tend to be those on which Americans pride themselves."
      2. Good will triumph over evil, courage will deter fear, strength will win over weakness—all are taught in westerns.

3. Western film takes advantage of the "open slate" of its historical time frame to create the perfect society in which good always defeats evil.
B. According to the magazine *Film Comment,* failure in a western film always equaled moral failure.
C. A recent western film, "Pale Rider," represents the moral lessons taught by westerns.
  1. According to a review in *Time* magazine of July 1, 1985, this film was typical of most westerns.
  2. "He saves the good folks, kills the bad folks, dodges a mother-daughter rivalry for his affection, and ends up in a showdown with a gunslinger."
  3. The hero in this film was typical of all western heroes because he followed his own "code," or moral values, in all decisions he made.
D. Best known of all cowboy figures was John Wayne.
  1. Last film he made was called "The Shootist."
  2. He played an aging gunfighter, dying of cancer.
  3. He told a young boy in the movie the code he had lived by.
  4. This was his own version of the golden rule.

Conclusion

I. As you can see, the western hero represents much of what we all hold as ideals.
II. That, plus the nostalgic look at history and the escapism possible, makes the western movie a valuable form of quality entertainment for the whole family.

References

Corliss, Richard. Review of "Pale Rider," *Time,* July 1, 1985, p. 63.
Durgnat, Raymond and Scott Simmon. *Film Comment,* September/October 1980, pp. 61–70.
Lejeune, Anthony. "The Rise and Fall of the Western," *National Review*, Dec. 31, 1989, pp. 23–26.
"The Shootist," Paramount Pictures Corp., 1979.
Waggoner, Glen. "Cowboy Hall of Fame," *Esquire*, June 1986, p. 332.

JOIN THE MILITARY: AN OUTLINE

Introduction

I. Attention Getter: Have you thought lately about just how lucky we are? We live in the greatest and strongest country in the world. Sometimes we don't appreciate that. We just take it for granted and don't really think about doing anything for our country. We just think about ourselves. Our late, great president, John F. Kennedy, once posed the question, "Ask not what your country can do for you, but what you can do for your country."

II. Need for Listening: Well, there is something we can do for our country, both men and women alike. We can show our loyalty and patriotism to our country by joining the military. I feel I'm qualified to speak on this because I devoted four years of my life to our country. But it's not just a matter of service to our country; we can better ourselves. I've asked all of the people in class and almost all of you feel it's a waste of time. I can truthfully say that the four years I spent in the military were definitely not a waste of time and can guarantee it won't be a waste of your time.

III. Thesis Proposition: Everyone who is mentally and physically capable of joining the military should join.
   A. Being in the military builds character.
   B. It gives us the tools we need to carry on a successful life.
   C. As Americans we should feel it's our duty to serve our country.

Body

I. Being in the military builds character.
   A. Experience things we've never before experienced.
      1. It gets us away from home and on our own probably for the first time.
      2. We're our own persons now.
      3. We make the decisions now.
      4. We are responsible for our own actions.
   B. See things we've never seen before. Almost everyone likes to travel.
      1. Get to go to other countries.
      2. Been above the Arctic circle.
      3. Floated the oceans on ships.

II. Being in the military gives us the tools we need to lead a successful life.
   A. Aids in paying our tuition.
      1. Get paid $100 a month for R.O.T.C.
      2. Get paid approximately $150 a month for being in the National Guard.
      3. Active duty pays more in the form of the G.I. Bill. One form is the VEAP program.
   B. Teaches discipline.
      1. Teaches discipline that, once learned, usually doesn't just go away. It stays with us.
      2. Makes us more serious about school or working. Makes us study harder or perform better at our jobs.

III. As Americans, we should feel it's our duty to serve our country.
   A. Nowadays, Americans think it's a waste of time to serve and protect our country. I'm glad our ancestors didn't feel the same way.

1. Our ancestors fought and died for the security of our freedom.
2. Just imagine if they hadn't. If they held the same attitudes that some of us hold now, there wouldn't be any America today.
3. It's going to take this same kind of loyalty and willing attitude to keep our country strong and free.

Conclusion

I. As we can now see, being in the military can help both us and our country. We can uphold the tradition of our ancestors by protecting our country and, at the same time, learn responsibility, see the world, and acquire the tools needed to live a successful life.

II. I would like to urge all of you to join the military. If you are ready to go in now, there's a recruiter's office located in town. If you want to finish college first, you may consider joining the National Guard. You can join now and go to boot camp this summer. If not, you can get in the R.O.T.C. program on campus and/or take some classes in military science that will be offered in the fall, and that will prepare you for doing active duty once you graduate.

Organizing and Outlining Your Speech

This unit presents a systematic process for organizing your messages and the guidelines for using a complete sentence outline for your speeches. The *process* for organizing informative and persuasive messages is the same. However, while the traditional outline format is appropriate for *all* informative messages, it is only appropriate for *some* persuasive messages.

The components of UNIT 10 are:

Organizational Patterns: Notes

Organizing Your Thoughts on a Topic

Process of Preparing a Speech

Outlining: A Method of Organization

Format for Informative Speeches

Comparison of Two Persuasive Outline Formats

Scrambled Outline Exercise

Scrambled Outline 1

Scrambled Outline 2

Problematic Outline Exercise

Problematic Outline 1

Problematic Outline 2

Outline Check for Informative Speeches

Outline Check for Persuasive Speeches

ORGANIZATIONAL PATTERNS: NOTES

Excellent organization in a speech is a result of several factors:

1. A carefully selected and narrowed *topic*.
2. A *specific purpose* that has been adapted to your *audience*.
3. A clearly worded central idea or *thesis*.
4. Well-developed *main points* with supporting materials adapted to your audience.
5. A carefully selected *pattern* or order for your main points.

There are five patterns or orders to select from when determining which is the most strategic order for your main points. Which pattern you should select depends on your particular topic and specific purpose.

Chronological Order: This pattern follows a time pattern. The main points are arranged in the order in which they occurred either historically or in a sequence of steps. For example:

Specific Purpose: To create understanding of conditioning in college basketball.

Thesis: Conditioning is especially important to a college basketball player.

Main Points:

   I.   Pre-season conditioning usually consists of six weeks of endurance exercises without drills.

  II. Season conditioning contains mostly drills with only a few endurance exercises.

 III. Post-season conditioning challenges the player to practice on his own.

Topical Order: This pattern follows no particular order beyond personal preference. The main points fall naturally into subtopics and the speaker decides which makes sense to cover first and to cover last. For example:

Specific Purpose: To inform the audience about what the customer-oriented approach to selling is and how they will benefit from it.

Thesis: The customer-oriented approach to selling focuses on meeting customer needs and providing benefits to us—the consumer.

Main Points:

   I.   The selling process is being tailored to first meet the needs of the customer.

  II. Consumers can use their knowledge of this approach to make better buying decisions.

Spatial Order: This pattern follows a direction or location order. When using this pattern, you can start at the top and progress down or go from east to west, or from front to back. For example:

Specific Purpose: To describe the beauty of Vermillion Park in south Louisiana.

Thesis: Vermillion Park is enhanced by three natural elements that are indigenous to Louisiana.

Main Points:

   I.   The entrance to the park is flanked by beautiful oak trees with Spanish moss.

  II. The center of the park contains many large magnolia trees.

 III. The back portion of the park is a lake, full of cypress trees.

Causal Order: This pattern presents a cause and then describes its effect. The main points illustrate an effect in relation to the proposition or central idea. For example:

Specific Purpose: To persuade the audience that raising the drinking age in Louisiana is unfair.

Proposition: The drinking age should not be raised to deter drinking.

Main Points:

    I.   It will violate personal civil rights and the constitutional rights of states.

   II.   Alcohol abuse among teenagers may increase.

  III.   It would increase unemployment.

Problem-Solution Order: This pattern first presents a problem and then offers a solution to that problem. For example:

Specific Purpose: To urge my audience to be more responsible in their selection of physicians.

Proposition: Because of the problem with drug-addicted physicians, we have to be more careful in selecting our physicians.

Main Points:

    I.   There is a growing problem of drug-addicted physicians.

   II.   We must be more responsible in selecting physicians.

ORGANIZING YOUR THOUGHTS ON A TOPIC

Objectives

1. To learn methods for organizing your thoughts on a topic.
2. To practice developing and organizing topics through rough draft outlines.

Instructions for Method 1

After selecting and narrowing your topic to a specific purpose statement by means of an audience analysis, you are ready to develop your topic and organize your thoughts. Working from your specific purpose, jot down, in any order, what you know or want to talk about. Keep your audience and purpose in mind as you do so. From that list, categorize your ideas into two or three connecting units. Refine and develop your ideas and write the main points that summarize each unit. Compose your thesis statement and your introduction and conclusion.

Example of First Draft: Method 1

General Purpose: To create understanding.

Specific Purpose: To create understanding of how to use a systematic process of preparing a speech.

1. Analyze audience and setting.

2. Select topic.

3. Know general and specific purposes.

4. Outline main ideas.

5. Research/gather supporting materials.

6. Compose final outline.

7. Practice aloud in conversational style.

Example of Second Draft: Method 1

  I. Planning.
    A. Analyze audience and setting.
    B. Select topic.
    C. Know general and specific purposes.
 II. Organizing.
    A. Outline main ideas.
    B. Research/gather supporting materials.
    C. Compose final outline.
III. Practicing.
    A. Practice aloud in conversational style.
    B. Practice from brief notes.

Instructions for Method 2

After selecting and narrowing your topic to a specific purpose statement through an audience analysis, you are ready to develop your topic and organize your thoughts. Working from your specific purpose, think of two or three main ideas or categories you want to talk about. Compose your thesis statement. From each of the general categories list the particulars or details you want to discuss. Refine your ideas. Compose your introduction and conclusion.

Example of First Draft: Method 2

General Purpose: To create understanding.
Specific Purpose: To create understanding of how to use a systematic process of preparing a speech.
Thesis: Speech preparation can be easy if you follow these steps.

1. Find out about audience, purpose, and topics.

2. Organize ideas into outline.

3. Practice your speech from your outline.

PROCESS OF PREPARING A SPEECH

Example of Final Draft: Methods 1 and 2

I. Planning the speech.
  A. Select and narrow topic.
    1. Knowledge and interest of speaker.
    2. Interesting and significant to audience.
    3. Limited in scope and purpose.
      a. For time limit.
      b. For audience understanding and expectations.
  B. Determine general and specific purposes.
    1. For general: answers why speaking.
    2. For specific: concrete goals to achieve.
  C. Analyze audience, occasion, and setting.
    1. Effective public speaking is audience centered.
      a. What does audience know about topic?
      b. What interests or attitudes does audience have toward topic?
    2. What are particulars about occasion and setting?
II. Organizing materials and ideas.
  A. Write a rough draft of thesis, main ideas, and subpoints.
    1. Thesis is direct, declarative statement expressing main point of speech.
    2. Main ideas explain or elaborate the thesis.
  B. Research/gather supporting materials relevant to audience.
    1. Examples.
    2. Statistics.
    3. Testimony.
  C. Compose final outline complete with examples, introduction, and conclusion.
    1. Address functions of introduction and conclusion.
    2. Write abbreviated speaking outline.
III. Working with presentational skills.
  A. Practice aloud for clarity and fluency.
  B. Practice aloud in conversational style.

Summary Discussion

1. Which method of organizing is most helpful for you? Why?

2. What would you include in the introduction and conclusion of this speech?

OUTLINING: A METHOD OF ORGANIZATION

Definition of an Outline

An **outline** is a brief compilation of the main points, subpoints, and developmental materials arranged to reflect the order of logical thought relationships. It is a blueprint of your speech.

Reasons for Using an Outline

1. It supplies you with an efficient method of preparation, a method that will be clear and orderly.
2. It assures you of having a specific purpose to achieve.
3. It aids you in distinguishing important and unimportant facets of your subject, thus helping to assure unity and coherence.
4. It aids you in selecting and strategically incorporating well-balanced and substantial amounts of supporting materials, thus maintaining the audience's interest and helping to assure acceptance of your message.
5. It helps you remember ideas and prevents you from making unnecessary, irritating, or embarrassing digressions.
6. It aids you in giving proper emphasis to important thoughts and feelings.
7. It provides you with a proven means for developing confidence in yourself and the speech situation.
8. It aids the audience by helping them comprehend the speaker's goal, follow the speech with ease, and retain main points, subpoints, and important supporting materials.

Requirements of a Complete Sentence Outline: A Planning Outline

1. Material placed within a complete sentence outline should be worded so that rather than giving the complete content of each piece of supporting material, each sentence carries merely the gist or essence of that material.
2. At the top of the first page, state the general purpose and the specific purpose of the speech.
3. Divide your outline into three distinct parts, capitalizing the words INTRODUCTION, BODY, and CONCLUSION and placing them in the center of the page.
4. The thesis statement is placed in the outline as the final main point in the introduction and indicated by writing the word "Thesis" before your sentence.
5. Use the standard outline symbols (see sample outlines).
6. Indent each symbol by placing it under the first word of the sentence it follows; never allow any sentence or part of a sentence to extend to the left-hand margin as far as the symbols do.
7. Follow each symbol with a *short, simple, declarative* sentence. Questions or quotations may not be used as main points, but it is acceptable to use questions as transitions between the main ideas.
8. Each symbol in the body should have *only one* short sentence.
9. Use only two or three main points in the body of a short speech (under fifteen minutes); in the body of a long speech, use from two to five points only. The only exception to this rule is the occasional use of more points when the subject matter absolutely demands it for clarity and when the time permits a more thorough development (fifty minutes).

10. Main points within any of the three divisions of the speech should be sufficiently subdivided to make each main point clear.
11. Main points and subpoints should be carefully worded to conform to a consistent organizational pattern, should be of equal importance, should never overlap, and, when possible, should be given parallel construction.

Functions of the Main Divisions of a Speech

1. Functions of the Introduction.
   a. To capture the attention and interest of the audience and to help them focus on the topic.
   b. To motivate the audience to listen; that is, to give the audience reasons to listen that are based upon their wants, needs, and desires.
   c. To establish rapport with the audience.
   d. To establish one's expertise and relationship to his/her subject.
   e. To lead smoothly into the thesis statement (the major point of the speech).
   f. To state the thesis and preview the main ideas.
2. Functions of the Body.
   a. To break the subject into its component parts of two or three main ideas.
   b. To develop the main ideas through supporting materials in the subpoints— examples, comparisons, explanation, etc.
3. Functions of the Conclusion.
   a. To reemphasize and summarize the main ideas.
   b. To end the speech climactically or to spur the audience to action if that is the speaker's goal.

FORMAT FOR INFORMATIVE SPEECHES

General Purpose:

Specific Purpose:

Introduction

   I. Attention-getting remarks.

  II. Need for listening.

 III. Thesis.

      A. Preview of main points.

      B.

Body

   I. Main point.

      A. Subpoint.

         1. Supporting materials.

         2.

      B. Subpoint.

         1.

         2.

  II. Main point.

      A. Subpoint.

         1.

         2.

      B. Subpoint.

         1.

         2.

Conclusion

   I. Summary.

  II. Clincher.

COMPARISON OF TWO PERSUASIVE OUTLINE FORMATS

Monroe's Motivated Sequence

Attention

   I. Attention-getting statement.
   II. Establish credibility.

   III. Audience predispositions/Survey.

Need

   I. Need (State the problem).
      A. Describe need.
         1. Evidence.
         2. Evidence.
      B. Illustrate need.
         1. Evidence.
         2. Evidence.

Satisfaction

   I. (State the solution.)
      A. Explain solution.
         1. Evidence.
         2. Evidence.
      B. Show how it meets need.
         1. Evidence.
         2. Evidence.

Visualization

   I. (Solution benefits.)
      A. Advantages if accepted.
         1. Evidence.
         2. Evidence.
      B. Disadvantages if not accepted.
         1. Evidence.
         2. Evidence.

Statement of Reasons

Introduction

   I. Attention-getting statement.
   II. Establish credibility;
      Audience predispositions/Survey.
      (Need for listening.)
   III. State proposition (Thesis).
      A. Preview main point I.
      B. Preview main point II.
      C. Preview main point III.

Body

   I. Main point.
      A. Explanation/Example.
         1. Evidence.
         2. Evidence.
      B. Explanation/Example.
         1. Evidence.
         2. Evidence.

   I. Main point.
      A. Explanation/Example.
         1. Evidence.
         2. Evidence.
      B. Explanation/Example.
         1. Evidence.
         2. Evidence.

   I. Main point.
      A. Explanation/Example.
         1. Evidence.
         2. Evidence.
      B. Explanation/Example.
         1. Evidence.
         2. Evidence.

Action

I. Action (Final commitment and call for action).

Conclusion

I. Summary (Review main points).

II. Clincher (Restate proposition).

SCRAMBLED OUTLINE EXERCISE

Objectives

1. To organize information in a coherent manner.
2. To apply concepts of organization and requirements for outline.
3. To develop a thesis from a body of a speech.
4. To develop an introduction and a conclusion from a body of a speech.

Instructions

1. Working in groups, unscramble one of the following scrambled outlines. Structure the statements into the *body* of a speech.
2. For each speech, there are three main points plus subpoints with examples.
3. Use correct outline format and requirements.
4. After unscrambling the statements into the body of a speech, write an introduction complete with attention-getter, need for listening, adaptation to audience, and thesis with preview of main points.
5. Write a conclusion.
6. Have a member or members of your group volunteer to deliver the introduction to the class. Use effective delivery skills.

Summary Discussion

1. Did all groups organize the statements in the same order? What were the differences?

2. Did the outlines follow the correct format? Were the outlines coherent and logical?

3. Were the introductions effective? Were they creative? Did they establish a need for listening?

4. Were the thesis statements direct, declarative, and assertive? Were the main points previewed?

SCRAMBLED OUTLINE 1*

1. Eye contact is an important skill for public speakers.
2. Speakers should establish eye contact with the entire audience.
3. Speakers can judge an audience's interest by its nonverbal behavior.
4. People distrusted Richard Nixon because he had "shifty eyes."
5. Speakers should talk from notes rather than manuscripts.
6. Three components of eye contact are essential to effective delivery.
7. Speakers should avoid "false" eye contact.
8. Speakers should look directly at the audience.
9. Looking over people's heads is not an effective way to establish rapport with an audience.
10. Staring at one person or one segment of the audience makes the rest of the audience feel excluded.
11. Speakers can ascertain the listeners' comprehension through their facial expressions.
12. Glancing at the audience does not allow a speaker sufficient time to establish eye contact.
13. There are three ways in which speakers can improve their eye contact with an audience.
14. Speakers should be familiar with their material so they don't have to look continually at notes.
15. Speakers should look at an audience frequently.
16. Eye contact allows the speaker to perceive audience feedback.
17. Juries may decide a person is guilty because he or she won't look at them.
18. People judge a speaker's honesty and trustworthiness partially through the speaker's use of eye contact.

---

*From J. C. Pearson, D. Yoder, and P. E. Nelson, *Instructor's Resource Manual for Understanding and Sharing*, 2nd ed. Copyright © 1982 Wm. C. Brown Communications, Inc., Dubuque, Iowa. All Rights Reserved. Reprinted by permission.

SCRAMBLED OUTLINE 2

1. A larger vocabulary can get you noticed in an interview.
2. The more words you have at your command, the clearer and more precisely you can express complicated ideas.
3. Two high school homeroom classes with students of similar vocabulary scores at the beginning of the year were selected.
4. A good command of words and wit is impressive.
5. The more confident you are about your language, the more likely you will be to take the initiative in conversation.
6. One class received systematic vocabulary lessons.
7. Increasing your vocabulary will increase your chance of success in business.
8. To share your thoughts and feelings with close friends, you need the words to express them.
9. A larger vocabulary allows you to read more complicated texts.
10. Misunderstandings occur when friends say the "wrong" things to each other.
11. One hundred young men who were studying to be industrial executives were surveyed.
12. A larger vocabulary may increase your chances of getting that job you want.
13. A study by Dr. O'Connor of the Education Department showed a connection between success in school and vocabulary power.
14. Language power can make you feel more confident when meeting new people.
15. Without the language power, you may lose a job to someone else.
16. A study by Dr. Johnson of the Management Department showed the connection between success in business and vocabulary power.
17. Increasing your vocabulary will enhance your social communication skills.
18. You increase your capacity for learning when you increase your vocabulary.
19. The class who received the vocabulary lessons made consistently higher grades in all their other classes.
20. Five years later, not a single man who received a vocabulary score in the lowest 25 percent was an executive.
21. Language power can help you express complicated feelings with friends.
22. Increasing your vocabulary will increase your chances of success in school.

PROBLEMATIC OUTLINE EXERCISE

Objectives

1. To recognize problems with organization and outlines.
2. To apply concepts of organization and requirements for outlines.

Instructions

The following two outlines were prepared for a six- to eight-minute informative speech assignment. Working in groups or alone, identify the problems with the following outlines. Then correct the problems by rewriting the outlines. Turn in a written copy of your work.

PROBLEMATIC OUTLINE 1

General Purpose: To create understanding.

Specific Purpose: To create understanding about the time period in which Americans consumed the most alcohol.

Introduction

I. I was drinking and decided the 1980s must be the time when Americans consumed the most alcohol.
   A. I was wrong.
   B. More alcohol was consumed during the time period after the Revolutionary War.
II. I thought this was interesting.
   A. Frontier people not just buffalo killers.
   B. Nation of drunks.
III. More alcohol was consumed between the years 1790–1840 than any other time period in American history.
   A. Liquor was thought healthful and nutritious.
   B. Grain surplus was effectively transposed into whiskey.
   C. Alcohol was part of diet.
   D. Alcohol relieved anxiety.
   E. It was used for pleasure drinking.

Body

I. A popular quote of the time was "Drink is in itself a creature of God, and to be received with thankfulness."
   A. There was belief that alcohol was nutritious and healthful.
      1. Used with food to break up meal monotony.
      2. Medication.
         a. Colds, snakebites, broken bones.
         b. Physician in Virginia.
      3. Relaxant for depression, tension, and camaraderie.
   B. These beliefs led to widespread drinking.
II. Cheap whiskey was a good cure for grain surplus.
   A. Fertile land caused surplus.
      1. Low prices.
      2. Glutted market.
   B. Technological improvements in stills.
   C. Farmers turned to distilling for better profits.
III. Whiskey and beer were parts of the American diet.
   A. Water from muddy rivers was no good.
   B. Milk was disease-ridden.
   C. Tea and coffee imports were expensive.
   D. Wine was expensive.
   E. People turned to beer and whiskey.
IV. Alcohol relieved anxiety.
   A. People with no customs, roots, or social ties (lumberjacks, stagecoach drivers) drank to ease loneliness.
   B. People with failed dreams and ambitions drank to relieve depression.

V. What better reason to drink is there than following the pursuit of happiness?
   A. Drinking in groups was popular.
   B. Drinking was a social event.

Conclusion

I. During the years 1790–1840, alcohol was considered nutritious, a cure for anxiety, and a way to pursue happiness.

II. Americans consumed more alcohol during that time period than they have in the 1980s.

PROBLEMATIC OUTLINE 2

General Purpose: To create understanding about Alpha Kappa Alpha sorority.

Specific Purpose: To create understanding about Alpha Kappa Alpha sorority by explaining its purpose, function, membership, and activities.

Introduction

I. Sorority, as defined by the Random House Dictionary, means "a society of women in college."
   A. Sorority comes from the Latin word "soror," meaning sister.
   B. Many sororities on I.W.U. campus.
      1. AOPi.
      2. SK.
      3. KD.
      4. Etc.
II. Alpha Kappa Alpha sorority is a service organization composed of black college women who have chosen this sorority as a channel of friendship and a means of self-fulfillment through community service.
III. Thesis: Because Alpha Kappa Alpha fulfills an important and vital role for society, more people ought to know about the sorority.
   A. Well-known members.
      1. Coretta Scott King.
      2. Ella Fitzgerald.
      3. Jane Addams.
      4. Ruth Love.
      5. Eleanor Roosevelt.
      6. Marian Anderson.
   B. Not here to persuade anyone to join but to tell the function, purpose, membership, and activities of AKA.

Body

I. Alpha Kappa Alpha, or AKA, is a sorority that functions as a service organization, which de-emphasizes the social aspect of Greek life.
   A. Instead of throwing lots of wild parties and having maybe one service activity, AKA is vice versa.
   B. AKA realizes that not all blacks have the opportunities of having a positive role model and tries to help.
II. AKA has three purposes.
   A. Cultivation of high scholastical and ethical standards.
      1. Scholarships.
      2. Fellowships.
      3. Support of NAACP.
      4. Negro College Fund.
      5. Tutorial programs.
   B. Promotion of unity and friendship among college women.
      1. Seminars.
      2. Rushes, workshops.
   C. Being of service by studying and alleviating social problems as they relate to women.

III. Because there is no one group dedicated to the cultivation of high scholastic and ethical standards, the promotion of unity and friendship among college women, and the study and alleviation of social problems through service, twenty women decided to incorporate a sisterhood of women to do this.

    A. Twenty juniors and seniors founded AKA in 1908.
        1. Incorporated on Jan. 23, 1913, at Howard University.
        2. Of the twenty founders, two are still alive.
    B. The symbols of AKA.
        1. The colors are salmon pink and apple green.
        2. The emblem is an oak leaf with the Greek letters AKA on each point and twenty pearls surrounding the leaf.
        3. The shield.
            a. Hands: friendship.
            b. Dove: peace.
            c. Globe: global issues and problems that AKA strives to change.
            d. Balance: justice and equality.
            e. Lamp: continuation of education.
        4. AKA.
            a. Abbreviation of a Greek word that, when translated in English, means "by culture and by merit," which is the motto of AKA.

IV. Presently there are over 70,000 members in AKA.

    A. Members are from the Bahamas, Africa, Haiti, and Jamaica as well as America.
    B. There are five types of members.
        1. Undergraduate.
            a. Women pursuing a degree in a college where a chapter is established.
        2. General.
            a. Undergraduates who have pledged AKA but attend a college where there is no chapter.
        3. Associate.
            a. An undergraduate who dropped out of college.
        4. Graduate.
            a. Women who were initiated as undergraduates and graduated.
            b. Women with degree(s) who were invited to join by the graduate chapter at a graduate school.
        5. Honorary.
            a. Highest honor, which has only been given to thirty-nine people.

V. Because AKA is a service organization, the members have to plan a program of community-oriented activities.

    A. Activities range from tutorial programs to health awareness to cotillions to job training.
    B. This year's program is targeted at education, health, civil rights, and voter registration.
    C. Specific programs initiated on the national level.
        1. Support of the NAACP.
        2. Voter registration drive.
        3. Certification in CPA and BSE.
    D. Specific programs initiated on a chapter level.
        1. Tutoring.
        2. Hospital volunteers.
        3. Fund raising for NAACP.

Conclusion

I. AKA is a sorority of black college women dedicated to community service.

II. Because AKA fulfills a vital function for the community and society, more people should know about the sorority's purpose, function, membership, and activities.

III. AKA believes that it is only through culture and merit that one can truly succeed in life and be happy.

OUTLINE CHECK FOR INFORMATIVE SPEECHES

Objectives

1. To systematically check your speech outline.
2. To get feedback on your speech outline from a classmate.

Instructions

Use the questions below to see if your speech outline meets the appropriate criteria. In addition, seek responses to the questions from a small group of your classmates.

Questions for Informative Outlines

1. Is the specific purpose clear and specific enough? Can it be covered in the time limit?

2. Is the thesis a single declarative sentence that summarizes the speaker's message? Does it express the speaker's main point or opinion?

3. Are the main points developed logically from the thesis? Explain.

4. Are the main points limited (two to four) and balanced?

5. Are the subpoints and the supporting materials developed logically from the main ideas? Explain.

6. Are the supporting materials relevant to the audience and the speech purpose? Explain.

7. What suggestions (other than those already made) do you have for improving the outline and the topic development?

OUTLINE CHECK FOR PERSUASIVE SPEECHES

Objectives

1. To systematically check your speech outline.
2. To get feedback on your speech outline from a classmate.

Instructions

Use the questions below to see if your speech outline meets the appropriate criteria. In addition, seek responses to the questions from a small group of your classmates.

Questions for Persuasive Outlines

1. What is the proposition of the speech? What exactly does the speaker want you to do, to think, or to believe?

2. What reasons (main points) does the speaker give for acceptance of the proposition?

3. Are the main points sound and logical reasons?

4. If the outline is in problem/solution (or Monroe's Motivated Sequence) format, is the problem clearly described? Explain.

5. Does the solution or satisfaction step directly address the problem? Explain.

6. Does the speaker provide convincing arguments and supporting materials to address the reasons for accepting the proposition or for describing the problem and accepting the solution? Why or why not?

7. How does the speaker address the audience's predispositions toward the topic or the proposition?

Preparing Introductions, Conclusions, and Transitions

This unit will help you identify and prepare effective introductions and conclusions. Speech preparation sometimes frustrates novice speakers because they attempt to begin with what to say first. However, experienced speakers know that the introduction should be the last consideration in preparation. Until you know the focus and direction of your topic, you cannot know how to interest the audience in your speech and provide an overview of direction.

In addition to the introduction and conclusion, transitions help focus and direct the audience on aspects of your speech. This unit provides practice activities on writing effective transitions.

The components of UNIT 11 are:

Functions of Introductions and Conclusions

Analyzing Effective Introductions and Conclusions

Introduction and Conclusion for Informative Speech on Asthma

Introduction and Conclusion for Informative Speech on Dolphins

Introduction and Conclusion for Persuasive Speech on Drugs and Physicians

Introduction and Conclusion for Persuasive Speech on Exercise and Stress

Writing Introductions and Conclusions: An Exercise

Spinning Kick: Informative Speech

Growing a Garden: Persuasive Speech

Increasing Your Vocabulary: Persuasive Speech

Writing Transitions

FUNCTIONS OF INTRODUCTIONS AND CONCLUSIONS

1. Functions of the Introduction.
   a. To capture the attention and interest of the audience and to help them focus on the topic.
   b. To motivate the audience to listen; that is, to give the audience reasons to listen that are based upon their wants, needs, and desires.
   c. To establish rapport with the audience.
   d. To establish one's expertise and relationship to his/her subject.
   e. To lead smoothly into the thesis statement (major point of the speech) or the proposition.
   f. For informative speeches, to state the thesis and preview the main ideas.
   g. For persuasive speeches, to address the audience's predispositions.
2. Functions of the Conclusion.
   a. To reemphasize and summarize the main ideas.
   b. To end the speech climactically or to spur the audience to action if that is the speaker's goal.

ANALYZING EFFECTIVE INTRODUCTIONS AND CONCLUSIONS

Objectives

1. To appreciate the importance of an excellent introduction.
2. To analyze introductions for their effectiveness.

Explanation

A well-composed introduction goes a long way in helping the speaker and the audience become immediately and directly involved with the speech topic and purpose. Excellent introductions for informative and persuasive speeches use vivid and concrete language to accomplish the tasks of getting the attention of the audience, stating the speaker's interest in the topic and its value to the listener, and providing an overview of the speaker's organizational approach. An effective conclusion summarizes the main ideas, restates the thesis or proposition, and provides a clincher or closing.

Instructions

In the following pages are examples of excellent introductions and conclusions. After reading them, use the questions below to discuss with your classmates why they are effective. In other words, what in particular makes them excellent and appealing.

Questions for Discussion

1. What type of attention-getter did the speaker use?

2. Why would the attention-getter work to capture the interest of the audience and to help them focus on the topic?

3. What reasons does the speaker give for presenting a speech on this topic? What are the speaker's qualifications, personal interest, and experience with the topic?

4. What reasons does the speaker give to motivate the audience to listen? Are they effective? Why or why not?

5. What is the thesis or proposition? Is it clearly and strongly stated?

6. How did the speaker summarize his/her ideas?

7. Is the clincher effective? Why or why not?

INTRODUCTION AND CONCLUSION FOR INFORMATIVE SPEECH ON ASTHMA

General Purpose: To create understanding.

Specific Purpose: To create understanding about what exercise-induced asthma is, how common it is, and how to help someone during an asthma attack.

Introduction

I. Attention-getting statement: Picture this: you are seven years old. It is a beautiful summer day and you are at Jungle Rapids Waterslide with several friends. Just as you are running up the hill, as you have been all morning, it hits you—you cannot breathe. No matter how hard you try you cannot get enough air. You are having an asthma attack.

II. Need for listening: I have exercise-induced asthma and this story did happen to me; it could happen to you. We all need to know what to do to help someone who is having an asthma attack. After all, I could be in your physical education class, and that could happen again.

III. Thesis: Exercise-induced asthma is a common condition, and everyone should know what to do to help someone during an asthma attack.

   A. Defining exercise-induced asthma.

   B. Establishing how common it is.

   C. Helping someone with the condition.

Conclusion

I. Summary: Exercise-induced asthma is a noncommunicable disease that affects two-thirds of the population.

II. Clincher: Now that you are familiar with what exercise-induced asthma is, you can use what you know to help others—maybe even me.

INTRODUCTION AND CONCLUSION FOR INFORMATIVE SPEECH ON DOLPHINS

General Purpose: To create understanding.

Specific Purpose: To create understanding about the beauty and intelligence of dolphins.

Introduction

I. Attention-getting statement: Picture a herd of 1,000 dolphins gracefully splashing and playing, clicking, squeaking, flipping, and slapping the surface of the water with their tails. They seem to be overjoyed at just being alive. This sight is unforgettable, and so is the remarkable dolphin.

II. Need for listening: Ever since I was a little girl growing up in the Midwest, I have been fascinated by dolphins. I read both fiction and nonfiction accounts of their uniqueness. I never passed up an opportunity to go to Sea World (a large fish tank) in my home town. Since I have moved here by the ocean five years ago, I have been able to view these creatures in their natural habitat.

III. Dolphins are beautiful mammals, intelligent and amazing.

    A. Their beauty.

    B. Their intelligence.

    C. Their abilities.

Conclusion

I. Summary: A dolphin's intelligence and beauty make it an amazing, unique mammal.

II. Clincher: Dolphins are common to this area and are a great source of beauty and entertainment. Do take advantage of this natural resource in our own backyards.

INTRODUCTION AND CONCLUSION FOR PERSUASIVE SPEECH ON DRUGS AND PHYSICIANS

General Purpose: To move my audience to action.

Specific Purpose: To convince or urge my audience to be more responsible in choosing and remaining with doctors, due to the problem of drug-addicted physicians.

Organizational Format: Monroe's Motivated Sequence.

Attention

   I.   Our speech class seems to be health conscious.
- A.   We learned from Dave to limit cholesterol intake.
- B.   We learned from Robin to watch the foods we eat.

  II.   Often when we do not watch our health, we get sick, panic, and go to the first doctor available without taking the responsibility to investigate the doctor.
- A.   Example of my mother's hematologist who became drug-addicted and caused paralysis in a patient.
- B.   Many do not investigate the doctor's reputation and end up with a drug-addicted physician.
    - 1.   My survey of this class indicated that many of you are not aware of the serious problem of drug-addicted physicians.
    - 2.   The survey also indicated that your families rarely seek second opinions.

 III.   We all need to be more responsible in choosing and remaining with a doctor.

Action

   I.   Start to be responsible now because in the long run you are only helping yourself by staying away from a drug-addicted physician.

  II.   It is up to you to write the American Medical Association to help yourself, other patients, and even the drug-addicted physicians.

INTRODUCTION AND CONCLUSION FOR PERSUASIVE SPEECH ON EXERCISE AND STRESS

General Purpose: To convince my audience.

Specific Purpose: To convince my audience that exercise will help relieve the stress felt during final exams.

Organizational Format: Monroe's Motivated Sequence.

Attention

    I.   Here we are exactly one week away from finals. We are all thinking about how many finals we are going to have, how many are going to be comprehensive, and how many we are going to have on a given day.

    II.   According to Hopkin's *Adolescent Psychology,* experts in psychology say, "During finals, students tend to seek some form of stimulation outside of the educational realm."

        A.   This means that we often occupy ourselves in activities that allow us to "escape" the pressures of finals.

        B.   Example of student who suffered severe stress during finals week.

        C.   We have all experienced test anxiety or stress about our performance in courses.

    III.   Experts in Hopkin's book also state, "The best form of outside stimulation while taking finals involves some type of physical exertion."

        A.   So, exercise is the best form of outside stimulation during finals.

        B.   With finals so close at hand, it is important that we understand the value of exercise for managing stress.

Action

    I.   Now, right before exams, is the time to engage in an exercise program.

    II.   Remember, studies reveal that your examination scores can then be much higher.

WRITING INTRODUCTIONS AND CONCLUSIONS: AN EXERCISE

Objectives

1. To understand the difference between a specific purpose and a thesis or proposition statement.
2. To write effective thesis and proposition statements.
3. To prepare effective introductions and conclusions.

Explanation

A **thesis** is a direct, declarative statement expressing the main point of your informative speech. It is an assertive statement and expresses your observation or conclusion about your topic. A specific purpose is exactly what you want the audience to understand about your topic. The thesis is similar to the specific purpose in content but it is different in form. For example, a specific purpose would be to describe the mental and physical benefits of aerobics. The thesis would be worded as: "Aerobic exercise has a positive affect on the mind as well as the body." It is important to have a strong, assertive thesis and not just a topic sentence, such as: "Today, I want to talk about the value of aerobics."

In a persuasive speech, the specific purpose states what you want your audience to think, to believe, or to do. The proposition, similar to the thesis, is the statement in your speech that asserts what you want your audience to do, to think, or to believe. Again it is similar to the specific purpose in content but different in form.

Instructions

For each of the following three speeches, prepare an introduction and a conclusion. Make sure that the thesis or proposition is a strong assertive statement. In addition, make sure that the introduction and conclusion fulfill the functions specified at the beginning of this unit.

SPINNING KICK: INFORMATIVE SPEECH

General Purpose: To create understanding.
Specific Purpose: To demonstrate the basic body movements of a spinning kick.

Introduction

Body

 I. Your stance should be balanced and comfortable.
  A. Balance is accomplished by keeping the body straight.
   1. Your body should stay loose.
   2. Your feet should be approximately shoulder-width apart and pointed slightly forward.
  B. Don't lean forward.
 II. The initial body movement should start with the upper body.
  A. Turn and look at target first.
   1. This automatically torques the body.
  B. Arms should be held close to the body.
   1. Helps protect head.
   2. Helps maintain balance.
 III. The hips are the pivotal point for entire body movement.
  A. Transfer point for the torque of the upper body to the power of the kick.
  B. Knees should be slightly bent to allow the maximum range of motion for the hips.
  C. Hip movement should continue to flow until the kicking leg returns to the starting position.
   1. Body movement should not stop on impact with target.

Conclusion

GROWING A GARDEN: PERSUASIVE SPEECH

General Purpose: To convince my audience.
Specific Purpose: To persuade my audience to grow their own vegetable gardens.

Introduction

Body

I. A garden should be grown because it is easy.
   A. It requires no special skill or talent to grow a garden.
      1. There are books and TV shows that can help.
      2. The local gardening store can help.
      3. Tools can be used.
   B. There are many vegetables that can be easily grown in Louisiana.
      1. Winter vegetables that can be grown include onions, lettuce, cabbage, and cauliflower.
      2. Summer vegetables that can be grown include tomatoes, corn, watermelons, beans, bell peppers, and peas.
   C. A garden does not require much time to maintain.
      1. According to *Money* magazine, a Gallup poll found that a typical backyard garden is slightly more than 650 square feet in area, produces an average of $460 worth of vegetables at a cost of only $19, and takes only a few hours of labor per week to maintain.

II. A garden should be grown because homegrown vegetables are much fresher and of better quality than vegetables found in the store.
   A. Freshness enhances taste, color, and vitamin content.
      1. Most vegetables are shipped from California and are not fresh.
   B. Quality is the condition of the vegetables.
      1. Water content.
      2. Degree of ripeness.
   C. Any surplus vegetables can be put in the freezer. Freshness and quality will be maintained.

III. A garden should be grown because it is economical.
   A. According to *U.S. News and World Report,* the broker is taking 65¢ of every food dollar.
   B. Except for the initial cost of getting started, there is very little cost involved.
      1. Garden tools.
      2. Seed.
      3. Chemicals.
   C. Another statistic found in the *Saturday Evening Post* stated that the average garden is 22' by 25' and will be valued at $425 for an outlay of $25 for seed and supplies.
      1. Some people with larger gardens sell their produce and make a nice profit.

Conclusion

INCREASING YOUR VOCABULARY: PERSUASIVE SPEECH

General Purpose: To convince my audience.

Specific Purpose: To convince my audience that increasing their vocabulary will be to their greater benefit.

Introduction

Body

I. Increasing your vocabulary will increase your chance of success in business.
  A. A larger vocabulary may increase your chances of getting that job you want.
     1. A larger vocabulary can get you noticed in an interview.
     2. Without the language power, you may lose a job to someone else.
  B. A study by Dr. Johnson of the Management Department showed the connection between success in business and vocabulary power.
     1. One hundred young men who were studying to be industrial executives were surveyed.
     2. Five years later, not a single man who received a vocabulary score in the lowest 25 percent was an executive.
II. Increasing your vocabulary will increase your chances of success in school.
  A. You increase your capacity for learning when you increase your vocabulary.
     1. A larger vocabulary allows you to read more complicated texts.
     2. The more words you have at your command, the clearer and more precisely you can express complicated ideas.
  B. A study by Dr. O'Connor of the Education Department showed a connection between success in school and vocabulary power.
     1. Two high school homeroom classes with students of similar vocabulary scores at the beginning of the year were selected.
     2. One class received systematic vocabulary lessons.
     3. The class who received the vocabulary lessons made consistently higher grades in all their other classes.
III. Increasing your vocabulary will enhance your social communication skills.
  A. Language power can make you feel more confident when meeting new people.
     1. A good command of words and wit is impressive.
     2. The more confident you are about your language, the more likely you will be to take the initiative in conversation.
  B. Language power can help you express complicated feelings with friends.
     1. To share your thoughts and feelings with close friends, you need the words to express them.
     2. Misunderstandings occur when friends say the "wrong" things to each other.

Conclusion

WRITING TRANSITIONS

Objectives

    1. To understand the importance of transitions in adding coherence to a speech.
    2. To practice writing transitions.

Instructions

Write transitions in the indicated places for the following speech.

Bats

General Purpose: To create understanding.

Specific Purpose: To create understanding about the misunderstood bats of the world.

Introduction

    I.   Attention-getting statement: The window is open, a creature flies in; is it a bird, or is it a flying mouse? Neither—it's a bat. I believe the majority of the class would be out that door—and in a hurry.
    II. Need for listening: I know that up until a few months ago I would have been out that door before anyone else. Now, after researching just what a bat really is, I realize my fears were undocumented.
    III. Thesis: A bat is a unique creature that has been given a bum rap through superstition.
        A.   Superstitions.
        B.   What a bat really is.

*Transition:

Body

    I.   Superstitions are undocumented folk tales, which have given the bat a bad reputation.
        A.   Bats get caught in your hair.
            1.   Lay eggs (Barney Fife).
            2.   Cut hair to get out.
            3.   Nonsense—quote by Merlin Tuttle, biologist, founder of Bat Conservation International: "Any creature which can catch a gnat in total darkness is not apt to get in your toupee."
        B.   Bats are blind (cliché—blind as a bat).
            1.   Only with their eyes closed.
            2.   They have good eyesight.
        C.   Bats give you rabies.
            1.   Like all mammals, they do.
            2.   No more than any other species.
        D.   Bats suck your blood.
            1.   Vampire bats, three species, Latin America only.
            2.   Do not live in coffins.

*Transition:

II. A bat is a mammal of the order *Chiroptera,* which, translated, means "flying hand."
  A. Skeletal structure—humanlike.
  B. Outward appearance.
    1. Like a flying mouse or shrew.
    2. Picture your fingers extended downward.
    3. Tough membrane attached.
    4. Most have fur, no feathers.
    5. Faces made for necessity, not beauty.
    6. *Picture*: Trumpet-nosed bat, Leach's Fruit bat, and Wrinkle-faced bat.
    7. *Jars*: Wrinkle-faced bat and Red bat.
  C. Food (perform vital function).
    1. The food they eat determines looks.
      a. Trumpet-nose—nectar.
      b. Fruit bats—fruit.
    2. Fruit and pollination in South America, mainly in the tropics.
    3. Others eat blood, fish, mice, lizards, fruit, and insects.
    4. The bat and the rain forest.
      a. Dr. Edward Stashko, a biologist, conducted research for the World Wildlife Fund and found that "bats are one of the main animals responsible for maintaining tropical rain forests due to pollination of species only adapted for the bat." Century Plant: Tequila; Avocado: Guacamole.
    5. U.S. insect eaters (Bug Zappers).
      a. Research performed by Merlin Tuttle (BCI) showed that in Texas, a colony of twenty million Mexican free-tailed bats eats a quarter of a million pounds of insects a night.

*Transition:

Conclusion

I. Summary: Bats, although not pleasant to look at, have been given a bum rap through the many superstitions handed down from generation to generation.
II. Clincher: Bats are a unique mammal serving an important duty that we all benefit from.

References

Barbour, R. and W. H. Davis. "Bats of America," Lexington, Ky: The University Press of Kentucky, 1979.

Cohn, P. "Applauding the Beleaguered Bat (Intelligent Creatures with Vital Ecological Importance)," *Americas,* November/December 1987, pp. 14–16.

Givens, K. T. "My Gentle Friend, the Bat," *Modern Maturity,* American Association of Retired Persons, November 1984, pp. 63–64.

Tuttle, M. D. "Harmless, Highly Beneficial, Bats Still Get a Bum Rap," *Smithsonian,* January 1984, pp. 75–81.

Using Language Effectively

This unit describes how your choice of language affects the meanings communicated in your message and shapes others' perceptions of you. In public speaking situations, it is particularly important to use language accurately, clearly, vividly, and appropriately. Oral language should be more conversational and informal than written language. Generally, oral language is more personal and direct. The activities and exercises in this unit will help you practice using language more effectively, especially in public speaking situations.

The components of UNIT 12 are:

Language Notes

Language Shapes Perceptions: An Analysis

Using Gender-Neutral Nouns and Pronouns

Using Concrete and Uncluttered Language

Using Language Clearly and Concretely

Using Colorful and Vivid Language

Using Language to Create Parallel Structure

Speech 1: Parallel Structure

Speech 2: Parallel Structure

LANGUAGE NOTES

I. To use language effectively, be aware of some of the common problems associated with language use.
   A. Avoid sweeping generalizations and vagueness:
      1. He is a fine speaker. (vague)
      2. He speaks with confidence and expresses his ideas clearly. (more concrete)
   B. Avoid clutter in your language:
      1. Uh . . . you know. . . .
      2. Okay . . . well. . . .
   C. Avoid cliches:
      1. He was fit as a fiddle.
      2. She's cool as a cucumber.
   D. Avoid offensive and inappropriate language:
      1. It was hot as hell.
      2. You chicks, gals. . . .
      3. The Amish people are somewhat backward, but nice.
II. Use language that will enhance understanding and your credibility:
   A. Accurate and free of jargon.
   B. Clear and concrete.
   C. Vivid.
   D. Appropriate to the audience and the situation.
III. You can use language to involve and adapt to your audience.
   A. Speak with, not to, audience by using personal pronouns.
      1. We all need to be concerned.
      2. This is an issue for all of us.
   B. Use rhetorical questions.
      1. Requires a mental rather than a vocal response.
         a. Would you like to know how to earn money in your spare time?
         b. When American hostages were freed from Iran, they became heroes. Were they really heroes? Or did the media make them heroes?
   C. Make reference to common experience.
      1. I'm sure we have all had experience with the effects of government bureaucracy, such as standing in lines to register for classes.
      2. If you have ever not been allowed to cash a check because you are a student, then you have some idea of discrimination.
   D. You can use language to emphasize a point in a speech. Consider the following:
      1. Amount of time spent on ideas.
      2. Transition—from one point to the next.
         a. Internal: "Therefore we can see that. . . ."
         b. External: By calling attention to organization of speech.
      3. Repetition—restatement of idea.

LANGUAGE SHAPES PERCEPTIONS: AN ANALYSIS

Objectives

1. To understand how language shapes perceptions.
2. To understand how one's choice of language reveals information about that individual.
3. To discuss language and differences in interpretation and perception.

Instructions

Read the following paragraphs and answer the questions below. After you have formulated your responses to the questions, compare your responses with two or three others' responses.

For Analysis

Life is a game of chess. One is bound to the board—an earthly existence—and to the regulations of the game—namely, ethics, mores, laws, and values one seeks to uphold. The opponent is the collective mass of external forces that threatens and degrades one's sanctity, one's happiness, and one's well-being. One's pieces symbolize one's resistance against these detrimental external factors. At the onset, one is fully equipped to withstand the turmoil of the dark forces encountered over the course of the game. The game pieces represent one's uniquely human ability to transcend situations that would otherwise be unbearable. One safely guards the king, the element upon which one's existence depends. The king may be related to the human soul, that quality which makes subsistence possible, that figure in which all our aspirations are contained. The secondary pieces, which serve only as a means to protect the king and to attack the enemy, represent the protective shell that man possesses, the complex methods that man has invented to ensure self-preservation and to conquer the enemy.

Every move one makes in response to a given situation is decisive in the unfolding of one's future. Seemingly insignificant moves or decisions later amplify into critical events that determine one's state of being. The way one reacts to even a single event affects all other sequences of moves. Thus, one attempts to make every move count and pursues an earthly version of perfection. The big question seems to be: How do you play the game? That can only be answered by the individual. Regardless of one's playing method, the aim remains constant: to conquer the opponent and, in turn, achieve victory.

Questions for Response and Discussion

1. What inferences can you draw about this individual in regard to gender, attitude, values, education, and so on? In other words, based on the use of language, how would you describe this individual?

2. What do you think is the overall meaning of these paragraphs? In other words, what do you think this individual is saying? Do you agree? Why or why not?

3. What observations can you make about how language shapes perceptions and reveals attitudes and values?

4. After discussing your responses above with a group of your classmates, what conclusions can you draw about differences in the interpretation of language?

USING GENDER-NEUTRAL NOUNS AND PRONOUNS

Objectives

1. To use gender-neutral nouns and pronouns.
2. To appreciate the value of using language appropriately.

Explanation

It is important to use language appropriately; this means using gender-neutral language. Use either the plural form or both "he" and "she" when making references to teachers, surgeons, and so on. In addition, change nouns such as "policeman" to "police officer."

Instructions

Change the following words and sentences to reflect the use of gender-neutral language.

Words:

fireman

mailman

seamstress

Sentences:

The teacher has a responsibility to his students.

The chairman cancelled the meeting for Friday.

We need a good leader. He will have to be someone we admire.

USING CONCRETE AND UNCLUTTERED LANGUAGE

Objectives

1. To practice using concrete language.
2. To practice using uncluttered language.

Instructions

Use the following suggestions for stories and tell a story to the class using concrete, descriptive language. In addition, tell your story without language clutter such as "uhm," "you know," or "OK."

Story Suggestions

1. The Three Little Pigs
2. Little Red Riding Hood
3. Jack and the Beanstalk
4. Cinderella
5. My favorite vacation
6. My favorite movie
7. My most embarrassing moment
8. My dream house

USING LANGUAGE CLEARLY AND CONCRETELY

Objectives

1. To analyze a passage for its use of clear and concrete language.
2. To practice rewriting a passage to reflect the use of clear and concrete language.

Instructions

Read the following passage and circle the words or phrases that are vague and clutter the passage. Edit the passage so that you eliminate the unnecessary words and substitute the vague words for words that are clear and concrete.

Passage for Analysis and Editing

This past weekend, there was this really strange and sort of neat event that happened in our dorms.

We were all, you know, gathered in the TV room, when this weirdo dude came in and just kind of

sat right in the center with us. I mean, gee, none of us knew him but we didn't realize it at the time.

All of us, we found out later were thinking that this dude was a friend or something of someone in

the room. Anyway, everything seemed sort of ordinary, you know—like just an afternoon of watch-

ing TV. Then this guy let out this huge noise and began to sing "Happy Birthday" sort of rock-and-

roll style to my kind of best friend, Sally. Boy were we all surprised.

USING COLORFUL AND VIVID LANGUAGE

Objectives

1. To identify language that is vivid and colorful.
2. To evaluate a speech for its effective use of language.

Instructions

Martin Luther King's "I Have a Dream" speech is abundant with language that is vivid, colorful, and concrete. In addition, he uses imagery and rhythm to emphasize his points. Identify the particular words or phrases that make the speech vivid or colorful. Also identify the imagery and the rhythmic phrases he uses. Finally, discuss with a small group of your classmates why his particular style of language is so effective in supporting his purpose. A copy of King's speech can easily be found in many public speaking texts or in other sources.

USING LANGUAGE TO CREATE PARALLEL STRUCTURE

Objectives

1. To appreciate the value of parallel structure to aid in retention.
2. To analyze speech outlines for their use of parallel structure.

Instructions

Analyze the two outlines on the following pages for their use of parallel structure. Note, in particular, the wording of the main points and the thesis. Try to use parallel structure in your speeches.

SPEECH 1: PARALLEL STRUCTURE

Introduction

I. It was Mr. Baseball himself, Bob Uecker, when asked how he stopped the wild pitch, who answered this way: "Usually I just wait till it stops rolling, go to the backstop, and then pick it up!"

II. As one of America's most-loved sports, baseball is something we can all relate to.
   A. I was a catcher for eight years in both little league and Home Talent baseball; for five years I was an All-Star.
   B. You can appreciate the game and the catcher's role by understanding the mastery involved in handling the wild pitch.

III. Thesis: Blocking the wild pitch is very important to the catcher, who must be:
   A. Fearless.
   B. Physically fit.
   C. Aware of the field.

Body

I. The catcher should be fearless, willing to sacrifice his or her body.
   A. The equipment helps take most of the fear out of the catcher.
      1. Mask.
      2. Chest protector.
      3. Cup.
      4. Shin guards.
   B. Catcher must not be afraid for the pitch to bounce in front of him or her.
   C. The body is an important tool in stopping the pitch.
      1. Face.
      2. Chest.
      3. Legs.

II. The catcher must be physically fit.
   A. Be as alive and instinctive as possible from the first through the ninth innings.
   B. A catcher can be large or small in build.
      1. For the big catcher, size is the asset used most in blocking the pitch.
      2. The smaller catcher relies on quickness.

III. The catcher must be aware of *all* situations on the field.
   A. Must know what pitch is coming and which position to take for that pitch.
      1. Fastball.
      2. Breaking pitch.
      3. Knuckleball.
   B. Must know the position of the baserunners.

Conclusion

I. The things usually found in the best catchers, those who are the best at blocking bad pitches, are:
   A. Fearlessness.
   B. Total awareness.
   C. Physical fitness.

II. As a catcher who blocked many pitches over eight years, I have found that these were the most exciting aspects of catching. If it hadn't been for this excitement, I doubt it would have been as fulfilling for me.

SPEECH 2: PARALLEL STRUCTURE

Introduction

I. Every day many of us go into the grocery store in search of fresh vegetables, only to find that the vegetables are either not ripe or overripe, dried out, or even rotten. On top of this, the store charges an outrageous price for these so-called good quality, fresh vegetables.

II. Fortunately, there is something most of us can do about this. We can go into our backyards and start our own vegetable gardens. I have done this for years.

III. Everyone who has access to land should grow their own vegetables.
    A. It is easy.
    B. The vegetables are fresher and of better quality than those bought in a store.
    C. It is very economical to grow your own garden.

Body

I. A garden should be grown because it is easy.
    A. It requires no special skill or talent to grow a garden.
        1. There are books and TV shows that can help.
        2. The local gardening store can help.
        3. Tools can be used.
    B. There are many vegetables that can be easily grown in Louisiana.
        1. Winter vegetables that can be grown include onions, lettuce, cabbage, cauliflower.
        2. Summer vegetables that may be grown include tomatoes, corn, watermelons, beans, bell peppers, and peas.
    C. A garden does not require much time to maintain.
        1. According to *Money* magazine, a Gallup poll found that a typical backyard garden is slightly more than 650 square feet in area, produces an average of $460 worth of vegetables at a cost of only $19, and takes only a few hours of labor per week to maintain.

II. A garden should be grown because homegrown vegetables are much fresher and of better quality than vegetables found in a store.
    A. Freshness enhances taste, color, and vitamin content.
        1. Most vegetables are shipped from California and are not fresh.
    B. Quality is the condition of the vegetables.
        1. Water content.
        2. Degree of ripeness.
    C. Any surplus vegetables can be put in the freezer. Freshness and quality will be maintained.

III. A garden should be grown because it is economical.
    A. According to *U.S. News and World Report,* the broker is taking 65¢ of every food dollar.
    B. Except for the initial cost of getting started, there is very little cost involved.
        1. Garden tools.
        2. Seed.
        3. Chemicals.
    C. Another statistic found in the *Saturday Evening Post* stated that the average garden is 22' by 25' and will be valued at $425 for an outlay of $25 for seed and supplies.
        1. Some people with larger gardens sell their produce and make a nice profit.

Conclusion

I.   As you can see, growing your own garden will present little difficulty and has many advantages, such as fresher, more flavorful, and much cheaper vegetables.

II. I would like to urge all of you who have access to land that can be used for a garden to do so. It will be worth it.

References

"Gardening Time Again," *Saturday Evening Post*, May/June 1982, p. 70.

"Growing Money in Your Garden," *Money,* March 1981, p. 144.

"Summer Gardening," *U.S. News and World Report*, June 1982, p. 65.

Delivery: Using Voice and Body Effectively

This unit will help you practice using your voice and body effectively in public speaking situations. If you feel confident about how you look and sound, then you will enjoy giving speeches and find the whole process less difficult.

The components of UNIT 13 are:

Methods of Presentation

Using Voice and Body for Effective Delivery

Tongue Twisters Exercise

Articulation and Pronunciation

Practicing Vowel Sounds

Practicing Vocal Emphasis

Reading Aloud for Effective Delivery

Content-Free Speech

Impromptu Speeches

Personal Experience Speech

The Modern Fairy Tale: Practice Speeches

Sample Modernized Fairy Tale: Ismerelda of the Forest

METHODS OF PRESENTATION

For the purposes of this course and for most public speaking situations you will encounter, the extemporaneous mode of delivery is the most appropriate and, in fact, superior mode of presentation. The extemporaneous mode of delivery is more spontaneous, flexible, and adaptable to the audience. It recognizes that communication is shared and that the meaning of messages is shaped by speakers as well as listeners. In an extemporaneous mode of delivery the audience's understanding is significant, feedback and adaptation are possible, ideas can be repeated, and examples can be altered as the need arises.

There are four recognized modes of delivery:

Impromptu presentation is an unplanned, spur-of-the-moment presentation. It frequently *appears* unplanned and can cause the speaker to ramble and fumble for ideas and words. This mode of delivery works for highly experienced speakers who speak on topics reflecting their knowledge and expertise. The impromptu mode of delivery is appropriate for very informal occasions and will be used periodically in labs to practice components of speechmaking.

Memorized presentation is a speech that has been committed to memory. It frequently produces a stilted, inflexible delivery in which the individual concentrates on remembering the exact wording rather than the meaning of the message. This mode of delivery is only effective for "performers" who have experience committing text to memory and can deliver it as if it were spontaneous. It is appropriate for highly experienced speakers and for very formal, ceremonious occasions. The only memorized portion of your speeches for this course should be your opening statement—the attention-getter.

Manuscript presentation is a presentation that is read from a written text. It diminishes spontaneity and adaptability. Like the memorized speech, this mode of delivery is only effective for those individuals who are highly experienced in reading a text aloud in a conversational mode. And, like the memorized speech, it is appropriate for very formal, ceremonious occasions. The only written portions of your speeches should be the thesis statement and the main ideas. The rest of your speech should be in outline form, identifying key words and phrases.

Extemporaneous presentation is a presentation that uses a carefully planned, systematically structured outline of thesis statement, main ideas, and key words and phrases. The exact wording is not predetermined. The speaker uses his or her notes as a reference rather than as a crutch.

The extemporaneous presentation involves a systematic series of steps that begins with your analysis of topic, audience, and purpose and ends with the delivery of the last word of your speech.

The extemporaneous delivery style resembles a polished dialogue or conversation with your audience. The following pages and activities can help you acquire an effective conversational delivery style for public speaking situations.

USING VOICE AND BODY
FOR EFFECTIVE DELIVERY

Explanation

The following speech outline specifies particular behaviors and attitudes that will help you develop an effective delivery style. Read the outline and practice these behaviors and attitudes in the impromptu and introductory speaking assignments in this unit.

Introduction

I. How much do you fear public speaking?
   A. Next to cancer, public speaking is most feared by Americans.
   B. Public speaking anxiety is very common and can be overcome or controlled.
II. As a public speaker and teacher of public speaking for fifteen years, I conceive of public speaking as:
   A. Essentially similar to interpersonal communication.
   B. Polished, refined dialogue with an audience.
III. Thesis: Public speaking becomes an art when you make it a dialogue or conversation with the audience.
   A. Use behaviors that make you look and feel confident.
   B. Adopt an attitude of concern for the audience's understanding.

Transition: How do you make that happen? Focus on behaviors.

Body

I. Demonstrate behaviors that make you look and feel confident.
   A. Use direct and frequent eye contact.
   B. Use relaxed facial expressions and gestures that do not distract from the meaning.
      1. It is essential to be natural.
      2. Focus on meaning and understanding.
   C. Your voice should respond to meaning by means of:
      1. Emphasis.
      2. Pace.
      3. Pause.
   D. Demonstrate purposeful use of space and movement.
      1. Stand near or on the side of the speaker stand.
      2. Use movement as transition between ideas.
   E. Use extemporaneous delivery.
      1. Not written out.
      2. Not memorized.
II. Portray an attitude of concern for the audience's understanding.
   A. Portray a sincere desire to communicate with the audience.
      1. Read audience feedback.
      2. Show enthusiasm and interest.
      3. Focus on the audience's understanding of your message.
   B. Think of your speech as a dialogue or conversation with your audience.
      1. Use nervous energy to engage audience in a dialogue—talk with, not *at* them.
      2. This can help you feel comfortable and build your confidence.

Conclusion

    I. Successful public speaking requires appropriate behaviors and attitudes.
       A. Behavior that makes you feel confident.
       B. An attitude of concern for the audience's understanding.
   II. Public speaking is at its best when it becomes art—a dialogue with your audience.

TONGUE TWISTERS EXERCISE

Objectives

1. To practice accurate articulation and pronunciation.
2. To learn to read aloud conversationally.

Instructions

Working in pairs or groups, students should practice selected sentences from the list below. Points can be awarded on the basis of demonstrated competency:

1. One point if the speaker flawlessly articulates the sounds and pronounces the words accurately.
2. One point if the speaker communicates the sentence in a conversational, meaningful manner.

Individuals in the group can each take a turn reading a sentence aloud while the other members record the number of points earned.

Tongue Twisters

1. Three gray geese in the green grass grazing; gray were the geese and green was the grazing.
2. The sun shines on the shop signs. (Repeat three times.)
3. The sixth sheik's sixth sheep's sick.
4. Fanny Finch fried five floundering fish for Francis Fowlar's father.
5. A big black bug bit a big black bear and made the big black bear bleed blood.
6. She stood at the door of Burgess's fish-sauce shop welcoming him in.
7. She stood at the door on the balcony, inexplicably mimicking him hiccupping, amicably welcoming him in.
8. Truly rural. (Repeat three times.)
9. He had sixty-six sick chicks.
10. Those are very strange strategic statistics.
11. Tie twine to three tree twigs.
12. Three new blue beans in a new-blown bean blower.
13. Six long slim slick slender saplings slid slightly southward.
14. Preshrunk shirts seldom shrink.
15. A bloke's back brake block broke.
16. Shy Sarah saw six Swiss wrist watches.
17. Does this shop stock short socks with spots?
18. Sheep shouldn't sleep in a shack, sheep should sleep in a shed.
19. Six sick soldiers sighted seven slowly sinking ships.
20. Washington's washwoman washed Washington's wash while Washington watched Wilson.
21. Blushing Barbara booed boisterously while blind Bobby brought brilliant birds bright barbs.

22. The chop shop stocks chops.
23. Double bubble gum bubbles double.
24. Thomas Tattertoot took taut twine to tie ten twigs to two tall trees.
25. Round and round the rugged rocks the ragged rascal ran.
26. Heinz skillfully seasoned spaghetti, scarlet sauce saturated, singularly satisfying.
27. Little Moses supposes his toeses are roses, but Moses supposes erroneously. For Moses he knowses his toeses aren't roses, as Moses supposes his toeses to be.

ARTICULATION AND PRONUNCIATION

Objective

1. To practice accurate articulation and pronunciation.

Instructions

Practice reading aloud the following pairs of words so that your classmates will be able to distinguish which word is which.

Words for Practice

1. accepted—excepted
2. secede—succeed
3. weather—whether
4. affect—effect
5. since—sins
6. willow—mellow
7. booths—booze
8. pictures—pitchers
9. wandered—wondered
10. stirred—third

PRACTICING VOWEL SOUNDS

Objectives

1. To practice pronouncing vowel sounds.
2. To practice vocal articulation.

Instructions

Practice reciting the following words accurately. Make sure the words are not pronounced with a "drawl" or "twang."

Words for Practice

1. tan, fan, ran, span, van
2. wean, clean, preen, lean, bean
3. ten, pen, wren, then, hen, men
4. bin, tin, din, fin, gin
5. lone, moan, tone, phone, bone
6. gang, clang, sang, bang, hang
7. ring, sing, bring, thing
8. along, bong, long, gong

PRACTICING VOCAL EMPHASIS

Objectives

1. To practice vocal expression and emphasis.
2. To develop effective delivery skills.

Explanation

Although words convey meanings, the particular meanings of words come from their use or expression. People give meaning to words as they speak them. Using the same words, you can change the meaning by just emphasizing different words.

In the following example, the italicized word connotes a different meaning. Practice reading the sentences aloud.

John is taking me to the ball. (John, not Sam)
John is *taking* me to the ball. (he is paying for everything)
John is taking *me* to the ball. (can you believe it, I'm so happy)
John is taking me to the *ball*. (wow, a real ball)

Instructions

Practice reading the following sentences aloud, emphasizing the italicized words. Ask your classmates: What was the meaning that you communicated in each sentence?

Sentences for Practice

1. *Sally* gave me her gown.
2. Sally *gave* me her gown.
3. Sally gave me her *gown*.

4. *I* don't care what you think.
5. I don't *care* what you think.
6. I don't care *what* you think.
7. I don't care what *you* think.

READING ALOUD FOR EFFECTIVE DELIVERY

Objectives

1. To develop effective vocal expression.
2. To practice effective gestures and posture.

Explanation and Instructions

Reading passages aloud can help you develop effective delivery skills. Select your favorite kinds of passages: a poem, a portion of a story, a clipping from a newspaper, magazine, or other source. Practice reading them aloud at home; then read one of your selections in front of the class. Use the following questions to receive feedback from your classmates.

Questions for Feedback

1. Describe the reader's use of eye contact.

2. Describe the reader's use of vocal expression (variety, emphasis).

3. Describe the reader's vocal quality (sound of voice, pitch).

4. Describe the reader's posture and stance.

5. Evaluate the effectiveness of the reading. What was the meaning conveyed by the reader?

CONTENT-FREE SPEECH

Objectives

1. To practice conversational delivery style by making sense out of nonsense.
2. To use voice, gesture, and bodily action to convey meaning.

Task

Each student will express an emotion without using words. You may use numbers, alphabet symbols, gibberish, or sounds along with gesture, facial expression, and bodily action to convey an emotion.

Instructions

Each student should allow approximately one to three minutes preparation time and one to three minutes delivery time. One student picks a slip of paper with an emotion listed on it and is allowed a maximum of three minutes for preparation time. While the first student is presenting his or her content-free speech, the second student can select an emotion and prepare a speech. The class should guess (much as in the game of charades) what emotion the student is presenting. The presenter should be allowed at least one minute delivery time before any guesses are allowed.

Suggestions for Preparation

After selecting your emotion, think of a situation in which you might experience that emotion or a person you might feel that way with or about. For example: If you select anger, you could recall the time you loaned your roommate your favorite sweater and he or she returned it to you dirty and with a cigarette hole burned in it.

Suggestions for Delivery

As you present this content-free speech, imagine yourself in that situation or talking to that person or group. For example: You might look directly at the audience (as your imagined roommate) in a stern manner and, with clenched teeth and fist, you could use numbers or alphabet symbols to vocally express anger through your tone of voice.

IMPROMPTU SPEECHES

Objectives

1. To practice behaviors and attitudes that make you look confident.
2. To develop effective delivery skills.

Instructions and Explanation

Working in small groups, select a topic from the list below and prepare a brief, two to three minute talk. All group members should contribute to the preparation of an outline containing an attention-getting introduction that states the topic, a body that has two main ideas or examples, and a conclusion that restates the main topic. Then review the outline in "Using Voice and Body for Effective Delivery" in this unit and select one group member to deliver the speech using effective delivery style.

Topics

1. The essentials of a successful interview
2. Counting calories
3. The best beaches
4. The best restaurants
5. Hunting dogs
6. Fashions in hair/dress
7. The art of babysitting
8. How to lose one's friends
9. My favorite TV show/film
10. My favorite book
11. My kid sister/brother
12. My favorite hero/actor
13. The art of surfing
14. A college survival kit
15. My favorite vacation
16. My favorite movie
17. My most embarrassing moment
18. The importance of participating in campus activities

PERSONAL EXPERIENCE SPEECH

Objectives

1. To use clear descriptive language.
2. To practice effective delivery skills.

Task

Prepare and present a speech based on personal experience to your group or to the class. Your goal is to use clear descriptive language to re-create the experience and to use effective delivery skills.

Suggestions for Preparation

1. Select a personal experience that had a significant impact on you. Possibilities might include:

   Your most embarrassing moment
   Your most exciting moment
   Your greatest accomplishment
   A car wreck
   Climbing a mountain
   An exquisite sunset
   The most delicious food you have ever tasted
   Your favorite vacation
   The most gorgeous man/woman you have ever seen
   Whatever you feel very strongly about or have *vivid* memories of

2. Develop and organize your speech by addressing these three questions: What? How? Why?

   a. If an event or experience, address:
      1. What happened or what you did.
      2. How you felt about it.
      3. Why you felt that way or why it was significant.
   b. If food, place, or person, address:
      1. What it/they look(s) like.
      2. How the food tastes; how that place or person makes you feel.
      3. Why you find it/them delicious or beautiful or wonderful.

3. Outline your speech in the most effective and logical order, addressing the three issues above. Use only key words or phrases.

4. Practice your speech aloud, concentrating on reliving the experience. Do not merely list things; use words to paint a picture of what happened or what you are describing. For example, if your speech is about the time you saved a drowning person, do not merely state, "I jumped in and pulled him out." Tell what he was doing; describe his struggles; tell how deep the water was; how far he was from shore; recount your fears and other feelings as you pulled him toward shore; tell how the current almost took you under; demonstrate the way you held him by the hair. Emphasize such items as your fatigue or exhaustion as you fought to stay afloat.

5. Prepare a brief introduction and conclusion.

Suggestions for Delivery

1. Do not use note cards or stand behind a podium. Be open and free to use gestures to relive the experience.
2. It may be appropriate to sit on a stool or lean on the end of a desk to create an intimate or relaxed atmosphere.
3. As you tell your story, concentrate on re-creating the experience for yourself and your listeners. Your attitude should be one that demonstrates a sincere and extreme desire to have the audience understand and share your experience.

Suggestions for Listeners

1. Allow yourself to partake in the experience created through the speaker's words.
2. Make note of particularly vivid words the speaker uses.
3. Find a way to unobtrusively record the vivid descriptive words and phrases the speakers in your group use. You might take turns sitting off to the side and writing down words and phrases that are particularly vivid or descriptive.
4. Turn in the list of words to your instructor and/or share the list of words aloud with the rest of the class.
5. Select one member to tell his or her story to the rest of the class.

THE MODERN FAIRY TALE: PRACTICE SPEECHES

Objectives

1. To practice effective delivery skills.
2. To practice using language fluently in a storytelling format.

Explanation

Fairy tales, fables, and traditional stories follow similar patterns. They begin with an introduction of characters and setting. The middle of the tale frequently consists of a feat to be proven, dilemma or riddle to be solved, or situation to be untangled. The tale concludes with a moral, truth, or insight about what occurred. The fairy tale or fable structure provides an excellent pattern in which to practice using language clearly and fluently. Too often we clutter our language with words and phrases such as "you know," "uhm," and "OK." The fairy tale format provides a familiar structure for you to practice effective language.

Instructions

Your goal is to tell a story or tale to the class using language effectively. Select one of your favorite fairy tales, fables, or traditional stories and modernize it. There are several approaches you might take:

1. Change the events or ending to reflect the modern female (make the princess be the hero or let her do the rescuing).
2. Change the events to reflect more modern stories (imagine Hansel and Gretel getting jobs of their own to help support the family, or Cinderella slowly poisoning her stepmother's and stepsisters' food).
3. Change the language or style to reflect the modern male (consider Michael J. Fox or Eddie Murphy awakening Sleeping Beauty, who turns out to be Whoopi Goldberg).

Suggestions for Preparation and Delivery

1. Consult your library (home, local, or university) for such works as Medieval and Early Modern Heroic Tales and Romances such as:

   Tales of King Arthur and the Knights
   Grimm's Fairy Tales
   The Arabian Nights
   Adventures of Robin Hood

   Or consult your memory and imagination for treasured fairy tales and fables of princesses, goblins, kings, dragons, wicked witches, and knights all living "once upon a time." The following sample modernized fairy tale is provided for your insight and inspiration.
2. Working in groups or alone, use the pattern below and sketch out your ideas and structure on a separate sheet of paper. When completed, turn in your outline to your instructor.
3. If prepared individually, tell your tale for your group. Then select one member to tell his or her tale to the class.
4. If composed or prepared as a group, decide how to present it to the class. The group can elect to tell it together or select one or two members to tell the tale.

5. It is important to relate your tale as a story; do not act it out as a performance.
6. Use vocal expression, gesture, and bodily action (as you would in a speech) to add meaning to your tale.

Fairy Tale Pattern

Title or Source of Original Tale:
Your Modernized Title Version:

    I. Introduction.
        A.   Setting.
        B.   Characters.
   II. The Action or Situation.
        A.
        B.
        C.
        D.
  III. Conclusion.
        A.
        B.   Moral, Truth, or Insight.

SAMPLE MODERNIZED FAIRY TALE: ISMERELDA OF THE FOREST

Adapted from the many tales of a princess who is given in marriage to the prince who can accomplish a feat.

Modernized Title: Ismerelda of the Forest

I. Introduction

    A. Setting—a castle near the forest.
    B. Characters:
        1. Princess Ismerelda (referred to as Emma by her papa)—a beautiful, kind-hearted young girl.
        2. The King—Ismerelda's father, a very traditional king who loves his daughter very much.
        3. Many potential princes who eagerly vie for Ismerelda's hand in marriage.

II. Action or Situation

    A. Ismerelda grew up a happy little girl playing in the forest, making friends with the animals.
        1. She especially loved to run with the deer.
        2. She was swift and graceful.
    B. When the King felt it was time for his lovely daughter to marry, he invited all the princes in the kingdom to a footrace.
        1. The fastest would win his daughter's hand.
        2. The King would celebrate with a big feast.
    C. The day before the footrace and feast, Ismerelda pleaded with the King to let her participate.
        1. The King felt it was "unprincess-like" or unlady-like to do so.
        2. She pleaded.
        3. He loved her very much, and so he consented.
    D. The morning of the feast, Ismerelda challenged her father with the following request:
        1. "If I win the race, can *I* choose?"
        2. The King, who loved his daughter very much, agreed.
    E. The footrace and feast were festive.
        1. The food and drink were delicious.
        2. The princes were colorfully attired.
        3. Princess Ismerelda appeared somewhat disguised for the race.
    F. Ismerelda, who had learned to run as swift as the deer, won the race.
        1. She talked with several of the princes, enjoying their company.
        2. However, she could not find that very special one.
    G. Ismerelda's choice, as she told her father, was to build a cottage in the forest.
        1. Many of the nearby village children enjoyed learning songs from her and listening to her read.
        2. She wanted to continue and start a small school.
    H. The King had never heard of a princess *not* marrying.
        1. But he loved his daughter very much.
        2. And she pleaded with him.
        3. So he agreed.

III. Conclusion

A. Ismerelda, the children, and the forest animals frolicked happily and learned much from each other.
   1. This continued for a while.
   2. Later, Ismerelda made another choice.
B. Moral, truth, or insight: Pick your own—
   1. Kings should never underestimate the will and determination of princesses.
   2. Boys should never assume that they can run faster than girls.
   3. Left to their own devices, young "princesses" can figure out survival tactics.
   4. Marriage is not the only road to happiness.
   5. Happiness is found within.

Using Presentational Aids

This unit provides you with a brief sketch of the kinds of presentational aids that can enhance your speech. This unit also provides you with suggestions for using presentational aids effectively. The activities in this unit can help you practice designing ways to enhance your speeches through the use of presentational aids.

The components of UNIT 14 are:

Kinds of Presentational Aids: Notes

Suggestions for Using Presentational Aids

Designing Presentational Aids: An Exercise

The Value of Scarfs: A Speech for Analysis

Understanding Bats: A Speech for Analysis

KINDS OF PRESENTATIONAL AIDS: NOTES

Presentational aids are very helpful in illustrating and clarifying ideas, in creating interest in ideas, and in supporting ideas. There are several kinds of presentational aids you can select from to enhance your speech. The list and the explanations below should help you in deciding which kinds of presentational aids you can use for your speeches.

Types of Presentational Aids

Objects
Models
Graphs
Charts
Videotapes
Photographs
Drawings
Transparencies

Descriptions of Presentational Aids

Objects: Using objects such as a twelve-string guitar or scuba diving equipment not only creates interest in your speech but can also help clarify your ideas. It is important to illustrate how the objects work or can be used. Do not just display your objects—make them an integral part of your speech.

Models: Sometimes it is not practical to bring in the actual objects because they are too large, not available, or would not work in a classroom setting. For example, one speaker created a model of a set of miniature snow skis made out of poster board. Thus he was able to place the skis in his hands and simulate the different moves that a skier makes. In this way the audience could vividly see the movements that he illustrated.

Graphs: Graphs are particularly useful in simplifying and clarifying statistics. For example, when an important part of your speech depends on whether or not your audience understands statistical patterns, use a bar, line, or pie graph to illustrate those patterns.

Charts: Charts are useful for summarizing and presenting large blocks of information. One speaker used a chart to present the batting averages of the top baseball players. Another speaker used a chart to list the essential equipment needed for a backpack trip into the wilderness. Because you can list items on a chart, they are useful for any type of speech. Many speakers find it helpful to list their main ideas on a chart and unveil them as they present their speech.

Videotapes: With careful editing and timing, videotapes can be very effective in illustrating your ideas. For a speech about Michael Jordan, a speaker was able to piece together some of his best basketball shots. The speaker used a brief clip of the video at the opening of his speech to create interest and then he used a slow-motion shot to illustrate Jordan's skills.

Photographs: A photograph, if large enough, can work very well to amplify or create interest in your message. Speakers have effectively used pictures of animals, scenery, or a city skyline that they found in oversized library books. These examples work well not only because they are large enough to be seen by their audience, but also they are colorful and vivid depictions. Regular size photographs will not work for speeches unless you have them enlarged. Passing photographs around the room will be distracting to your presentation.

Drawings: A viable alternative to photographs are drawings. These can be done fairly inexpensively using poster boards and colored pens. These drawings do not need to be of artistic quality; in fact, simplicity and clarity should be the guiding factors in your drawings.

Transparencies: Transparencies are easy and inexpensive to create. They are shown on an overhead projector which is usually standard equipment in most classrooms. You can easily convert photographs, drawings, graphs, and charts to transparencies. In addition, different color transparencies are available.

SUGGESTIONS FOR USING PRESENTATIONAL AIDS

1. The entire speech situation must be thought of as visual. A visual aid is merely an aid; it is not to be the speech.
2. The visual aid must be needed—it must furnish clarity and understanding beyond the spoken word.
3. The aid must be clear and uncluttered, including only those details and features that are essential to clarity.
4. The aid must be large enough for all to see it easily.
5. The aid should be attractive and pleasing to the eye.
6. The aid must be relatively easy to operate, manipulate, and handle, keeping in mind that all must be able to see and follow.
7. Avoid circulating visual aids among your audience. The chalkboard, because of time constraints in class, should not be used.
8. The visual aid should only be seen when being used. (Handouts are only appropriate *after* the speech and do not meet the requirements of a visual aid.)
9. Use eye contact with audience rather than visual aids.

DESIGNING PRESENTATIONAL AIDS: AN EXERCISE

Objectives

1. To understand the value of using presentational aids.
2. To anticipate types of presentational aids that would work to enhance particular messages.

Instructions

Working individually or in small groups, discuss what types of presentational aids would be useful for the following two speech outlines. In your discussions, be sure to consider the feasibility of the aid as well as the appropriateness of the aid.

THE VALUE OF SCARFS: A SPEECH FOR ANALYSIS

General Purpose: To create understanding.
Specific Purpose: To present a humorous and informative perspective of the usefulness of scarfs.

Introduction

I. Have you ever been excluded from someplace because you weren't dressed appropriately?
II. You'll never know when you might need a scarf or need to know how to use it creatively.
III. A scarf can be a lifesaver.
   A. How it is functional for a man.
   B. How it is functional for a woman.

Body

I. A scarf can "save" a man's face.
   A. Bandanna scarfs worn in old days by cowboys.
      1. Kept dust away from face.
      2. Worked to hide bandits.
      3. Popularized as fashionable.
         a. Roy Rogers.
         b. Gene Autry.
   B. Scarfs work as neckties for modern man.
      1. Some restaurants require neckties.
      2. Story of friend, Harry, who forgot his tie.
II. A scarf can "save" a woman's hairdo and fashion.
   A. Scarfs used throughout history to cover a woman's head.
      1. In biblical times, women covered their heads as a sign of modesty.
      2. Peasant women frequently wore scarfs while working in the fields.
      3. Fifties and sixties—scarfs were used to protect a woman's teased hairdo.
      4. Seventies—the hippie generation woman re-created the "peasant earth woman" look.
   B. A scarf can add life to a drab outfit or hairdo.
      1. Can fashionably save or hide unsightly hair.
      2. Can add style and color to a drab dress.
         a. At neck or around shoulders.
         b. At waist.

Conclusion

I. Remember a scarf can save a man's face and a woman's fashion.
II. So never throw away a scarf. Keep it handy for its many creative uses in face- and neck-saving times.

UNDERSTANDING BATS: A SPEECH FOR ANALYSIS

General Purpose: To create understanding.

Specific Purpose: To create understanding about the misunderstood bats of the world.

INTRODUCTION

 I. Attention-getting statement: The window is open, a creature flies in; is it a bird, or is it a flying mouse? Neither—it's a bat. I believe the majority of the class would be out that door—and in a hurry.

 II. Need for listening: I know that up until a few months ago I would have been out that door before anyone else. Now, after researching just what a bat really is, I realize my fears were undocumented.

 III. Thesis: A bat is a unique creature that has been given a bum rap through superstition.

  A. Superstitions.

  B. What a bat really is.

Body

 I. Superstitions are undocumented folk tales, which have given the bat a bad reputation.

  A. Bats get caught in your hair.

   1. Lay eggs (Barney Fife).

   2. Cut hair to get out.

   3. Nonsense—quote by Merlin Tuttle, biologist, founder of Bat Conservation International: "Any creature which can catch a gnat in total darkness is not apt to get in your toupeé."

  B. Bats are blind (cliché—blind as a bat).

   1. Only with their eyes closed.

   2. They have good eyesight.

  C. Bats give you rabies.

   1. Like all mammals, they do.

   2. No more than any other species.

  D. Bats suck your blood.

   1. Vampire bats, three species, Latin America only.

   2. Do not live in coffins.

 II. A bat is a mammal of the order *Chiroptera,* which, translated, means "flying hand."

  A. Skeletal structure—humanlike.

  B. Outward appearance.

   1. Like a flying mouse or shrew.

   2. Picture your fingers extended downward.

   3. Tough membrane attached.

   4. Most have fur, no feathers.

   5. Faces made for necessity, not beauty.

   6. *Picture:* Trumpet-nosed bat, Leach's Fruit bat and Wrinkle-faced bat.

   7. *Jars:* Wrinkle-faced bat and Red bat.

  C. Food (perform vital function).

   1. The food they eat determines looks.

    a. Trumpet Nose—nectar.

    b. Fruit bats—fruit.

2. Fruit and pollination in South America, mainly in the tropics.
3. Others eat blood, fish, mice, lizards, fruit, and insects.
4. The bat and the rain forest.
   a. Dr. Edward Stashko, a biologist, conducted research for the World Wildlife Fund and found that "bats are one of the main animals responsible for maintaining tropical rain forests due to pollination of species only adapted for the bat." Century Plant: Tequila; Avocado: Guacamole.
5. U.S. insect eaters (Bug Zappers).
   a. Research performed by Merlin Tuttle (BCI) showed that in Texas, a colony of twenty million Mexican free-tailed bats eats a quarter of a million pounds of insects a night.

Conclusion

I. Summary: Bats, although not pleasant to look at, have been given a bum rap through the many superstitions handed down from generation to generation.
II. Clincher: Bats are a unique mammal serving an important duty that we all benefit from.

References

Barbour, R. and W. H. Davis. "Bats of America," Lexington, Ky: The University Press of Kentucky, 1979.

Cohn, P. "Applauding the Beleaguered Bat (Intelligent Creatures with Vital Ecological Importance)," *Americas,* November/December 1987, pp. 14–16.

Givens, K. T. "My Gentle Friend, the Bat," *Modern Maturity,* American Association of Retired Persons, November 1984, pp. 63–64.

Tuttle, M. D. "Harmless, Highly Beneficial, Bats Still Get a Bum Rap," *Smithsonian,* January 1984, pp. 75–81.

Preparing Informative Speeches

This unit highlights the essential components of informative speaking, has exercises on organizing informative speeches, and provides example student informative speech outlines. The major difference between informative and persuasive speeches is in your general purpose for speaking. It is important to understand this difference and to develop your topics and speeches accordingly.

The components of UNIT 15 are:

Informing Audiences: Notes

Organizing Informative Speeches

Format for Informative Speeches

The Wild Pitch: Informative Outline 1

Rock 'n' Roll and Blues: Informative Outline 2

Gospel Music: Informative Outline 3

The Journalist: Informative Outline 4

INFORMING AUDIENCES: NOTES

Purposes for Informative Speeches

The general purpose for your informative speeches will be "to create understanding." More specifically, your purpose or reason for speaking will be to create understanding about a particular topic rather than just "to give information" or "to inform." Too often, beginning speakers prepare speeches as if their goal was to provide all the information they know about a topic or to merely tell audiences something they do not already know. It is essential for informative as well as persuasive speeches that you adapt your topic to your audience. Therefore, you must begin with what your audience knows about your topic and what aspect they would be interested in learning about—or learning more about. In this way, you will be guided by your general purpose of "creating understanding with your audience." To accomplish that purpose or goal it will be necessary for you to consider the knowledge, interests, and needs of your audience throughout your preparation and delivery.

Understanding purposes and determining specific goals for speeches is one of the most important steps in preparing speeches that are adapted to particular audiences.

Essential Characteristics of Informative Speaking

The characteristics of informative speaking are those qualities or standards that you strive to achieve. The standards that you should strive for in your informative speeches are:

1. Clarity and concreteness of message.
2. Coherence and simplicity.
3. Association and adaptation of ideas and examples to audience.
4. Motivation of audience to listen and want to know.

ORGANIZING INFORMATIVE SPEECHES

Objectives

1. To apply effective organizational skills in preparing a speech.
2. To practice developing an informative speech topic.

Task

Each student prepares, in class, an informative speech that demonstrates effective organization style (see "Requirements" below) and topic development. Students should deliver their speeches to their groups; each group should select one member to present his/her speech to the class.

Instructions

Select a topic provided by your instructor or one of your own choosing. Take approximately thirty to forty minutes to prepare an informative speech outline that illustrates the principles of effective organization and topic adaptation. Scribble out your ideas on a sheet of paper. Remember to develop your attention-getter, need for listening, and conclusion *after* you develop your thesis and main points. Identify the pattern order used for the main points. Use the outline form on page 227 for your final copy. Turn in your final copy to your instructor.

You might find that a sense of humor or wit is appropriate to apply in developing your topic. Humor is not a requirement; it may not work for some topics. You determine your general and specific purposes in preparing your speech. You may select either of the following general purposes:

1. To create understanding.
2. To share a funny experience or sense of humor.

Requirements for Effective Organization

Your impromptu demonstration speech must contain:

1. Attention-getting remark(s) that creates interest in the topic and a need for the audience to listen.
2. A thesis that is direct, declarative, and assertive.
3. A preview of main points.
4. Two main points that explain or elaborate on the thesis.
5. Examples or explanations of the main points.
6. A thesis and the two main points in complete sentences. (Limit the subpoints and examples to essential words and phrases.)

FORMAT FOR INFORMATIVE SPEECHES

Note: Using this as a guide, compose an outline that fulfills the necessary requirements.
See the following example outline. Fill in the blank areas with supporting materials.
General Purpose:
Specific Purpose:

Introduction

    I.   Attention-getting statement.

   II.   Need for listening.

  III.   Thesis.

       Preview of main points.

       A.

       B.

Body

    I.   Main point.

       A.   Subpoint.

          1.

          2.

       B.   Subpoint.

          1.

          2.

II. Main point.

    A. Subpoint.

        1.

        2.

    B. Subpoint.

        1.

        2.

Conclusion

    I. Summary.

    II. Clincher.

THE WILD PITCH: INFORMATIVE OUTLINE 1

Note: Contains excellent attention-grabbing thesis, parallel construction of main ideas, and brief preview of main ideas. This specific purpose lends itself to demonstration or use of visual aids.

General Purpose: To create understanding.

Specific Purpose: To create understanding of how to stop the wild pitch when catching in baseball.

Introduction

I. It was Mr. Baseball himself, Bob Uecker, when asked how he stopped the wild pitch, who answered this way: "Usually I just wait till it stops rolling, go to the backstop, and then pick it up!"

II. As one of America's most-loved sports, baseball is something we can all relate to.
   A. I was a catcher for eight years in both little league and Home Talent baseball; for five years I was an All-Star.
   B. You can appreciate the game and the catcher's role by understanding the mastery involved in handling the wild pitch.

III. Thesis: Blocking the wild pitch is very important to the catcher, who must be:
   A. Fearless.
   B. Physically fit.
   C. Aware of the field.

Body

I. The catcher should be fearless, willing to sacrifice his or her body.
   A. The equipment helps take most of the fear out of the catcher.
      1. Mask.
      2. Chest protector.
      3. Cup.
      4. Shin guards.
   B. Catcher must not be afraid of the pitch bouncing in front of him or her.
   C. The body is an important tool in stopping the pitch.
      1. Face.
      2. Chest.
      3. Legs.

II. The catcher must be physically fit.
   A. Be as alive and instinctive as possible from the first through the ninth innings.
   B. A catcher can be large or small in build.
      1. For the big catcher, size is the asset used most in blocking the pitch.
      2. The smaller catcher relies on quickness.

III. The catcher must be aware of *all* situations on the field.
   A. Must know what pitch is coming and which position to take for that pitch.
      1. Fastball.
      2. Breaking pitch.
      3. Knuckleball.
   B. Must know the position of the baserunners.

Conclusion

I. The things usually found in the best catchers, those who are the best at blocking bad pitches, are:

  A. Fearlessness.

  B. Total awareness.

  C. Physical fitness.

II. As a catcher who blocked many pitches over eight years, I have found that these were the most exciting aspects of catching. If it hadn't been for this excitement, I doubt it would have been as fulfilling for me.

ROCK 'N' ROLL AND BLUES: INFORMATIVE OUTLINE 2

Note: Contains strong thesis statement that reflects the observation or conclusion of the speaker.
General Purpose: To create understanding.
Specific Purpose: To create understanding about the effect blues has had on rock 'n' roll.

Introduction

    I.   Here in Lafayette, it is easy to hear live blues.
   II.   Musical taste and interest is a personal choice.
       A.   I know that we represent all kinds of musical interest in this class.
       B.   After listening to different kinds of music since age six, I have come to prefer rock 'n' roll and blues over other types of music.
       C.   I find the connections between these two types of music fascinating and hope you will also.
  III.   Thesis: Today's rock 'n' roll is a direct result of the blues.
       A.   Originated in Mississippi.
       B.   Filtered out of Chicago.
       C.   Resurgence during the 60s.

Body

    I.   Blues originated in Mississippi during the 20s.
       A.   Blues was created by blacks in response to bad times.
       B.   People called it "the devil's music."
           1.   Robert Johnson.
           2.   William Christopher Beale.
       C.   Blues is not just a style of music; it is a language used to express emotions.
   II.   Chicago becomes center of blues during 40s and 50s.
       A.   By way of Mississippi River, people leave the South for the opportunity of the North.
       B.   From Chicago, blues begins to spread throughout nation.
           1.   New Orleans.
           2.   Memphis.
       C.   Transition takes place. Rock 'n' roll appears at this time.
           1.   Chuck Berry.
           2.   Buddy Holly.
 III.   British invasion during 60s causes resurgence of blues.
       A.   Rock 'n' roll is well established in U.S. and England.
       B.   However, the phase doesn't last as long in England.
           1.   In England, blues becomes big and in turn hits U.S.
           2.   Rolling Stones.
           3.   The Who.

Conclusion

    I.   Blues originated in Mississippi, developed in Chicago, and was brought back to life in the 60s.

    II.   Throughout history different types of music like reggae, jazz, pop, and rock 'n' roll have all appeared on the social scene. If searched hard enough, their roots will eventually lead to the blues.

GOSPEL MUSIC: INFORMATIVE OUTLINE 3

Note: Excellent topic development.

General Purpose: To create understanding.

Specific Purpose: To help audience understand the history of gospel music.

Introduction

I. Gospel music is sung around the world.
   A. Gospel music is sung in many different churches.
   B. Gospel music is sung differently in every religion.
      1. Baptist.
      2. Catholic.
      3. Comparison between the two.
II. I have been singing and studying gospel music for many years.
III. Thesis: Gospel music reflects the history and culture of African-Americans.
   A. History of gospel music.
   B. Feelings of gospel music.
   C. Religious style.

Body

I. The history of gospel music is a unique story.
   A. Slaves brought true meaning to gospel music:
      1. While in the fields.
      2. While sitting at home.
   B. Great names brought about the major spread of gospel music.
      1. Martin Luther King.
      2. Mahalia Jackson.
      3. Rev. James Cleveland.
II. Gospel music is music, based on feelings of the heart.
   A. The words of the gospel songs are words from past experiences.
      1. Many songs are emotional: "Soon I Will Be Done."
      2. Most songs are, or are spring-offs of, folk songs: "Chariot Is a Coming."
   B. Modern gospel music is based more on a fast beat.
      1. The clapping of the hand and rocking is a more acceptable part of the choirs.
      2. The modern music is composed by the younger generation.
   C. More instruments are brought into gospel than before.
      1. The drums play a major part in gospel music.
      2. The bass guitar and different horns are used more frequently now.
III. Gospel music is sung differently in each religion.
   A. Baptists are more adapted to the "hallelujah" style of singing gospel.
      1. The large rocking choirs.
      2. The clapping hands.
   B. Catholics are more adapted to soft congregational-type music.
      1. Simple forms of "Amazing Grace" (no harmony).
      2. Sing more original old-time music.
   C. The words of the music are the same in both religions but are sometimes arranged differently.

Conclusion

I. The arrangement, the emotional aspect, the big names, and the spread of gospel music help to make up the unique history that involves us all.

II. Gospel music is music that is applied to us all.

THE JOURNALIST: INFORMATIVE OUTLINE 4

Note: Contains example of use of research and bibliography.

General Purpose: To create understanding.

Specific Purpose: To create understanding about a journalist's job and how he or she goes about doing it.

Introduction

I. Have you ever dreamed about being an ace reporter in search of the "big story"? You see yourself sneaking past police barricades for an exclusive interview with bomb terrorists. Maybe you envision yourself on a movie set talking with Mel Gibson and Kim Bassinger or perhaps covering a Super Bowl or NBA finals.

II. Although this famous, dangerous lifestyle may appeal to you, sadly a journalist's job is far from glamorous. In fact, it is hard work that requires patience, dedication, and diligence.

III. As a four-year columnist and editor for the weekly student paper, *The Seahawk,* I hope to share my knowledge on what a reporter's job entails and how they go about doing it.

IV. Thesis: Journalism is the art of good detective skills and writing skills.
   A. A reporter must be aggressive and thorough in gathering the facts.
   B. A reporter must write simple and concise to be fully understood.

Transition: So how does a journalist do this? How does he or she use these skills to capture a story?

Body

I. Selecting and covering a story requires aggressiveness and thoroughness.
   A. Choosing an article requires aggressiveness. (David Burke, "A Reporter's Guide to Working at the Seahawk")
      1. Stories assigned by the editor.
      2. Beat reports:
         a. Knows who to talk to.
         b. Visits area at least three times a week.
         c. Investigates any rumors.
      3. Recycled stories—new information with old.
      4. Personal choices.
   B. Covering a story requires thoroughness. (Eric Nalder, *The Art of Reporting*)
      1. On-the-scene work.
         a. Factual Accounts.
         b. Interviews.
      2. Telephone book, specialized business listing.
      3. Door-to-door.
      4. Research.
         a. Public records.
         b. Freedom of Information Act.
II. Writing a story requires thoroughness, simplicity, and objectivity.
   A. Thoroughness.
      1. Verify sources and facts at least twice before writing. Quote: Nalder, *The Art of Reporting,* "You say your mother loves you? Check it out."
      2. Update or eliminate new or old information.

B. Simplicity—Melvin Mencher, *News Reporting and Writing*.
   1. Opening statement should answer at least three of the five W's.
      a. Billboard paragraph.
      b. Inverted pyramid.
   2. Avoid wordiness and jargon.
      a. Fifth-grade reading level, newspapers today.
      b. Check for grammar and spelling mistakes.
C. Objectivity—unbiased tone, fairness.

Conclusion

I. Successful reporting requires good detective skills and writing skills.
   A. Where to look for stories.
   B. Whom or what to gather story facts and details from.
   C. How to write clearly and fairly.
II. So next time you see a newspaper article, a radio voice, or a news blip on TV, think of the work and time the journalist put into the piece and maybe you'll appreciate the story more.

References

Burke, David E. "A Reporter's Guide to Working at the Seahawk," *The Seahawk,* 1991, pp. 1–7.

Mencher, Melvin. *News Reporting and Writing,* Wm. C. Brown Communications, Inc., 1987, pp. 26–50.

Nalder, Eric. "The Art of Reporting," *Seattle Times,* 1990, pp. 1–4, 8.

Preparing Persuasive Speeches

This unit highlights the essential components of persuasive speaking, contains exercises for practicing persuasive strategies, and provides sample student persuasive speech outlines. The persuasive outlines presented in this unit use either Monroe's Motivated Sequence or the Statement of Reasons method for an organizational pattern. It is important to note that there are other persuasive patterns that are appropriate to use. However, these two are the most common.

The components of UNIT 16 are:

Persuading Audiences: Notes

Organizing Persuasive Speeches

Monroe's Motivated Sequence

Comparison of Two Persuasive Formats

Adapting Topics to Audience's Predisposition

Organizing Persuasive Speeches: Selling a Product or Person

Organizing Persuasive Speeches: Influencing Ideas, Attitudes, or Actions

Growing Vegetable Gardens: Persuasive Outline 1
    (Statement of Reasons Method)

The Drinking Age: Persuasive Outline 2
    (Statement of Reasons Method)

Exercise Relieves Stress: Persuasive Outline 3
    (Monroe's Motivated Sequence)

Learning a Second Language: Persuasive Outline 4
    (Monroe's Motivated Sequence)

PERSUADING AUDIENCES: NOTES

Persuasion Defined

Persuasion is a complex, fascinating process that permeates our lives. Essentially (or eventually) it involves *change*. The purpose of persuasive speaking is to change or alter people's beliefs, concepts, values, or attitudes toward certain persons, processes, or phenomena. Another directed purpose of persuasive speaking is to motivate people to action. For example, they may already believe in your concept or belief but are not doing anything about it, so the purpose of your speech would be to motivate them to action.

For your persuasive speech, you must select a specific purpose that will require some sort of change on the part of your audience. To convince your audience to get a college degree does not involve change; however, to convince them to make their college education work for them could potentially involve a change in attitude or action. If you do a thorough audience analysis about your specific topic, then you can avoid an embarrassment such as trying to convince your audience not to smoke cigarettes when no one does.

Essential Characteristics of Persuasive Speaking

The essential characteristics of persuasive speaking are the qualities or standards you should strive to achieve in the preparation and presentation of your persuasive speech:

1. Logical and emotional appeals adapted to the audience.
2. Change by degrees.
3. Credibility and sincerity.
4. Ethical arguments and motives.

Selecting a Topic

The selection of a topic is particularly important. In preparing the persuasive speech, you follow essentially the same process as the preparation for an informative speech. Because the general purpose is to convince or move your audience to action, you must select a specific purpose you feel strongly about or you are convinced about—in fact, one that you feel passionate about. You cannot convince others if you are passive or apathetic toward a subject or purpose. Furthermore, you cannot convince others if you have scant knowledge of or experience with the topic.

Once you select a topic you feel strongly about, you need to conduct an audience survey and an analysis to discover the audience's predisposition (attitude) toward your topic and their knowledge of the topic. There are five general predispositions to a topic that your audience might hold:

1. Favorable but not aroused to act.
2. Apathetic toward the situation.
3. Interested but undecided what to do or think about it.
4. Interested but hostile to the proposed attitude, belief, or action.
5. Hostile to any change from present state of affairs.

Your survey of the audience's attitude toward and knowledge of your topic will be essential in shaping a message that seeks change. Your speech must deal directly with your audience's predisposition toward your topic and must seek a change from them.

ORGANIZING PERSUASIVE SPEECHES

The two most common persuasive formats (logical approaches to persuading) are:

1. **Statement of Reasons method**. In this approach you make a claim (the proposition) and state the reasons (your main points) *why* the audience should believe or consider to do what you propose. See the following Sample Speech Outlines 1 and 2 for examples of the Statement of Reasons method of persuasion prepared by students in public speaking classes.

2. **Monroe's Motivated Sequence**** (like the problem-solving method). In this structure you describe a problem (convincing your audience that this is a serious problem and one that deserves their attention), and then you present a solution that addresses that problem. You provide a way for the audience to think or act in order to alleviate the problem in some way. You also predict the results of the solution by visualizing for your audience how the solution will solve the problem. See the following Sample Speech Outlines 3 and 4 for examples of students' use of Monroe's Motivated Sequence as a structure for persuasion.

**Note that the outline using Monroe's Motivated Sequence follows a different outline format. Instead of the traditional three-part outline (the Introduction, Body, and Conclusion), Monroe's format uses five parts (Attention, Need, Satisfaction, Visualization, and Action). As with the traditional outline, each part is numbered separately.

MONROE'S MOTIVATED SEQUENCE

Note: Alan Monroe's* design of the motivated sequence was influenced by John Dewey's reflective thinking sequence (a problem-solving method) and Abraham Maslow's hierarchy of needs (addressing human motivation). The motivated sequence is a very popular and useful method for organizing messages that seek to influence audiences or move them to action. If you select the motivated sequence for your persuasive speech, use the information below to guide you in developing and structuring your topic. You need to address all of the functions under each step to assure potential persuasion of your audience.

I. **Attention**

The functions of the attention are to create interest in the topic and desire to attend to the problem, to establish your credibility and connection to the topic, and to address the audience's psychological states or predispositions to the topic.

II. **Need**

The purpose of the need step is to create or develop the problem. It is an analysis of what is wrong and how these wrongs affect the individual's interests and desires. In this step you relate your subject to the vital concerns and interests of your audience. The need step should:

A. *State need*—a clear statement of need or problem.

B. *Illustrate*—use examples that describe the need.

C. *Elaborate*—use additional examples and supporting materials (statistics and testimony) to show extent of need; you must show your audience how this is a severe problem.

D. *Point*—use convincing demonstrations of how the need directly affects the audience's health, happiness, welfare (motivational appeals work well here).

III. **Satisfaction**

The purpose of this statement is to state the proposition (what you want audience to think, believe, or do) that will alleviate the problem and satisfy individuals' interests, wants, desires. In this step you should:

A. State the proposition.

B. Explain your proposal.

C. Show how it meets the problem pointed out in the need step.

D. Give examples showing how the proposal (your idea) has worked or can work effectively—use facts, figures, and the testimony of experts.

IV. **Visualization**

The function of the visualization step is to intensify desire and seek belief or action from your audience. To accomplish this you need to project into the future and describe the results of your solution (the satisfaction step). The visualization step should vividly describe either:

A. What the world would look like and/or feel like if the proposition was believed or followed;
or,

B. What the world would look like if the proposition was not believed or followed. You *must* state the benefits of the proposition; it is optional to describe the dangers of not accepting the proposition.

---

*Alan H. Monroe, in *Principles and Types of Speech* (Chicago: Scott, Foresman, 1935).

V. **Action**

This step is a final call for commitment or a call to action. As in the conclusion of an informative speech, you should restate the proposition or thesis and end with a clincher-type statement. The action step may use one or more of the following devices:

A. Challenge or appeal.
B. Quotation.
C. Illustration.
D. Summary of proposition.
E. Steps to achieving proposition.

COMPARISON OF TWO PERSUASIVE FORMATS*

This comparison can be helpful in the following ways:

1. *As a learning device.* It may be easier for you to understand Monroe's Motivated Sequence (a persuasive outline) by comparing it with the traditional outline (used for your informative speeches).
2. *As an alternative outline choice for your persuasive speech.* If you decide to use the problem/solution approach in your speech, then you may follow the outline format below (Monroe's Motivated Sequence) or you may follow the example of outlines 3 and 4. It is important to note that whichever of the two outline formats for Monroe's Motivated Sequence you select, the approach is the same; that is, first you describe the problem, then you present the solution.

Monroe's Motivated Sequence
Attention

   I.   Attention-getting statement.
   II. Establish credibility.

   III. Audience predispositions/Survey.*

Statement of Reasons method
Introduction

   I.   Attention-getting statement.
   II. Establish credibility.
        Audience predispositions/Survey.*
        (Need for listening.)
   III. State proposition (Thesis).
        A.   Preview main point I.
        B.   Preview main point II.
        C.   Preview main point III.

Need

   I. Need (State the problem).
      A. Explanation/Example.
        1. Evidence.
        2. Evidence.
      B. Explanation/Example.
        1. Evidence.
        2. Evidence.

Body

   I. Main point.
      A. Explanation/Example.
        1. Evidence.
        2. Evidence.
      B. Explanation/Example.
        1. Evidence.
        2. Evidence.

Satisfaction

   I. (State the solution.)
      A. Explanation/Example.
        1. Evidence.
        2. Evidence.
      B. Explanation/Example.
        1. Evidence.
        2. Evidence.

   I. Main point.
      A. Explanation/Example.
        1. Evidence.
        2. Evidence.
      B. Explanation/Example.
        1. Evidence.
        2. Evidence.

---

*This idea (comparing two outlines) was contributed by Cindy Sawicki.

Visualization

I. (Solution benefits.)
  A. Explanation/Example.
    1. Evidence.
    2. Evidence.
  B. Explanation/Example.
    1. Evidence.
    2. Evidence.
       etc.

I. Main point.
  A. Explanation/Example.
    1. Evidence.
    2. Evidence.
  B. Explanation/Example.
    1. Evidence.
    2. Evidence.
       etc.

Action

I. Action (Final commitment and call for action).

Conclusion

I. Summary (Review main points).

II. Clincher (Restate proposition).

ADAPTING TOPICS TO AUDIENCE'S PREDISPOSITION

Objectives

1. To understand how the audience's predisposition to a topic guides the development of a topic.
2. To practice adapting persuasive topics to audiences.
3. To practice using logical and emotional appeals to persuade audiences.

Instructions

Working alone or in groups, review the five general predispositions toward topics (see "Persuading Audiences: Notes" in this unit). For each predisposition pick a topic that might fit that predisposition. For example, seat belts is a good example of predisposition two. That is, your audience will probably feel apathetic toward the topic because they have heard so much about the importance of wearing seat belts. Your audience could also feel favorable toward seat belts (they agree in theory that they save lives), but they don't wear them—predisposition one.

Once you pick an example topic for each predisposition or combination of predispositions, select a specific purpose or proposition for that topic. Make sure that the specific purpose of your topic fits the definition of persuasion. It must seek change from your audience. The proposition is what you want the audience to believe or do. Next, briefly explain what motivational and logical appeals you will use to address your audience's predisposition.

This activity requires that you make some educated inferences about your audience. This can only be done with an audience you know fairly well. By the time you approach your persuasive speech assignment, you should have a fairly extensive understanding of your audience's background. However, it is still essential to survey your audience specifically about your persuasive topic. You need to find out what they know about the topic and how they feel about your proposal.

Turn in to your instructor a copy of your example topics with propositions and an explanation of how you will use logical and motivational appeals to adapt them to your audience's predisposition.

ORGANIZING PERSUASIVE SPEECHES: SELLING A PRODUCT OR PERSON

Objectives

1. To understand the similarities and differences between two persuasive patterns for organizing speeches.
2. To practice developing and shaping impromptu persuasive messages.

Task

Each group will select an object or topic from the impromptu collection and spend approximately twenty minutes developing that topic in two different ways: (1) the Statement of Reasons method and (2) Monroe's Motivated Sequence. The group will then elect two members to deliver one- to three-minute persuasive messages that will potentially sell their product or topic.

Instructions

Select an object or topic from the impromptu collection (clock radio, camera, Michael Jackson, Lee Iacocca, pizza, etc.). Working in groups, decide on your proposition—what you want your audience to do with the product or with your topic. Do you want your audience to buy a 35mm camera? Believe that Michael Jackson is the greatest rock star of all time? Believe that pizza is nutritious and should be eaten weekly? Once your group decides on the proposition, develop two one- to three-minute speeches using Monroe's Motivated Sequence for one and the Statement of Reasons method for the other. Your group might elect to divide and conquer: dividing the group in half, each working with one of the methods. Select two members to deliver the speeches.

Summary Discussion

1. What are the similarities and differences between the two persuasive strategies?

2. Which one worked better for your topic and proposition? Why?

ORGANIZING PERSUASIVE SPEECHES: INFLUENCING IDEAS, ATTITUDES, OR ACTIONS

Objectives

1. To understand the similarities and differences between two persuasive patterns for organizing speeches.
2. To practice developing and shaping more complex topics and messages.

Task

Each group will choose a topic in which all members are fairly well versed. The group will then decide on the best strategy for developing that topic and spend approximately forty-five minutes preparing an outline. One member will deliver the group's persuasive message to the class. The group will turn in a copy of their outline to the instructor.

Instructions

Selecting a Topic

In selecting a topic, the group might consider previous informative speeches. For example, an informative speech on exercise might have a specific purpose such as how to exercise without straining muscles or the best kind of exercise for older citizens. A persuasive speech on the same topic, exercise, would need to have a different purpose. It would need to seek change. In Speech Outline 3 "Exercise Relieves Stress" in this unit, the student used the topic of exercise to seek change in her audience. She discovered, through audience analysis, that her audience of college juniors and seniors believed in and followed an exercise program, but let it slide during finals week. Since she knew the value of exercise during stressful times, she worded her specific purpose as "to convince my audience that exercise will help relieve the stress felt during final exams." She found that Monroe's Motivated Sequence was the best method for the structuring of her persuasive message.

The group might also consider controversial issues in their lives. Refer back to the brainstorming exercise you did at the beginning of the course entitled "Self-Analysis for Speech Topics." You might select problems or issues that you feel strongly about. The tough part of this assignment could be deciding on a topic. Do not expect to initially agree on a topic and do not waste too much time deciding on a topic. Just select something your group members know something about and are willing to work with for this exercise.

Once you have selected your topic, analyze your audience's predisposition toward that topic. Use educated inference based on previous information about your audience. After you have analyzed your audience's predispositions toward your topic, you are ready to word your specific purpose to determine what you want them to believe or do.

Next, your group should decide which organizational strategy would best accomplish your specific purpose. Briefly try both to make your decision. After selecting either Monroe's Motivated Sequence or the Statement of Reasons method, compose an outline of your persuasive message. Select one member to deliver that message to the class. Turn in a copy of your outline to your instructor.

Summary Discussion

1. What are the similarities and differences between the two persuasive strategies?

2. Explain why your group selected the pattern they did. Why was it a better choice than the other?

GROWING VEGETABLE GARDENS: PERSUASIVE OUTLINE 1 (STATEMENT OF REASONS METHOD)

General Purpose: To convince my audience.

Specific Purpose: To persuade my audience to grow their own vegetable gardens.

Introduction

I. Every day many of us go into the grocery store in search of fresh vegetables, only to find that the vegetables are either not ripe or overripe, dried out, or even rotten. On top of this, the store charges an outrageous price for these so-called good quality, fresh vegetables.

II. Fortunately, there is something most of us can do about this. We can go into our backyards and start our own vegetable gardens. I have done this for years.

III. Everyone who has access to land should grow their own vegetables.
   A. It is easy.
   B. The vegetables are fresher and of better quality than those bought in a store.
   C. It is very economical to grow your own garden.

Body

I. A garden should be grown because it is easy.
   A. It requires no special skill or talent to grow a garden.
      1. There are books and TV shows that can help.
      2. The local gardening store can help.
      3. Tools can be used.
   B. There are many vegetables that can be easily grown in Louisiana.
      1. Winter vegetables that can be grown include onions, lettuce, cabbage, cauliflower.
      2. Summer vegetables that can be grown include tomatoes, corn, watermelons, beans, bell peppers, and peas.
   C. A garden does not require much time to maintain.
      1. According to *Money* magazine, a Gallup poll found that a typical backyard garden is slightly more than 650 square feet in area, produces an average of $460 worth of vegetables at a cost of only $19, and takes only a few hours of labor per week to maintain.

II. A garden should be grown because homegrown vegetables are much fresher and of better quality than vegetables found in a store.
   A. Freshness enhances taste, color, and vitamin content.
      1. Most vegetables are shipped from California and are not fresh.
   B. Quality is the condition of the vegetables.
      1. Water content.
      2. Degree of ripeness.
   C. Any surplus vegetables can be put in the freezer. Freshness and quality will be maintained.

III. A garden should be grown because it is economical.
  A. According to *U.S. News and World Report,* the broker is taking 65¢ of every food dollar.
  B. Except for the initial cost of getting started, there is very little cost involved.
      1. Garden tools.
      2. Seed.
      3. Chemicals.
  C. Another statistic found in the *Saturday Evening Post* stated that the average garden is 22' by 25' and will be valued at $425 for an outlay of $25 for seed and supplies.
      1. Some people with larger gardens sell their produce and make a nice profit.

Conclusion

I. As you can see, growing your own garden will present little difficulty and has many advantages, such as fresher, more flavorful, and much cheaper vegetables.
II. I would like to urge all of you who have access to land that can be used for a garden to do so. It will be worth it.

References

"Gardening Time Again," *Saturday Evening Post,* May/June 1982, p. 70.
"Growing Money in Your Garden," *Money,* March 1981, p. 144.
"Summer Gardening," *U.S. News and World Report,* June 1982, p. 65.

THE DRINKING AGE: PERSUASIVE OUTLINE 2 (STATEMENT OF REASONS METHOD)

General Purpose: To convince my audience about an issue.

Specific Purpose: To persuade the audience that raising the drinking age is unfair and will not deter drunk driving.

Introduction

I. As most of you know, the Louisiana State Legislature is in the process of deciding whether or not to raise the minimum drinking age to twenty-one.

II. Drinking and driving is a serious problem.
   A. It affects everyone to some extent because everyone must travel on roads.
   B. Some of you may have confusion about certain issues concerning whether or not to raise the drinking age.
   C. After careful consideration, I believe that the drinking age should not be raised from eighteen to twenty-one as a means to deter drunk driving.

III. Proposition: The drinking age should not be raised to deter drinking because:
   A. It will violate personal civil rights and the constitutional rights of state governments.
   B. It may actually increase alcohol abuse among teenagers.
   C. It will increase unemployment.

Body

I. The drinking age should not be raised because it will violate personal civil rights and the constitutional rights of states.
   A. On a personal basis, civil rights will be violated because the law discriminates against a sector of the adult population from eighteen to twenty-one years old.
      1. Vote.
      2. Take out loan in own name.
      3. Get married.
      4. Be drafted.
   B. On a national basis, the constitutionality of the mandate to raise the drinking age to twenty-one is questionable.
      1. Federal mandate:
         a. State time limit—October 30, 1985.
         b. Fiscal year 1986–87, cut 5 percent highway federal funds.
         c. Fiscal year 1987–88, cut 10 percent highway federal funds.
         d. Total—$45 million.
         e. Money put in escrow account.
         f. Money retrievable when state raises drinking age.
      2. Reagan administration long opposed.
         a. Sale of alcohol—state responsibility.
         b. Suddenly changed mind.
      3. Mandate is clearly a threat.
         a. Blackmail quote by Wyoming Governor Ed Herschler.
         b. States filing suit against Congress.

II. The drinking age should not be raised because alcohol abuse among teenagers may increase.
   A. New drinking laws will not deter student thrill-seekers from drinking.
      1. Recent research by the psychology department of University of Wisconsin suggests this.
      2. Extroverted risk-takers welcome change and novelty.
      3. Reject rules and regulations—abuse may increase by flaunting law.
   B. Controlled drinkers will be tempted to drink in an uncontrolled environment.
      1. Present—drinking in licensed liquor establishments (controlled environment).
      2. Future—older friends buy liquor, drinking in uncontrolled environment.
         a. Cruising cars.
         b. Private homes.
         c. Parks.
         d. Beaches.
III. The drinking age should not be raised because, if it were raised, it would increase unemployment.
   A. Unemployment would primarily affect thousands of college students.
      1. College students (18–20), part-time jobs in restaurants and bars (considered ideal job).
         a. Flexible hours (not 9–5).
         b. Tips—additional funds.
      2. Loss of job from raising drinking age.
         a. Unemployment difficult to draw on part-time job.
         b. If one could draw unemployment, it would not be enough to live on.

Conclusion

I. To conclude, I am going to give you something to think about. Anybody of any age is liable to cause problems if he/she drinks and drives. Why stop at twenty-one? If drunk driving were to be deterred to decrease accidents and fatalities, then tougher drunk driving laws should be passed with strict penalties that should be enforced for all violators, regardless of age.

References

"Ahead: Minimum Drinking Age of 21," *U.S. News and World Report,* June 25, 1984, p. 8.
"Making It Tougher to Drink and Drive," *Newsweek,* July 9, 1984, p. 23.
"Minimum Age for Drinking at 21?" *U.S. News and World Report,* June 4, 1984, p. 88.

EXERCISE RELIEVES STRESS: PERSUASIVE OUTLINE 3 (MONROE'S MOTIVATED SEQUENCE)

General Purpose: To convince my audience.

Specific Purpose: To convince my audience that exercise will help relieve the stress felt during final exams.

Attention

I. Here we are exactly one week away from finals. We are all thinking about how many finals we are going to have, how many are going to be comprehensive, and how many we are going to have on a given day.

II. According to Hopkin's *Adolescent Psychology,* experts in psychology say, "During finals, students tend to seek some form of stimulation outside of the educational realm."
   A. This means that we often occupy ourselves in activities that allow us to "escape" the pressures of finals.
   B. Example of student who suffered severe stress during finals week.
   C. We have all experienced test anxiety or stress about our performance in courses.

III. Experts in Hopkin's book also state, "The best form of outside stimulation while taking finals involves some type of physical exertion."
   A. So exercise is the best form of outside stimulation during finals.
   B. With finals so close at hand, it is important that we understand the value of exercise for managing stress.

Need

I. Due to daily social stresses, 52 percent of females and 60 percent of males have moderate to high anxiety.
   A. According to Comb's *An Invitation to Health,* studies reveal that these figures increase by 15–20 percent among college students during final exam period.
   B. Comb also states that this "excessive amount of anxiety is known to interfere with concentration, productivity, and sleep."
      1. Less can be accomplished with the increase of anxiety.

II. Hopkin's *Adolescent Psychology* says that the average student gets approximately three to four hours of sleep a night during final exam week.
   A. This decrease in the amount of sleep can result in suppression of the immunity system, which fights back against disease, infection, and illnesses.
   B. Studies reveal that the common cold/flu is the most prevalent among illnesses due to inadequate sleep.

III. Hopkin also states that "there is an astronomical increase in irritability and moodiness during final week preparation."
   A. This irritability results in abrupt or explosive behaviors toward others that would not occur under normal circumstances.
   B. Example of mother or father asking to do work around the house.

Satisfaction

I. "Exercise is by far the most practical and elemental activity that should be engaged in to relieve excess anxiety," says Comb in *An Invitation to Health*.
  A. It is beneficial in that it provides a means for burning off excess fats and sugars that have accumulated during periods of anxiety.
     1. Example of how we have much excess energy that needs to be released.
  B. Exercise can be a form of productivity.
     1. Example of how we can mentally visualize and study our notes while exercising.

II. Hopkin states that regular exercise is needed to maintain consistent and more relaxing patterns of sleep.
  A. Exercise enables us to be more relaxed and thus sleep more easily.
  B. Experiment done by Sampson:
     1. Three weeks with control and experimental groups.
     2. Control group—no exercise but mental stimulation, such as TV and cards.
     3. Experimental group—exercise daily for twenty to thirty minutes of strenuous activity, such as jogging, walking, cycling, swimming.
     4. Results indicated:
        a. Experimental group—no problems related to inadequate amount of sleep.
        b. Experimental group—scored high on final exams.

III. Moodiness and irritability are alleviated through exercise by giving a positive feeling of accomplishment.
  A. This positive feeling from exercises is carried over into our studying.
  B. Example: "Exercisers' High"—beta endorphines are released in the brain, which suppress pain sensations; lasts for two to three hours following activity—much studying accomplished during this time.

Visualization

I. You can see how exercise can alleviate much of the anxiety, sleeplessness, and moodiness that is associated with taking finals and its preparation.
  A. You become more relaxed.
  B. You will perform better.

II. If you choose an exercise that is strenuous enough, just imagine how you can help yourself better prepare for final exams.
  A. Picture a stress-ridden student attempting to release stress by playing cards.
  B. Picture a stress-ridden student engaging in twenty to thirty minutes of vigorous swimming.
  C. The person exercising will be refreshed and more ready to handle the pressures involved in taking finals.

Action

I. Now is the ideal time to engage in an exercise program.
II. When you feel any of the pressures described earlier, go out and engage in some sort of physical exertion.
III. Studies reveal that your examination scores will be much higher.

References

Comb, Richard. *An Invitation to Health,* Chicago: McGraw-Hill, 1980.
Hopkin, Samual. *Adolescent Psychology,* New York: Westwood, Inc., 1979.

LEARNING A SECOND LANGUAGE: PERSUASIVE OUTLINE 4 (MONROE'S MOTIVATED SEQUENCE)

General Purpose: To influence and convince the audience.
Specific Purpose: To convince the audience of the utility and value of learning a second language.

Attention

I. Illinois Representative Paul Simon published a book in 1980 entitled *The Tongue-Tied American*. His suggestion: "Welcome to the United States. We cannot speak your language."
II. Our campus is full of students who have faced this initial and ongoing problem of language. How does it feel?
III. Not only do we make bad hosts, but we make bad tourists as well.
   A. Both when Nixon visited China and when Carter was visited by the Chinese, we were unable to provide our own interpreters.
   B. When we do provide interpreters, they are often not qualified.

Need

I. The problem we face is apathy toward learning a second language.
   A. Recent statistics state that of the eleven million U.S. students seeking graduate and undergraduate degrees:
      1. Fewer than 1 percent are studying the languages used by three-fourths of the world's population.
      2. Only a small number of these students will ever achieve a reasonable degree of competence.
II. In order to appreciate the problem, let us examine its effects on our country.
   A. We face problems in the international market.
      1. The Task Force on Inflation of the Budget Committee in 1979 recommended expansion of exports and stimulation of language study.
      2. We don't know our customers.
         a. We try to sell doormats to the Japanese.
         b. We label Coke products in Chinese to say "Coke brings your ancestors back from the grave."
      3. A Japanese businessman said, "Sir, the most useful international language in the world is not necessarily English, but rather it is the language of your client."
   B. We face a problem of national security.
      1. A 1979 study showed that forty-three positions in the State Department required professional proficiency in Russian.
      2. We don't have the language capacity to communicate with world leaders.
         a. Only one school in the U.S. even offers a masters degree in Russian.
         b. We are uninformed about what is happening in other countries.
   C. We face a problem of culture and isolation.
      1. A student explains, "Our isolation goes deeper than our ears and tongues. It is really an isolation of the soul. Our ignorance of language keeps us nationally from making the kind of contact that ties people together, which enables

individuals to talk to individuals, and which can, in the long run, prevent embroilment, misunderstanding, and violence."
2. Concept of globalization:
   a. We can travel better than ever.
   b. Worldwide communications are better than ever.
   c. The age of information leaves us hungry for knowledge.
3. The Rockefeller Commission Report says, "We need to emphasize the humanities for the development of our mental capacities and historical knowledge."
4. Knowledge for:
   a. Improved English skills.
   b. Art appreciation.
   c. Increased awareness.
   d. Analysis and assessment of ethical problems.
   e. Questions of value in public policy and science and technology.

Satisfaction

I. Increased understanding in dealing with other people can be achieved by learning other languages.
II. Language skills can benefit trade, foreign policy, and ourselves as individuals.
   A. In trade:
      1. Follow the example of Japanese—combine foreign language skills with business training.
         a. The president of a large international company says, "There are only about 1,000 U.S. students each year to graduate in International Trade. There are jobs for 200,000!"
      2. Our products will be more appealing.
      3. Our business relationships will be more genuine.
   B. In security and foreign policy:
      1. Appropriate funding to language instead of "arms" in order to communicate with Russia.
      2. Learning other languages gives us the chance to read literature and journals from other countries.
   C. In culture:
      1. Communication with other cultures brings awareness of ourselves and appreciation of others.
      2. We can balance the material wonders of technology with the spiritual demands of human nature.
      3. We can achieve knowledge for our cultural hunger.
      4. Practical education:
         a. Speak English better.
         b. Appreciate other cultures through their art and literature.
         c. Understand our own positions in the world (personal and global).

Visualization

I. Language is a tool.
II. Learning other languages exposes us to new sources of knowledge.
III. Our only tool for achieving true and effective communication is language.

IV. "We are the children. We are the world."

Action

I. We have a responsibility to the peoples of the world.
II. Language communication is the means to our "end."
III. If world peace is our responsibility, then our action should demonstrate a willingness to learn a second language.

References

"Languages, Learning, and Change," *The Ram's Horn,* Summer/Spring 1982–83, p. 5.
Simon, Paul. "The Tongue-Tied American: Confronting the Foreign Language Crisis," New York: Continuum Publishing Corporation, 1980.

Preparing Special Occasion Speeches

In addition to understanding how to prepare informative and persuasive speeches, it is valuable to understand the different kinds of special occasion speeches. This unit provides you with exercises that will help you prepare speeches for particular situations. In addition, it provides you with two excellent examples of special occasion speeches.

The components of UNIT 17 are:

Types of Special Occasion Speeches

Speeches of Introduction: An Exercise

Speeches of Awards and Acceptance: An Exercise

Analyzing Special Occasion Speeches

A Eulogy

A Speech of Tribute

A Ceremonial Speech

TYPES OF SPECIAL OCCASION SPEECHES

Everyday life offers many opportunities to give a speech, say a few words, or give a tribute to someone. Such occasions occur at banquets, award ceremonies, graduation ceremonies, weddings, retirements, welcoming ceremonies, and funerals. At such times, individuals may present well-prepared manuscript or memorized speeches, or they may just speak "off the cuff" and present an impromptu speech.

The most common types of special occasion speeches are:

Speeches of Introduction
Speeches of Awards and Presentations
Speeches of Acceptance
A Eulogy
A Speech of Tribute
A Ceremonial Speech

SPEECHES OF INTRODUCTION: AN EXERCISE

Objectives

1. To prepare and organize a speech of introduction.
2. To practice and observe speeches of introduction.

Instructions

The class will divide into partners and prepare, organize, and deliver speeches of introduction that are 2 to 4 minutes in length. The goal is to introduce one of your classmates as a unique individual.

Gathering the Information: An Interview

Select a partner (one of your classmates that you did not know well before this class) and interview him or her. The purpose of the interview is to find out particular and interesting information about that individual so that you can introduce him or her to the class. Your partner will interview you for the same purpose. Since you will be introducing each other to the class, finding out about your partner's hometown, major, hobbies, and similar kinds of information will be important. In addition, you will need to find out something valuable, important, or unique about that individual. Your goal is to go beyond a list of information and provide a description of a particular individual.

Organizing the Information

After the interviews are complete, organize your information from the particulars (name, major, hometown, etc.) to the general description of something unique, special, or important about the individual you are introducing. Remember to include that person's name in your opening and closing remarks. The speech should be a brief two- to four-minute presentation.

Delivering the Speeches of Introduction

As you practice your delivery, remember that you are asking your classmates to greet or welcome the uniqueness of your partner. You want your classmates to remember his or her name and something particular about that individual. So your tone of voice and your enthusiasm must suggest these qualities.

SPEECHES OF AWARDS AND ACCEPTANCE: AN EXERCISE

Objectives

1. To prepare a speech of awards or presentation.
2. To deliver and observe speeches of awards and speeches of acceptance.

Task

The class will divide into partners and prepare and deliver speeches of awards and speeches of acceptance that are two to four minutes in length.

Instructions: Step One

Working with a partner, decide on a particular situation in which one person can present an award or recognition to the other and the second person can accept the award or the recognition. It will probably be necessary to create realistic, hypothetical situations such as (1) recognizing athletes for their abilities or their cooperative teamwork; (2) recognizing particular individuals for their accomplishments or contributions to the department (i.e., the excellent acting skills or journalistic skills of particular individuals); (3) recognizing individuals for the accomplishment or contributions to particular organizations (i.e., leadership award for student government, membership award for a fraternity); or (4) any other university- or community-based situation based on a real or realistic situation that could be role-played by you and your partner.

Instructions: Step Two

Once you decide on a situation with your partner, work together to prepare the award and the acceptance presentations. Make sure you each know the particulars of why the award or the recognition is being made. The organization, its goals, and the accomplishment of the individual will need to be presented. After the speeches are prepared, practice with your partner using a delivery that demonstrates praise for the recognition speech and honor and sincerity for the acceptance speech.

ANALYZING SPECIAL OCCASION SPEECHES

Objectives

1. To recognize excellence in different types of special occasion speeches.
2. To read and analyze different types of special occasion speeches.

Explanation and Instructions

An excellent method for learning how to prepare effective special occasion speeches is to read or listen to these types of speeches. Your library will have a number of excellent sources for such speeches. Consult some of the following: *Representative American Speeches, Vital Speeches of the Day,* or *Winning Orations*.

Three examples of special occasion speeches are provided in the remainder of this unit. They have been included as examples of particular types of speeches. They are reprinted as they appear in the original manuscript; therefore, the language is not always gender-neutral.

First read these speeches for enjoyment or interest and then analyze them according to the type of speech and the occasion. Note how each speaker addresses the audience and how the content is developed and organized.

A EULOGY

An Instrument of Revelation*

Elizabeth Langer

1.   Arturo Toscanini led his farewell concert on April 4, 1954. Carnegie Hall overflowed with his admirers and his life-long friends. As the lights began to dim, a dignified man walked slowly to his earned position at the center of the stage. He was short of stature; but walked with a confidence reminiscent of a once bursting energy. His long-flowing white hair, deep-set moist eyes, expressive thin fingers, suggested the lovable quality of the true artist. His manner was serene and unpretentious. Throughout the performance of Wagner, one of the Maestro's favorite composers, a loving audience wept shamelessly as it watched the quality of the Maestro's work deteriorate before its eyes. His strength was gone, and he had no heart for his music. A few times he gripped a nearby rail for support. And the concert ended with Toscanini only beating time. He had once said to his close friends, probably those in the audience at that very moment, "When the baton trembles in my hand, I shall conduct no more." The baton did tremble that night, and Arturo Toscanini never conducted again. And on January 17 of this year, the great Maestro died at fourscore and nine.

2.   What of the origins of this man whom we honor today? Arturo Toscanini was born in Parma. As a child he studied at the Conservatory. At the age of nineteen he had earned the colossal title of Maestro by performing the incredible task of conducting the opera *Aida* from memory. At thirty-one, the boyhood dreams and aspirations of one who was destined to become the greatest music genius of our age were realized when he lifted his baton to conduct at La Scala in Milan, the highest culmination to which any musician can aspire in Italy. In 1907 Toscanini came to the Metropolitan Opera House, where for seven years he thrilled music patrons. In the later 20s he toured the United States, bringing beauty and happiness to the lives of millions who needed inspiration during the disastrous depression. And in 1937, he conducted the first of his concerts with the NBC Symphony in Radio City. Here, through the miracle of radio, the electrifying music of Arturo Toscanini was heard and appreciated by the poor as well as by the rich.

3.   The Maestro was an indefatigible and even a fanatical perfectionist. To watch him conduct was to experience his joy in carefully interpreting the score as the composer envisioned it and the joy coming from his unbounded love for good music.

4.   There were those of small discernment who thought of him as a tyrant. There were those who placed undue emphasis upon the extravagance of his manner. Had the Maestro disciplined his musicians for personal attainment, he might justifiably have been called a tyrant. But the reason for his uncompromising methods was one of humility. The Maestro believed that the revelation of the composer's intent was the musician's sole reason for being. His personal integrity required him honestly to recreate with his orchestra the composer's meaning. The composer was his master and his disciplinarian.

5.   Several years ago, Lawrence Gilman paid a tribute to the Maestro which I pray will never be forgotten:

> Arturo Toscanini is among the foremost prophets of that subliminal world of indestructible beauty and reality. He is no visionary who has merely slept and dreamed there. He is creatively alive there—an active *instrument of revelation.*

---

*From *Winning Orations*, 1957, pp. 50–52. Reprinted by permission of Larry Schnoor, Executive Secretary, Interstate Oratorical Association.

A SPEECH OF TRIBUTE

Martin Luther King—A Man for All Seasons*

By C. Eric Lincoln, Professor of Religion and Culture
Duke University

Delivered at the Martin Luther King Memorial Banquet,
Morehead Planetarium, the University of North Carolina,
Chapel Hill, North Carolina, January 17, 1986

1.   Among the reasons for the promise of America is a man named Martin Luther King. A man of peace, a man of courage, a man of goodwill, a man of forgiveness. A man for all seasons. A man for America in her time of trial, and in her hour of need. That was the King we knew. That was the King who rescued America from ignominy and gave her a chance for greatness.

2.   By some miracle of Divine Providence, the world survived World War II, almost in spite of itself, but the quality of that survival is not one of civilization's most creditable accomplishments. Somewhere in the undefinable agonies of stress and counter-stress produced by that latest signal of our resurgent depravity, the world lost sight of its moral lode star, and the human qualities by which our species had always been defined slipped into critical declension. We were numbed by the impossible spectacles of Buchenwald and Hiroshima, and we were hardened by a creeping moral callousness that not only made the impossible possible, but threatened to make it acceptable as well. Thereon hangs a tale, and the telling of it reveals a lot about the postwar state of mind of America, and the uniqueness and the value to America of Martin Luther King. For if Buchenwald and Hiroshima could happen, what is the meaning of Western civilization? What is the meaning of three thousand years of moral philosophy? Two thousand years of Christian experience? A thousand years of academic and intellectual development and debate? It is no wonder that there emerged a school of theologians after World War II who concluded that God is dead. They were wrong of course, God is not dead. God is alive and well and living in St. Elsewhere. It is man who has contracted a certain sickness unto death.

3.   This was the world into which Martin Luther King was thrust. It was an impossible world numbed by the excesses of war, confused by the awesome possibilities of future war, and frightened by the new burdens of human responsibility. We had despaired of the human potential to recover, to regroup and to attempt once again humanizing our sick and decadent social order. And our beloved country was ripe, as ripe as it has ever been for a social and political implosion that may well have destroyed this civilization that began with such dreams of human perfection 350 years ago. Certainly, it was not an era of optimism.

4.   There were men who had been brutalized in Europe and in Southeast Asia, who had killed and were ready to kill again. Blood was no stranger, and death was to many less traumatic than the anxieties of change, or lack of change; or to the muddled uncertainty of what it meant to be "American" in the new world after Buchenwald and Hiroshima. There were men under color of law in cruisers and on horseback, with dogs and guns and cattle prods. There were men outside the law in pick-up trucks and the hateful regalia of intimidation and murder, men who scavenged the night in search of human prey. And there were other men and women who cached guns and burned buildings, and vowed to claim their rightful share of America "by any means necessary." There were perennial political posturers standing in the Schoolhouse door and on the Courthouse steps, whose fearsome determination to arrest change and abort progress was engraved on their psyches even as it was emblazoned in their faces. The forces of law and order had a massive attack of confusion that often made duty and responsibility a victim of personal affinity; and our chief inves-

---

*From *Vital Speeches of the Day,* vol. 52, April 1, 1986, pp. 381–384. Reprinted with permission.

tigative organizations were often in collusion with the people they were directed to investigate. And there was Vietnam with its ominous and tragic implications for our political image, and for our private peace of mind.

5. No, it was not an auspicious time for America. It was a time of gravity and doubt and apprehension. It was a time when we needed a man for all seasons. It was a time when only a man like Martin Luther King could save America. Thank God for Martin Luther King. He came late, but he came in time. That is our hope.

6. Two hundred years ago the American founding fathers gave to the world "a new nation, conceived in liberty, and dedicated to the proposition that all men are created equal." They also laid it down in the record of establishment that every man was endowed by his Creator with certain "inalienable rights," among which were life, liberty and the pursuit of happiness. Two long centuries have come, and two long centuries have gone, and we who now stand trembling in the room our fathers left, search frantically for some clue that the legacy bequeathed to us is reasonably possible of realization.

7. In our confusion and our doubt we do remember that this country had its beginning in a commitment to moral and religious perfection, and that the pre-eminent American heritage is the promise implicit in the cause and the courage and the ethic which brought an intrepid band of Christian zealots to the bleak and hostile shores of Massachusetts Bay. They came with the notion of empire, but what they had in mind was a *righteous empire,* a city to be set on a hill, as it were, to be the model of faith and practice for all people of good will for all time to come. So pervasive and so enduring has been this notion of America's religious and moral commitment, that fully 300 years after it was first voiced President Woodrow Wilson could announce to the World without a trace of a blush that "America was born a Christian nation for the purpose of exemplifying to the nations of the world the principles of righteousness found in the Word of God."

8. Today in our assessment of American history we are somewhat less certain of the innocence of our birth, and we worry that our national development may be even less reflective of the brave intentions of our pilgrim fathers. We ask ourselves: What happened to the promise that was America? Seldom has a nation been so certain of the sure hand of God on the tiller of its destiny, or committed itself so irrevocably to divine guidance and precept. And seldom has any nation found itself in such wretched default of its own avowed principles.

9. In the language of the faith we claim to cherish, America has sinned—mightily, consistently, and with conscious deliberation. Our cardinal sin is idolatry—the worship of self; the worship of class; the worship of race. This is our national disease, and from this malignancy there oozes a corruption which poisons and contaminates everything it touches: the schools, the churches, the courts, the military, the places where we work, the communities where we live, our politics, our economics—every level of social and personal intercourse. It is our common sickness and our common legacy. It is endemic to the culture and so pervasive that there are no islands of immunity, only varying degrees of contamination. The contagion that infects the one of us afflicts the other. Every day of our lives we must deal with the consequences of our recalcitrance, our refusal to deny the myths we have elected to live by, and to accept the responsibilities of the men and women we claim to be in the fantasies we cherish and strive to project onto others. We know in our hearts that God will not be mocked, and that the wanton distortion of history, the cheap retreat from political and social responsibility, the cynical evasion of the implications of the fatherhood of God and the brotherhood of man must at some point in human experience accumulate a formidable burden of consequence.

10. By a hindsight born of centuries of pain and orgies of blood, we know too that no Christian community worthy of the name can be built on the bondage and oppression of one human being by another, whether with chains, or whether with laws, or whether with the fetters of ignorance, the mysteries of doctrine, or the threat of power. So it was that the political experiment in the West addressed itself to failure before it was scarcely begun. But God is gracious, and though man is weak he is still the subject of God's love and redemption. Man is a creature of free will, and if

he is able to make the conscious decisions which promote evil, then he can make a conscious decision to undo that evil. God will not have it any other way. Man cannot have it any other way. And this is the premise upon which Martin Luther King staked his life.

11.   Three times since this land was first blessed by a firm commitment to the high ideals of a nation under God, and cursed in turn by the refusal to honor that commitment in the breach, an historic occasion to relent, to repent and accept redemption has been granted America. The first was at the very birth of this nation when we had the very unique opportunity to rid ourselves of the pestilence of slavery by excluding that supreme barbarism from the new nation we determined to fashion on the high principles of human equality with liberty and justice for all. The choice ought to have been to use the occasion of our new independence to restore our own integrity by restoring freedom and dignity to the captives we held enthralled. We chose a meaner path, and the insistent rhetoric about liberty and freedom and justice, like the pious commitment to nationhood under God, rang hollow against the pitiful cries of the black man and woman whose freedom never reached the agenda of serious deliberation.

12.   The Civil War presented a unique second occasion for the realization of our moral and political commitments to God and society, but again we defaulted. The war was fought; the slaves were freed; the mentality that made slavery possible remained intact. In time it would spread, adapting itself to our new requirements of respectability. That mentality has never restricted itself to any single region of the country. It is not "Southern." It is not "Northern." It is "American," and it persists with a tenacity that bodes no good for the future of this country.

13.   Another hundred years have passed, and we have not yet developed the internal strength and the fortitude to address seriously the convictions on which this civilization is so tenuously underpinned. That is what Gunnar Myrdal defined as "the American dilemma" forty years ago—the awesome gap between the way we see ourselves, and the way we are. The tragic disfunction between perception and performance. We swab at the symptoms of our ailment; we have yet to address the disease.

14.   In the aftermath of World War II, many of the conventions the world had lived by were suddenly obsolete. In Africa, in colonial Asia, in the United States there was a revolutionary spirit abroad which threatened to delay indefinitely the return to normalcy and business as usual. The world as it was before the Hitlerian era would never be reconstructed. For us at home, the possibility that the blood we left on the beaches of Europe and the atolls of the Pacific would be replicated on the streets of New York and Chicago and Atlanta became the pre-eminent concern of the guardians of the establishment. The military was alerted; the federal agencies of intelligence and investigation were staked out among the citizenry. New "reception centers" were secretly prepared for the disaffected, and an amazing array of mobile armor and sophisticated weaponry was purchased at great cost by the local governments to use against some mysterious "enemy" who was never identified. We were on the way to a "final solution" of the problem by the only means in which we seem to have confidence. Extermination. If it worked once, it could work twice. Why not?

15.   It was at this juncture that for the third time in our national existence Divine Providence offered a way out—a higher way in perfect consonance with all our professions of Christian love and brotherhood in a just and humane society. From the legions of the disinherited God raised a prophet, a black man, who had known the jackboot of oppression, but whose chosen response was a gospel of love. He was a lowly man, humble, but full of hope; sagacious, but full of dreams. Dreams for the future of America, the country he loved and longed to see put right. His name was Martin Luther King, Jr. He came teaching peace, preaching forgiveness, and showing by precept his own full commitment to all he asked America to do. He came neither to the Jews, or yet to the Gentiles, but to all who stand in the fear of judgment, saying "This is the way." Wherever he went those who had reached the end of their endurance found new strength; and those who had so lately given themselves to violence on behalf of their country, laid down their arms and accepted the violence heaped upon them at the hands of their countrymen. In simple faith and hope and prayer they

sustained each other. Those who abused them were confounded by the peace they knew as they offered their bodies to be brutalized, and their lives to be a symbol of their determination that *men among men should be men,* and so received. Black and white they were. Men and women of all faiths bound by the common faith that "we shall overcome." One unity of believers in the fatherhood of God and the brotherhood of man, they marched, they bled and they died until the agents of denial and intimidation and death convulsed by the enormity of their own behavior finally leashed their attack dogs, sheathed their cattle prods, turned in their riot guns and retired from public view.

16.   Thank God for Martin Luther King. Thank God for the courage and the determination of black-and-white-together who finally brought the country they loved so much, first kicking and screaming, but finally in sullen compliance to the very edge of the fountain of redemption.

17.   We have not overcome because America has not overcome. But America gained in Martin Luther King a true father of his country. We have not overcome because America has not overcome. But we are still a young nation, and now there is hope. In Martin Luther King America gained a new founding father, and to honor him with a special day on the calendar is an appropriate gesture of national appreciation and pride. Just as George Washington was the father of our political identity, so was Martin Luther King the father of our moral and spiritual identity. George Washington gave us a nation, and because he did we have been able to give political leadership to the world. But Martin Luther King tried to humanize America, and because of him our political order took on credibility. Because of King, we can speak to the world about terrorism in Libya, or barbarism in South Africa, or militarism in Russia, and the world will give us a hearing. We have not always merited that respect, for our own hands were less than clean, and our own house was in serious disarray.

18.   We have not overcome. The forces of hatred and bigotry and fear still stalk our bastard peace. We have not overcome, but there are signs of overcoming.

> Come Back
> Martin Luther King
> Pray with me
> and hold my hand
> and
> help me still the turbulence
> the agitation that shakes me
> when
> I walk the streets of Boston
> Where once you drew your strength.
>
> O see how quickly there
> the people have forgot
> the eloquence of outrage
> that freedom in the South
> was such a paltry thing
> And
> see how strangely there
> the people now resent
> that freedom in the North
> should put them to the test.
>
> Have you seen
> the hunger in the streets?
> Do you hear
> the crying in the night?
> Doors do not open

Eyes turn away
Lips do not smile
Who will
give the people jobs?
Who will
give the children bread?
Where is love?

Come Back
Martin Luther King
for
down in your native Georgia
where your name
and where your dream
and
where your doctrine
made a Georgia peanut farmer
thirty-ninth president
of the United States
see how coldly
the Christians in his church
turned the locks
and fired the preacher
and split that twice-born congregation
when your dream
knocked at the church-house door.

Come Back
Martin Luther King
teach us
as once you taught us
to endure.
Teach us
as once you taught us
that love
is the price of freedom.

For we are not assured.

The friends we used to know
have long since quit the scene.
The responsible people
the proper Bostonians
whose names
gild the log of the Mayflower
are silent and remote
in retirement from the cause.
Who marched with you
in Selma
keep to their tents
in Boston
and
in a hundred other cities
where

hunger is
and
jobs are not.

There are not voices raised
to give the people hope
or point the way.
There are no shelters raised
for respite from the strife.

Come Back
Martin Luther King.
See how
the great cathedrals
that seized your public moment
to gild their own pretensions
are shuttered
from the cause
are silent now
and voiceless.

Come Back
Martin Luther King.
The dreamers you left with your Dream
wake not to the task of the dreaming.
The Dream languishes
The cock crows
I hear the tolling of the bells.
There is no sound of trumpets!
When shall we overcome?

A CEREMONIAL SPEECH

The Impertinent Questions—Star Wars and Skepticism*

by Garry Trudeau, Satirist

Delivered at the Commencement, Wake Forest University,
Winston-Salem, North Carolina, May 19, 1986

1.   LADIES AND GENTLEMEN of Wake Forest: My wife, who works in television, told me recently that a typical interview on her show used to run 10 minutes. It now runs only five minutes, which is still triple the length of the average television news story. The average pop recording these days lasts around three minutes, or, about the time it takes to read a story in *People* magazine. The stories in *USA Today* take so little time to read that they're known in the business as "News McNuggets."

2.   Now, the average comic strip only takes about 10 seconds to digest, but if you read every strip published in the *Washington Post,* as the President of the United States claims to, it takes roughly eight minutes a day, which means, a quick computation reveals, that the Leader of the Free World has spent a total of 11 days, 3 hours and 40 minutes of his presidency reading the comics. This fact, along with nuclear meltdown, are easily two of the most frightening thoughts of our time.

3.   There's one exception to this relentless compression of time in modern life. That's right—the graduation speech. When it comes to graduation speeches, it is generally conceded that time—a generous dollop of time—is of the essence.

4.   This is because the chief function of the graduation speaker has always been to prevent graduating seniors from being released into the real world before they've been properly sedated.

5.   Like all anesthetics, graduation speeches take time to kick in, so I'm going to ask you to bear with me for about a quarter of an hour. It will go faster if you think of it as the equivalent of four videos. (If you put up with Jimmy Carter for 4 years, you can put up with me for 15 minutes.)

6.   I want to speak to you today about questions. About pertinent questions and impertinent questions. And where you might expect them to lead you.

7.   I first learned about pertinent questions from my father, a retired physician who used to practice medicine in the Adirondacks. Like all parents racing against the clock to civilize their children, my father sought to instruct me in the ways of separating wheat from chaff, of asking sensible questions designed to yield useful answers. That is the way a diagnostician thinks. Fortunately for me, his own practical experience frequently contradicted his worthiest intentions.

8.   Here's a case in point: A man once turned up in my father's office complaining of an ulcer. My father asked the pertinent question. Was there some undue stress, he inquired, that might be causing the man to digest his stomach? The patient, who was married, thought about it for a moment and then allowed that he had a girlfriend in Syracuse, and that twice a week he'd been driving an old pick-up down to see her. Since the pick-up frequently broke down, he was often late in getting home, and he had to devise fabulous stories to tell his wife. My father, compassionately but sternly, told the man he had to make a hard decision about his personal priorities if he was ever to get well.

9.   The patient nodded and went away, and six months later came back completely cured, a new man. My father congratulated him and then delicately inquired if he'd made some change in his life. The man replied, "Yup. Got me a new pick-up."

10.   So the pertinent question sometimes yields the impertinent answer. In spite of himself, my father ended up teaching me that an unexpected or inconvenient truth is often the price of honest inquiry. Of course, you presumably wouldn't be here if you didn't already know that. I'm confident that your education has been fairly studded with pertinent questions yielding impertinent answers.

---

*From *Vital Speeches of the Day,* vol. 52, August 1, 1986, pp. 619–622. Reprinted with permission.

11. But how many of you have learned to turn that around—to ask the impertinent question to get at that which is pertinent?

12. I first came across the impertinent question in the writings of that master inquisitor, Studs Terkel. He himself claims to have adopted it from the physicist Jacob Bronowski, who once told him, "Until you ask an impertinent question of nature, you do not get a pertinent answer. Great answers in nature are always hidden in the questions. When Einstein in 1905 questioned the assumption held for three hundred years that time is a given, he asked one of the great impertinent questions: 'Why? How do I know that my time is the same as yours?'"

13. The impertinent question is the glory and the engine of human inquiry. Copernicus asked it and shook the foundations of Renaissance Europe. Darwin asked it and is repudiated to this day. Thomas Jefferson asked it and was so invigorated by it that he declared it an inalienable right.

14. Daniel Defoe asked it and invented the novel. James Joyce asked it and reinvented the novel, which was promptly banned.

15. Nietzsche asked it and inspired Picasso, who restated it and inspired a revolution of aesthetics.

16. The Wright Brothers asked it and their achievement was ignored for five years. Steven Jobs asked it and was ignored for five minutes, which was still long enough for him to make $200 million.

17. Whether revered or reviled in their lifetimes, history's movers framed their questions in ways that were entirely disrespectful of conventional wisdom. Civilization has always advanced in the shimmering wake of its discontents. As the writer Tristan Vox put it, "Doubt is precisely what makes a culture grow." How many of what we call our classics were conceived as the breaking of laws, exercises in subversion, as the expression of doubts about the self and society that could no longer be contained?

18. The value of the impertinent question should be self-evident to Americans, for at no time in human history has it been asked more persistently and to greater effect than during the course of the American experiment. It is at the very core of our political and cultural character as a people, and we owe our vitality to its constant renewal.

19. Today, the need for that spirit of renewal has never seemed more pressing. There is a persistent feeling in this country that many of our institutions have not measured up, that with all our recourses and technology and good intentions we as a nation are still a long way from fulfilling our own expectations. The social programs that have failed to eliminate poverty, an educational system which has seen its effectiveness seriously eroded, the chemical breakthroughs that now threaten man's environment, the exploding booster rockets, malfunctioning nuclear power plants—these are but some of the images that have shaken our confidence. According to a recent poll, the only American institution that still enjoys the trust of a majority of college students today is medicine; only 44 percent of those polled trust educational institutions, 29 percent trust the White House, 23 percent trust the press and only 21 percent say they trust religion.

20. It's difficult to think of an institution in this country that has not had to re-examine its agenda, to ask impertinent questions about the purpose and the means of its mission. Society's leaders, whose numbers you join today, face a wall of public cynicism. As professionals, they have to speak more clearly about what they can do. As citizens, they have to speak clearly about what they *should* do.

21. Nowhere is the need for [accountability] more [urgent] than in what is shaping up to be the largest co-ordinated national undertaking of your generation—the Strategic Defense Initiative. It may well become the most fiercely contended issue of your times. Already 6,500 college scientists, including a majority of professors in 109 university physics and engineering departments, have declared their opposition to SDI and have signed a "pledge of non-participation" in a project they have called "ill-conceived and dangerous." The group, including 15 Nobel Prize winners, maintains that the weapons system is inherently destabilizing and that further pursuit of its development is likely to initiate a massive new arms competition.

22. The actions of these scientists constitute an extraordinary repudiation of the amorality of indiscriminate weapons research. Science, since it leads to knowledge, has all too frequently led its practioners to believe that it is inherently self-justifying, that there is nothing dangerous about splitting atoms in a moral vacuum. These attitudes are held in abundance by some of the brightest people of your generation, who are already hard at work on what nearly all of them concede is a dangerous fantasy.

23. Listen to these comments from the young Star Warriors still in their 20s working on particle beams and brain bombs at Lawrence Livermore National Laboratory.

24. This from the inventor of the atomic powered x-ray laser: "Until 1980 or so, I didn't want to have anything to do with nuclear anything. Back in those days I thought there was something fundamentally evil about weapons. Now I see it as an interesting physics problem."

25. His co-worker, another brilliant young physicist, says he has doubts about the wisdom of SDI but concurs that "the science is very interesting."

26. A third member of the team had this to say: "I think that the great majority of the lab's technical people view the President's [Star Wars] speech as somewhat off the wall and the programs being proposed as being, in the end, intrinsically rather foolish. But obviously, the lab is benefiting right now and will continue to benefit, and everybody's happy with the marvelous new work."

27. Marvelous new work, indeed. As a TRW recruiting brochure put it recently, "We're standing on the first rung of a defense development that will dominate the industry for the next 20 years." Why? Because weapons manufacturers think Star Wars will work? On the contrary, at a recent trade show, McDonnell Douglas boasted on one wall of its Star Wars hardware while on a facing wall, it displayed proposed Star Wars countermeasures, including a "maneuvering re-entry vehicle" and a "defense suppression vehicle." GA Technologies is already marketing the latest in "survivable materials" to protect American missiles from a Soviet defensive system.

28. No one in the defensive industry seriously believes in a "peace shield"; in fact they're betting against it. If an American SDI is big business, then the hardware needed to overcome the anticipated Soviet response is even bigger business. The industry is further encouraged by the mindless momentum of the program, as evidenced by the recent admission of Reagan's undersecretary of defense that he pulled the $26 billion price tag out of the air.

29. Said the official, "I tried to figure out what the hell we're talking about. [Congress] wanted a number and kept on insisting on having a number. OK. First year was $2.4 billion, and I figure, OK, best we could handle is maybe a 20 percent–25 percent per growth."

30. Little wonder that during the program's first year, the money could not be spent fast enough to use up the yearly appropriation. Undeterred, the following year the Administration asked for $2.5 billion, greater than its request for all the basic research financed by the National Science Foundation and Department of Energy combined.

31. It should not surprise us that so many in the scientific establishment find this obscene. Said computer scientist David Parnas, who recently quit an SDI advisory panel, "Most of the money spent will be wasted; we wouldn't trust the system even if we did build it. It is our duty . . . to reply that we have no technological magic (that will make nuclear weapons obsolete). The President and the public should know that."

32. To question the rationale of the SDI enterprise should be, as Mr. Parnas suggests, a question of simple duty. It shouldn't have to be an impertinent question, but that's exactly what it's becoming. The Star Wars juggernaut may already be unstoppable. Sixty-nine billion dollars will be spent by 1994. A representative of Hughes Aircraft recently predicted, "By 1988, it may be institutionalized." Lobbies are already being mobilized, interests are becoming entrenched, foreign governments are already being involved, on the sound theory that Star Wars will be harder to stop if it becomes part of Allied diplomacy. And all around the country, some of the most talented men and women of your generation are being recruited to solve "an interesting physics problem."

33. The impertinent question. We need it now more than ever.

34. And yet, sadly, healthy skepticism is at odds with the prevailing sentiment of our times. As Tristan Vox sees it, "arguments abound to the effect that a nation does not grow great by doubting itself, indeed that self-criticism was the trap that American democracy had laid for American greatness."

35. We've been here before. It was called the '50s. This supposedly conservative doctrine holds that the very qualities from which this country has traditionally drawn its strength— idealism, openness, freedom of expression—are naive and dangerous in a cold war struggle. It maintains that America's raucous squabbles, our noisy dissent—in short, its very heritage—have weakened us as a nation and caused it to lose its unchallenged supremacy.

36. As the *New Republic's* Mike Kinsley put it, "Talk about blaming America first."

37. In such an atmosphere, the impertinent question comes with risks. Ask the two engineers at Morton Thiokol who protested the launch of the doomed Challenger space shuttle. Ask any Pentagon procurement whistle-blower. Ask David Stockman. The mere fact of this president's widespread popularity casts suspicions on the motives of even the loyalest of oppositions. There is, of course, no question that this president seems to have fulfilled a deep yearning in many Americans to feel positively about their country. And yet, the Reagan Presidency often reminds me of a remark made by a woman to sportscaster Heywood Broun following the victories of the great racehorse Secretariat in the Triple Crown. After the trauma of Vietnam and Watergate, she told Broun, Secretariat had "restored her faith in mankind."

38. I would submit to you that Ronald Reagan is the Secretariat of the '80s. He has restored our faith in ourselves, and for that, we are all in his debt. It does not, however, exempt his Administration from criticism from concerned citizens who love their nation as much as he does. One of the things that has always distinguished this country from most others is that we've always challenged ourselves to do better. As a satirist, I can't foresee any Administration, Republican or Democratic, under which the basic message wouldn't be the same—that it's possible to do better.

39. This is the true glory of America. This hope is what stirs me as a patriot—not a winning medal count at the Olympics, not the ability to drop 9,000 servicemen on a Caribbean golf course, not jingoistic commercials that tell me that the pride is back, America, when for many of us the pride never left, and certainly not by the fantasy of 1,000 laser rays criss-crossing the heavens in software-orchestrated precision, obliterating a swarm of supersonic projectiles.

40. Skeptical? You bet. You're looking at a man who has attended 16 graduations, at four of which, including one technical college, the microphone failed.

41. The impertinent question. The means by which we reaffirm our noblest impulses as a people. But what about the impertinent question as it pertains to us as individuals? Bronowski had an addendum to his comments on the subject. "Ask the same kind of question," he charged Studs Terkel, "not about the outside, but the inside world; not about facts but about the self."

42. This is impertinence of the gravest sort. The inner life finds very little currency in this, the age of hustle. David Stockman has written of a leadership circle which is intellectually inert, obsessed by television, bored by introspection and ideas of substance. Meanwhile, all across town, the sad stories of sleaze abound, 110 to date, all pointing to the new prevailing ethic of corner-cutting and self-advancement, whose only caveat is the admonition not to get caught.

43. It can seem a pretty grim picture. Indeed, as you look around you, you see very little to distract you from this narrow path. And yet that is exactly what your liberal education— with its emphasis on ideas, on inquiry, on humanist values—sought to do. As the president of my alma mater once observed, "The whole point of your education has been to urge you to see and feel about the connectedness among things and how that connectedness must be fostered so that civilization is sustained."

44.　Our understanding of the interdependencies of the human experience is the only force which keeps a society from fragmenting. The extent to which you seek that understanding is the extent to which you will be strong enough to repudiate the callousness you see around you.

45.　This won't please you, but let me share a little of what one of the more astute voices of your generation, 24-year-old David Leavitt, has written about his peers: "Mine is a generation perfectly willing to admit its contemptible qualities. But our contempt is self-congratulatory. The buzz in the background, every minute of our lives, is that detached, ironic voice telling us: At least you're not faking it, as they did. It's okay to be selfish as long as you're up-front about it."

46.　This is a pretty bleak portrait of the values of a generation, and my guess is I'm staring at hundreds of exceptions. My further guess is that the yearning for moral commitment is as intense as it always was, but that the generation with no rules, the generation that grew up in the rubble of smashed idealism, fallen heroes and broken marriages is deeply suspicious.

47.　Columnist Ellen Goodman has speculated that this is why apartheid and the soup kitchen have emerged as the causes of choice; they offer that stark unambiguous clarity that World War II offered their grandparents, that sense that there is no good news about the other side of the argument. But Goodman, being incorrigibly of her era, also believes that micro evolves into macro; that to be involved inevitably leads to decisions between imperfect options; that many of you will take risks, make mistakes, and become citizens in spite of yourselves.

48.　I'm afraid there's simply no other way. If ours becomes a society intolerant of failure and uncompassionate in the face of suffering, then surely we are lost. With the uncertainties of the future hedging in on you, you need to assess your commonalities. You need to say how you would treat other people, and how you would have them treat you back.

49.　The best your college education can do for you now is to remind you that it's one thing to be self-absorbed and quite another to be self-aware. It comes down to a matter of being open, of seeing. It comes down to a matter of remaining intrigued enough by life to welcome its constant renewal. In short, it comes down to the impertinent question.

50.　From those of us floundering out here in the real world, to those of you preparing to enter it, may I just say, welcome. We need you.

Thank you and good luck.

Speech Assignments and Evaluation

This unit contains the specific requirements for a variety of speech assignments for an introductory course in public speaking. It also contains forms that specify particular criteria and expectations used to evaluate and grade classroom speeches. In addition, it contains forms that will enable you to receive feedback from your classmates and to respond to your videotaped speeches. The criteria and expectations specified on these forms should guide your speech preparation.

The components of UNIT 18 are:

Values/Belief Speech Assignment

Demonstration or Visual Aid Speech Assignment

Informative Speech Assignment

Persuasive Speech Assignment

Persuasive Presentation/Debate Assignment

Essay Assignment: Self-Evaluation

Evaluation Form: Values/Belief Speech

Feedback Form: Values/Belief Speech

Video Self-Evaluation: Values/Belief Speech

Evaluation Form: Demonstration or Visual Aid Speech

Feedback Form: Demonstration or Visual Aid Speech

Video Self-Evaluation: Demonstration or Visual Aid Speech

Evaluation Form: Informative Speech

Feedback Form: Informative Speech

Video Self-Evaluation: Informative Speech

Evaluation Form: Statement of Reasons Persuasive Speech

Evaluation Form: Monroe's Motivated Sequence Persuasive Speech

Public Speaking Debate Ballot

Feedback Form: Persuasive Speech

Video Self-Evaluation: Persuasive Speech

Evaluation Form: Self-Evaluation Assignment

Outside Speech Critique Assignment

VALUES/BELIEF SPEECH ASSIGNMENT

Objectives

1. To practice conversational extemporaneous speaking.
2. To practice using voice, gesture, and bodily action to convey meaning.

Instructions

Select an excerpt from a poem, an essay, or a speech that reflects your values, beliefs, or philosophy of life. Use that excerpt to guide you in preparing your introductory speech.

Requirements and Expectations

Content (ingredients)

1. Brief summary on author's thesis of the poem, essay, or speech.
2. Your connections to it, that is, *why* it is important to you or why you value the idea or hold the same belief.
3. Read an excerpt.

Organization

The three ingredients will be organized in the way you deem most appropriate or effective. For example, you may begin reading an excerpt (manuscript mode), then summarizing the author's ideas, and explaining your connections to the values or ideas in the excerpt (extemporaneous mode), and conclude by reading another portion of the excerpt (manuscript mode).

Style

The purpose of the speech is to practice effective delivery. Your grade will be based on the effectiveness of your delivery style based on the following:

1. Sincere desire to communicate, establishing "dialogue with audience."
2. Direct and inclusive eye contact.
3. Voice, gestures, and bodily action used to convey meaning of message rather than nervousness.
4. Extemporaneous delivery (brief reference to notes; reading allowed for quotes only and must be done in a "speaking" voice).
5. Clear evidence of preparation and organization (including time limit).

DEMONSTRATION OR VISUAL AID SPEECH ASSIGNMENT

General Purpose: To inform.

Specific Purposes:

1. To demonstrate the essential characteristics of informative speaking.
   a. Clarity and concreteness of message.
   b. Coherence (organizing principles) and simplicity.
   c. Association and adaptation of ideas and examples to audience.
   d. Motivation of audience to listen and to want to know.
2. To create understanding about *(complete with specific topic).*

Evaluation (in the categories of)

1. Content.
2. Organization.
3. Delivery.
4. Adaptation of message to audience.
5. Effective demonstration or use of visual aid.

Requirements

1. You must use a visual aid or demonstrate some aspect of your speech.
2. Speak from an outline on notecards or regular size paper.
3. A copy of your speaking outline must be turned in after you speak. It will not be graded; however, points will be subtracted if your speaking outline is not turned in.
4. Only primary research (your own knowledge) is required. Secondary resources and knowledge may be included.

Criteria for Visual Aid Use

1. The whole speech situation must be thought of as a visual. A visual aid is merely an aid; it is not to be the speech.
2. The visual aid must be needed—it must furnish clarity and understanding beyond the spoken word.
3. The aid must be clear and uncluttered, including only those details and features that are essential to clarity.
4. The aid must be large enough for all to see it easily.
5. The aid should be attractive and pleasing to the eye.
6. The aid must be relatively easy to operate, manipulate, and handle, keeping in mind that all must be able to see and follow.
7. Avoid circulating visual aids among your audience. The chalkboard, because of time constraints in class, may *not* be used.
8. The visual aid should only be seen when being used. (Handouts are only appropriate *after* the speech and do not meet the requirements of a visual aid.)
9. Use eye contact with audience rather than visual aid.

INFORMATIVE SPEECH ASSIGNMENT

General Purpose: To inform.

Specific Purposes:

1. To demonstrate the essential characteristics of informative speaking.
   a. Clarity of and concreteness of message.
   b. Coherence (organizing principles) and simplicity.
   c. Association and adaptation of ideas and examples to audience.
   d. Motivation of audience to listen and to want to know.
2. To create understanding about *(your specific topic)*.

Evaluation (in the categories of)

1. Content.
2. Organization.
3. Delivery.
4. Adaptation of message to audience.
5. Written outline in required format.

Requirements

1. You must turn in two copies of a typed outline the day of your speech. It will be graded for correct format and requirements.
2. For specific requirements of outlines, refer to your text or to the examples in this workbook.
3. Speak from a copy of your outline or less. You may use notecards with a brief outline. Your instructor retains the right to request your speaking notes.
4. Primary source (your own knowledge) and secondary sources (research) are required.
5. Include at least two secondary sources (research) in your speech as part of your supporting materials. Include the bibliographic information at the end of your outline.
6. Use of a visual aid to clarify an idea or help create understanding is optional.

PERSUASIVE SPEECH ASSIGNMENT

General Purpose: To persuade.

Specific Purposes:

1. To demonstrate the essential characteristics of persuasive speaking.
   a. Logical and emotional appeals adapted to the audience.
   b. Change by degrees.
   c. Credibility and sincerity.
   d. Ethical arguments and motives.
2. To convince your audience to (complete with your specific topic).

Evaluation (in the categories of)

1. Content.
2. Organization.
3. Delivery.
4. Adaptation of message to audience's psychological states.
5. Use of secondary sources (research) as part of supporting materials.
6. Written outline in required format, complete with bibliographic references.

Requirements

1. You must use either Monroe's Motivated Sequence or the Statement of Reasons method to develop and organize your message.
2. You must turn in two copies of a typed outline the day of your speech. It will be graded for correct format and requirements.
3. Speak from a copy of your outline or less. You may use notecards with a brief outline. Instructor retains the right to request your speaking notes.
4. Must directly address, in your speech, your audience's predisposition to your topic as discovered through survey and analysis.
5. Primary source (your own knowledge) and secondary sources (research) are required. Credibility is essential and established through a speaker's knowledge of and experience with the topic.
6. Include at least two secondary sources (research) in your speech as part of your supporting materials. The bibliographic information for these materials should be a part of your speech and included at the end of your written outline.
7. Use of a visual aid to help clarify an idea or support your proposition is optional.

PERSUASIVE PRESENTATION/DEBATE ASSIGNMENT*

General Purpose: To persuade.

Specific Purposes:

       1. To demonstrate the essential characteristics of persuasive speaking.
         a. Logical and emotional appeals adapted to the audience.
         b. Change by degrees.
         c. Credibility and sincerity.
         d. Ethical arguments and motives.
       2. To convince your audience to (*complete with your specific purpose*).

Evaluation (in the categories of)

       1. Content.
       2. Organization.
       3. Delivery.
       4. Adaptation of message to audience predispositions.
       5. Use of evidence (research) as part of supporting materials.
       6. Typed outline in required format, complete with research and bibliographic references.

Instructions

Selection of Debate Topics:

The class as a whole will brainstorm and select five or six topics (depending on the size of the class). Four people will debate one topic. The topics will be selected based on their knowledge and interest for class members as well as on the accessibility of research for the topics. After the class selects the top five or six choices, each student turns in a preference for topic(s) to debate. Each student should select a first, second, and third choice providing a justification (knowledge, experience, interest) as to why he/she should be put in the topic of their choice. Students with no preference or equal preference among several topics should indicate so. Students will be placed in groups according to their topic preferences.

Preparing the Presentation/Debate:

In the initial stages of preparation, each group of four students will meet to determine the focus of their topic and to word the topic as a resolution to be debated. Students should then decide which two will debate the affirmative position and which two will debate the negative position. Example resolutions for debate are: (1) Resolved: Cigarettes should be illegal, and (2) Resolved: The drinking age should be lowered to age eighteen. The next step is for the group to survey their audience to find out the audience's predispositions to their resolution by wording several questions to ask the rest of the class members. The responses will prove valuable in structuring their arguments. After the surveys are completed, the group should break into their affirmative and negative pairs to continue their preparation. Each individual should determine which arguments they will cover to avoid any duplication. Then each individual of the pair is responsible for his/her own research and outline preparation.

---

*This assignment was adapted from a debate assignment by Frank Trimble.

Delivering the Presentation/Debate:

Two people (the affirmative) will present their arguments for acceptance of the resolution and then two people (the negative) will present their arguments for rejection of the resolution. Each presentation will have a 7- to 9-minute time limit. After the four presentations (each graded individually), there will be a rebuttal time (15–20 minutes) for the presenters and the audience. The rebuttal portion will not be graded; however, class members will vote by ballot which side they think won the debate based on the logic of the arguments, the evidence presented, convincing delivery, use of logical appeals, and use of emotional appeals. Individual presentation will be graded on the same aspects plus the strength of your arguments (reasons why we should agree with you), credibility of evidence, fully developed typed outline, etc. (see evaluation form on persuasion in this unit).

ESSAY ASSIGNMENT: SELF-EVALUATION

Task

Describe and evaluate what you have learned in this course about speaking in public situations. Address the following issues in your essay:

1. *Your confidence as a speaker:* Has it improved? What have you learned to do to control your nervousness when speaking in public?
2. *Your strengths and weaknesses as a speaker:* What did you intend to learn/ accomplish in this class? What were your strengths and weaknesses, what are they now, and what can you do in the future to improve—that is, what do you know (knowledge) to improve?

Requirements

Two to four typed pages; must be typed and meet standards for style (organization, grammar, spelling).

In analyzing yourself as a public speaker, use the relevant concepts from your text and other relevant sources. To evaluate, you need to use concepts applied *specifically* to you and include examples to illustrate your points.

Your essay should demonstrate your best efforts in understanding the principles of public speaking—the making of rhetorical choices—and the best in evaluation, which deals with specific, concrete examples. In other words, the essay should reflect you as an individual and not be so general that it could refer to anyone. You need to thoroughly analyze yourself as a public speaker. To achieve this thoroughness, do not attempt to cover all the categories. You will end up with a superficial surface analysis that lacks detail and depth, or you will end up with a paper that far exceeds the maximum limit. Be sure you address the issues above. Select your strengths (one or two) and your weaknesses (one or two) and dwell on those. Separately deal with the issue of confidence.

EVALUATION FORM: VALUES/BELIEF SPEECH

Speaker _____

Scale: E = Excellent; VG = Very Good; S = Satisfactory; F = Fair; P = Poor

_____Sincere desire to communicate (Dialogue with audience; interested in audience and topic)

_____Direct and inclusive eye contact

_____Voice, gestures, bodily action used to convey meaning of message

_____Extemporaneous delivery (Brief reference to notes, reading quotes only and in speaking voice)

_____Clear evidence of preparation and organization (including time limit)

FEEDBACK FORM: VALUES/BELIEF SPEECH

_____   _____
Name   Respondent

1. Did the speaker seem to have a sincere desire to communicate with his/her audience? Give examples to support your answer.

2. Describe the speaker's use of eye contact.

3. Describe the speaker's use of voice, gesture, and bodily action.

4. Did the speaker seem well-prepared and the message well-organized? Give examples to support your answer.

5. What suggestions do you have for the speaker to improve the effectiveness of his/her delivery style?

VIDEO SELF-EVALUATION: VALUES/BELIEF SPEECH

Name

1. Describe your voice, gestures, and bodily action. What message(s) did they seeem to communicate?

2. Did your use of voice, gestures, and bodily action enhance or detract from the message of your speech? What might you do to reinforce or change your use of your voice, gestures, and bodily action in a public speaking situation?

3. Did you seem to establish a dialogue with your audience? Did you appear sincerely interested in the topic and in your talking with your audience? Give examples to support your answer.

4. Describe, in detail, what specific things you plan to do to improve your delivery style for your next speech.

EVALUATION FORM: DEMONSTRATION OR VISUAL AID SPEECH

_____   _____

Time   Speaker

Scale: E = Excellent; VG = Very Good; S = Satisfactory; F = Fair; P = Poor

Content

____Time limit adhered to

____Topic: knowledge and interest clear
     and adapted to audience

____Main points clear and well-developed

____Supporting materials (and sources)
     enhanced message

____Use of demonstration or visual aid
     enhanced clarity of message

Organization

____Introduction: engages interest and
     motivation of audience

____Stated thesis

____Previewed main points

____Body: coherence of main ideas
     developed from thesis

____Effective use of transitions

____Conclusion: reviewed main points

____Final clincher

Delivery

____Direct and inclusive eye contact   _enthusian_

____Effective use of voice and body

____Extemporaneous delivery: Not read
     or memorized
     AID USED CORRECTLY

Total Score_____

FEEDBACK FORM: DEMONSTRATION OR VISUAL AID SPEECH

_____   _____
Name   Respondent

1. What was the speaker's thesis (main point)? What were the supporting ideas for the thesis?

2. How did the speaker create understanding (or confusion) in the *content* of the speech? Give examples to support your answer.

3. How did the speaker create coherence in the *organization* of the speech? Give examples to support your answer.

4. How did the speaker make it easy or difficult to listen to him or her? In other words, comment on aspects of *delivery*. Give examples to support your answer.

EVALUATION FORM: INFORMATIVE SPEECH

_____   _____
Time   Speaker

Scale: E = Excellent; VG = Very Good; S = Satisfactory; F = Fair; P = Poor

Content

_____Topic: knowledge and interest clear
and adapted to audience

_____Main points clear and well-developed

_____Supporting materials (and sources)
enhanced message

_____Explanation or visual aid enhanced
clarity of message

Organization

_____Introduction: engaged interest and
motivation of audience

_____Stated thesis

_____Previewed main points

_____Body: coherence of main ideas
developed from thesis

_____Effective use of transitions

_____Conclusion: reviewed main points

_____Final clincher

_____Typed outline in correct format with
bibliography (2 copies)

Delivery

_____Direct and inclusive eye contact

_____Effective use of voice and body

_____Extemporaneous delivery: Not read
or memorized

Total Score_____

FEEDBACK FORM: INFORMATIVE SPEECH

Name _____   Respondent _____

1. What was speaker's thesis (main point)? What were the supporting ideas for the thesis?

2. How did the speaker create understanding (or confusion) in the *content* of the speech? Give examples to support your answer.

3. How did the speaker create coherence in the *organization* of the speech? Give examples to support your answer.

4. How did the speaker make it easy or difficult to listen to him or her? In other words, comment on aspects of *delivery*. Give examples to support your answer.

VIDEO SELF-EVALUATION: INFORMATIVE SPEECH

_____
Name

1. How did you adapt your message to your audience's knowledge and interests? What relevant examples did you use?

2. Did you communicate your message clearly in an organized manner? Why or why not? Give examples to explain your answer.

3. Did you seem to establish a dialogue with your audience? Did you appear sincerely interested in the topic and in talking with your audience? Give examples to support your answer.

4. How has your delivery style improved since your previous speeches? What specific aspects of delivery are you still working on? Give examples of your successes and areas that still need improvement.

EVALUATION FORM: STATEMENT OF REASONS METHOD PERSUASIVE SPEECH

_____

Speaker

Scale: E = Excellent; VG = Very Good; S = Satisfactory; F = Fair; P = Poor

Content and Organization

_____Gained attention and interest in problem/topic

_____Directly addressed audience's predispositions
      (knowledge/attitudes)

_____Clearly stated proposition (thesis) and
      previewed main points

_____Knowledge, experience, preparation (credibility)
      evident

_____Sufficient evidence (supporting materials)
      provided to support claims (main points)

_____Sources of evidence stated

_____Logical and motivational appeals used to provide
      convincing argument

_____Evidence interpreted to support claim

_____Conclusion summarized main ideas and restated
      proposition

_____Outline typed in correct format, including
      bibliographic information

Delivery

_____Direct and inclusive eye contact

_____Persuasive, convincing use of voice, gestures,
      movement

_____Extemporaneous delivery: Not read or memorized

Total Score_____

EVALUATION FORM: MONROE'S MOTIVATED SEQUENCE PERSUASIVE SPEECH

_____

Speaker

Scale: E = Excellent; VG = Very Good; S = Satisfactory; F = Fair; P = Poor

Content and Organization

_____ATTENTION: gained attention and interest in topic/problem

_____Directly addressed audience's predispositions (knowledge/attitudes)

_____NEED: clearly explained and illustrated

_____Sufficient evidence; sources stated

_____Convincing arguments (logical and motivativational appeals) demonstating how problem affects audience

_____SATISFACTION: proposition clearly stated and explained

_____Sufficient evidence to show how speech will address problem/need

_____Effective use of logical and emotional appeals related to audience

_____VISUALIZATION: vividly and clearly described the benefits of adopting propostion and/or disadvantages of not adopting it

_____Directly related benefits to audience

_____ACTION: calls for a final commitment

_____Specified what audience should do, think, believe

_____Knowledge, experience, preparation (credibility) evident

_____Outline typed in correct format, including bibliographic information

Delivery

_____Direct and inclusive eye contact

_____Persuasive, convincing use of voice, gesture, movement

_____Extemporaneous, conversational delivery: Not read

Total Score_____

PUBLIC SPEAKING DEBATE BALLOT

Judge's Name:_____   Topic:_____

Aff:_____   Vs. Neg:_____

    5 = Excellent   3 = Satisfactory   1 = Poor

Use of evidence	1 2 3 4 5	Use of evidence	1 2 3 4 5
Convincing delivery	1 2 3 4 5	Convincing delivery	1 2 3 4 5
Clear organization	1 2 3 4 5	Clear organization	1 2 3 4 5
Use of logical appeals	1 2 3 4 5	Use of logical appeals	1 2 3 4 5
Use of emotional appeals	1 2 3 4 5	Use of emotional appeals	1 2 3 4 5

        TOTAL_____   TOTAL_____

In my opinion, the debate was won by_____on the

_____side of the issue. I reached this decision because:

PUBLIC SPEAKING DEBATE BALLOT

Judge's Name:_____   Topic:_____

Aff:_____   Vs. Neg:_____

    5 = Excellent   3 = Satisfactory   1 = Poor

Use of evidence	1 2 3 4 5	Use of evidence	1 2 3 4 5
Convincing delivery	1 2 3 4 5	Convincing delivery	1 2 3 4 5
Clear organization	1 2 3 4 5	Clear organization	1 2 3 4 5
Use of logical appeals	1 2 3 4 5	Use of logical appeals	1 2 3 4 5
Use of emotional appeals	1 2 3 4 5	Use of emotional appeals	1 2 3 4 5

        TOTAL_____   TOTAL_____

In my opinion, the debate was won by_____on the

_____side of the issue. I reached this decision because:

FEEDBACK FORM: PERSUASIVE SPEECH

Name _____   Respondent _____

1. What was the speaker's proposition?

2. What reasons did the speaker give for acceptance of his or her proposition? Give examples of speaker's use of logical and emotional appeals.

3. Were the speaker's reasons for acceptance of proposition or solution convincing? Will you consider changing your mind, attitude, or behavior? Why or why not?

4. What would you suggest for the speaker to do in order to improve the content, organization, or delivery of his or her speech?

VIDEO SELF-EVALUATION: PERSUASIVE SPEECH

Name _____

1. How did you adapt your message to your audience's knowledge and attitudes about your topic? What logical and motivational appeals did you use?

2. Did you communicate your message clearly in an organized manner? Why or why not? Give examples to explain your answer.

3. Did you seem to establish a dialogue with your audience? Did you appear sincerely interested in the topic and in talking with your audience? Give examples to support your answer.

4. How has your delivery style improved since your first speech (values/belief speech)? What specific aspects of delivery are you still working on? Give examples of your successes and areas that still need improvement.

EVALUATION FORM:
SELF-EVALUATION ASSIGNMENT

(Number of possible points for each category indicated in parenthesis)

_____Used concepts from text and other sources relevant to purpose of paper; demonstrated understanding of concepts

_____Used descriptive, specific examples from own classroom speeches; descriptions were accurate reflections

_____Addressed issues (confidence; strengths and weaknesses) completely and integrated concepts with examples

_____Demonstrated critical thinking through a thorough in-depth analysis of concepts and issues pertinent to your own abilities as a public speaker; the essay clearly and specifically gave a reflection of you as a public speaker

_____Met requirements of two to four pages typed; received on time; met standards for style: organization, grammar, spelling

Total Score_____

OUTSIDE SPEECH CRITIQUE ASSIGNMENT

Observe a speech outside of class and evaluate it according to the following:

I. *Describe* briefly:
    A. Title, where held, setting time, audience (approximately how many, what type).
    B. Speaker's name, credentials, what kind of speaking (manuscript, notes, etc.), what distance, use of podium.
    C. The point or thesis of the speech.
    D. The main ideas used to develop or support the thesis.

II. *Evaluate* (using the checklist given below):
    A. The speaker.
    B. The message.
    C. Without responding to all categories.

Requirements for Written Critique

These critiques will be written in essay form, using proper English and spelling. They are to be *typed,* double spaced, and clean. Paper should be two to three pages in length. In your essay, describe specific actions or comments that made the speaker effective or ineffective and explain why the speaker or message was effective or not effective. Use concepts and terminology from your public speaking text and workbook to analyze the effectiveness of speaker and message and the effect on the audience.

Checklist for Critique

Did the speaker:

_____Use direct eye contact

_____Appear interested in topic and audience

_____Appear confident and sincere

_____Use a conversational tone of voice

_____Use an expressive voice

_____Have purposeful gestures and facial expressions

_____Have vivid expressive language

_____Have clear concrete language

Did the message:

_____Have an introduction that captured your interest

_____Have a clear purpose

_____Have clear and easy-to-follow main ideas

_____Include examples and explanations tailored to the audience

_____Include effective concluding statements

Group Discussion

This unit contains activities and assignments that challenge you to learn to work cooperatively in small groups to accomplish tasks and to solve problems.

The components of UNIT 19 are:

Student Information Form

Learning to Work Cooperatively in Groups

Conflict in Small Groups: A Student's Testimony

The Frustrations of Working in Groups

Establishing Criteria for Making Decisions: The Scholarship Case

Decision-Making Case Study: The Harris Scholarship

Small-Group Project

Evaluation for Small-Group Project

Participant Rating Scale

Participant Rating Scale: Student Examples

The Reflective Thinking Sequence

Problem-Solving Project

Evaluation: Problem-Solving Project Report and Presentation

Analysis Paper of Problem-Solving Project

Evaluation: Analysis Paper

Sample Analysis Paper

STUDENT INFORMATION FORM

Name_____
     Last, First

Address_____

Phone: Work_____Home_____

Classification_____

Major_____ Minor_____

Area of interest/emphasis_____

Why are you taking this class? Specifically list or describe what you want and/or need to learn from this course.

Describe your experience in working in groups or committees in the past.

What do you enjoy most about group work? Least?

Why are groups effective? Ineffective?

LEARNING TO WORK COOPERATIVELY IN GROUPS

Objectives

1. To appreciate the value of group cohesiveness.
2. To analyze conflict in groups.
3. To manage conflict in groups.

Explanation

Learning to work cooperatively with others is an essential part of group work. Cooperative groups find their work more satisfying and frequently produce better decisions and products. Some combinations of individuals in particular situations just work well together. But when things do not get off to a smooth start or when the group begins to split apart, it is important to know what to do.

Instructions

Read the following two essays about conflict and frustrations in small groups. Discuss the situations with your group members, using the following questions as a guide.

Questions for Discussion

1. Describe the conflict or the problem in each situation.

2. What could have been done to avoid the conflict or the frustration?

3. What would you do if you were in that group?

4. What suggestions would you have for the group members for handling the conflict or frustration more effectively?

CONFLICT IN SMALL GROUPS: A STUDENT'S TESTIMONY

According to our text, one way in which conflict occurs is when members disagree on goals to be achieved. With this in mind, our group began with conflict in deciding between two topics on which to base our project (athletics or environment). I believe Ted wanted to do research about the job market for college students, which wasn't one of our choices. Sam said he didn't care what topic he worked on. Anne and Donna, being members of athletic teams, wanted to "attack" the athletic department, which left me in a position to try and persuade the others to research ways to improve recycling efforts at the University. I knew the athletic situation would be difficult to address due to the fact that Anne and Donna would be biased. They both had some pretty heated words to say about the athletic program. I felt the research that needed to be covered should be a topic that we knew little about. It just seemed like common sense to me that in order for our group to produce a quality product, we should pick a neutral topic (one in which no one had severe emotional ties).

This was not to be the case. My opinion on a topic was shot down in flames before I even opened my mouth. I remember Donna saying, "Who the hell picked environment? I'm tired of hearing about the environment." I didn't even want to address the environment. I wanted to find ways to improve recycling efforts at the University. The text points out that one negative effect of conflict is the creation of bad feelings among group members. If this is true, it is easy to see that, in addition to the usual primary tensions associated with small groups, substantive conflict (conflict involving what a group should do) was the monkey on our backs from the starting line.

Once a topic was chosen, I began noticing as well as feeling the effects of procedural conflict (conflict which represents disagreement about how we should reach our goals) during the group meetings. I noticed Anne and Donna wanted to divide our main topic into four or five subtopics covering such things as neglect for out-of-state athletes, where should all the money go, whether athletes receive equal treatment in the classroom, and other topics as these that really didn't seem to be problems that we could find solutions to, but rather chances for Anne and Donna to complain. I can't explain why I didn't tell anyone how I felt. By doing this, I was experiencing the second dimension of a conflict situation, emotion. The text states there are four elements present in a conflict situation—perception, emotion, behavior, and interaction. Looking back, I remember feeling mad about the lack of organization and, quite possibly, failed to let this be known for fear of starting some kind of hostile verbal exchange.

Once again, substantive conflict was beginning to affect our group in negative ways. Meeting after meeting went by, and we were no closer to a defined goal than we were on the first day. Certain members stopped attending meetings. I remember one instance when our group made plans to meet at five o'clock in the old Student Union. No one showed up. I was shocked. I stayed there for an hour thinking they were just tied up at the moment. I was quite upset. An hour passed, and I missed Star Trek! If this isn't an example of low cohesion, I don't know what is.

I felt as though no one had read the directions or knew what the objective was in doing this project. Eventually—maybe a week before the presentation—I suggested we concentrate on one thing since we were getting nowhere. Up until this point, Donna had taken the role of leader. This was a big step I had to overcome, sort of like a mutiny; but, at this point, the group was desperate for ideas. "How to increase student support and attendance at athletic events" was my suggestion. Everyone agreed, but I could tell from the nonverbals that some weren't too happy. This would be the first dimension of conflict, perception.

At this point, there wasn't much procedural conflict. We all took roles to accomplish this goal and decided to meet in two days with our results. However, the only person who showed at this meeting was Ted. Quite possibly, the others had taken offense at what I had done. Ted and I began working on the Reflective Thinking Sequence (RTS) with the information we had. We became the leaders of the group and took the incentive to do this project with or without the others' help. Ted has a computer at his place so he typed our product and printed it out. We figured that if the others eventually came up with some information, we would just add it in. I felt, at the time, that we were going to be the only ones doing the work. This created what the text calls inequity conflict. This occurs when group members do not have equal work loads and do not make equal contributions to the group. Inequity reduces satisfaction with the group and is associated with higher levels of conflict. This is what happened. Ted and I felt the others weren't doing their parts. Personally, I didn't care if the others contributed at all. I knew Ted and I could finish this alone.

To my amazement, two days before the presentation, my roommate informed me that a group meeting had been scheduled. At this meeting, things seemed to take a turn for the better; everyone showed up. Not only that, but all had input for our product. They had heard of the work Ted and I were doing; and, I guess, in some way, wanted to repent. In six hours, we had completed a rough draft of the RTS and began planning for the presentation. Had we achieved cohesion? In my mind, NO! Ted and I were still left with the task of actually producing a final copy of the RTS, which we had to delay until the night before due to personal conflicts. Again, this is an example of inequity conflict. The morning of the presentation, I made it known to the others that Ted and I had stayed up working on this RTS outline until one in the morning and that it was me who went to Sir-Speedy Printing to get copies made.

Although I was pleased with the quality of our final product, as a group we failed to work cohesively together and did not learn to use time efficiently and effectively. In no way was our time spent wisely. According to the text, highly cohesive groups have greater rates of interaction, and members express more positive feelings for each other and report more satisfaction with the group and its product. Certain behaviors are associated with high cohesive groups:

1. Teamwork and giving credit to the group are stressed.
2. Contributions to the group made by members are recognized.
3. Human concern for group members is shown.
4. Freedom of expression and openness are encouraged.
5. Clear, attainable goals are set.

From my previous discussion, it is clear that our group did not meet any of these criteria, especially number four above. There were several instances when people from other groups had said they heard some negative things about our group. This, obviously, meant that members of our group had some unfavorable remarks to express. I was also guilty of doing this, but only after I had heard others. This was a very difficult group to work with, and I am not sure what we could have done to avoid or manage the conflict we experienced.

THE FRUSTRATIONS OF WORKING IN GROUPS

Our group had a dual focus of task accomplishment within an atmosphere of social compatibility and cooperation. Cohesiveness was not an end in and of itself, but rather the means to achieving the ultimate outcome of effectiveness. When it became apparent that cohesiveness was eluding us, it took on greater importance as a desired goal to be achieved as the semester wore on. Two group members, Sally and myself, were very task-oriented, tending to steer the group in the direction of task accomplishment rather than emphasizing the socialization aspect. The factors at work in our lives outside the class perhaps magnified the impatience we felt with the more frustrating aspects of the group interaction. I had too much to do, too many other demands on my time to waste precious time due to several group members' absences and failures to complete assignments. Valuing and respecting each other should have encouraged optimal participation and equitable contributions. I found that I had tremendous respect for Sally, although toward the end, as deadlines became more imminent, maintaining positive attitudes toward other group members became increasingly difficult for me. Superficially, another goal was to avoid the *appearance* of dichotomy between the two interest groups that emerged when we could not reach consensus on our topic. Sally and I were the teacher-student "faction," while Mary, Steve, and Sam were the supervisor-employee "faction." I wanted cohesiveness yet really did not want to be affiliated with an inferior outcome. On one occasion, Sally commented to me after a meeting was over and the others had left that "at least our part of the report will be good." We could not really impose our concept of what constituted a quality report on the rest of the group without further splitting the group apart, thus destroying what cohesiveness we had managed to develop.

Not all the group goals were met, in my opinion, which only reflects reality. According to our text, "Seldom, if ever, are all the goals met all the time, so that most people learn to live with a constant sense of ambiguity and frustration in their work." This could not have been more true for me. I had to consciously overrule my prevailing philosophy, "If you want something done right, you have to do it yourself!" In previous group experiences, I have usually been the formal leader (chairperson of committees), responsible for directing the group, establishing agendas, and ensuring accomplishment of goals; thus, it was extremely difficult for me to "let go" and allow ambiguity to exist without becoming overly frustrated. I was anxious over a lack of direction, a topic that was too vague for my taste, and was frustrated that I couldn't impart (or impose) my standards for performance on the group members who did not necessarily share my need for achievement. The goal of a quality project was not met in my estimation or, at least, not in the part of the report that was not my responsibility. I had to accept the reality that I could not force the group to do the report "MY WAY." Once, when Sally suggested that we no longer "worry" about the quality, which we could not control anyway, I was able to relax and concentrate on the relationships and interactions. Although I believe quality was sacrificed for the sake of cohesiveness—an artificial cohesiveness, at that, because I never really felt the comradery I expected to enjoy in this group except with Sally—I suppose the outcome was acceptable. What a delight it would have been had we produced an excellent report and enjoyed the process as well!

SMALL-GROUP PROJECT

Objectives

1. To work cooperatively (cohesively) in a small-group situation.
2. To use the principles of small-group theory to produce a quality product.
3. To increase individual understanding of small-group theory and experience.
4. To present an excellent group presentation based on the group members' findings.

Task and Purpose

The task of each group is to investigate (research) the effectiveness of small groups to increase understanding of the principles and use of small groups in a variety of contexts. The end result of this investigation will be a 30-minute group presentation that should increase the audience's understanding of the principles and use of small groups. The presentation should contain an explanation of theory (the components of small groups) and practice (a description of particular small groups, how they operate, and how effective they are).

General Questions or Issues to be Investigated and Addressed

1. What are the important principles of small-group theory that relate to your presentation? Use text and beyond.
2. How are small groups used in particular professions, sororities or fraternities, other formal social organizations, student government, community groups, and educational institutions? What is the function, composition, and value of these groups?
3. How effectively do these groups work? What particular factors make them effective or ineffective?
4. What suggestions do you have for improving the use of small groups or increasing the effectiveness of small groups?

Note: It is the task of each small group to select a particular focus for their presentation. For example, one group might look at the concept of group roles (task and maintenance) in sorority/fraternity committees; another group might look at how groups function in different professions (training teams in banks, problem-solving teams in hospitals, teaching or resource teams in the elementary or secondary schools).

Guidelines for Accomplishing the Task and Maintenance Goals/Roles

1. First, get to know group members (names, etc.) and their backgrounds in relation to the kinds of groups they work with.
2. Select a focus for your investigation and presentation; decide what groups you will investigate and what library sources you will use to provide additional principles of small-group theory (or team work or participative decision making); decide what questions you will ask and to whom.
3. Decide who will do what (divide up the tasks). In addition, you should set up explicit rules and procedures (and deadlines) so your group can accomplish the tasks efficiently, cohesively, and thoroughly.
4. Agree to have all information collected by a certain date so the group can focus on the presentation.

EVALUATION FOR SMALL-GROUP PROJECT

Group Members

Content

____Principles of small-group theory selected clearly understood and relevant to focus/theme of presentation

____Examples of small-group function and value described thoroughly

____Presentation organized and coherent with principles connected to examples

Delivery

____Overall understanding created; transitions used and moderator connected ideas

____Conversational, professional mode of delivery; notes used but not read; all members used vocal expression and eye contact

____Overall professional presentation: time limit adhered to; group directly included audience through questions or participation

Total Score_____

PARTICIPANT RATING SCALE

Instruction: Rate each member of your group, including yourself, according to the scale and definitions below. It is expected that most members will be rated in the "2" category; provide examples (reasons why) you rated each person as you did.

Dependability: regular and complete attendance at planning sessions; arrangements made if he or she had to miss a session; reliable about doing share of work and having it done on time, cooperative in attitude, listens to others' ideas; group-centered, agreeable, and easy to work with

Contribution: well prepared for meetings; interested in quality problem analysis; actively participated in discussions, decisions, agenda planning, etc.; contributed relevant comments, ideas, and suggestions; did share of research/interviews, *contributed individual powerpoint*

Scale:

1	2	3
Below expectations: absences, failed to call, late in work, lack of contributions to discussion, did not do share of research	Excellent, met expectations specified above	Exceptional, exceeded expectations; did work above and beyond rest of group

Meetings outside of class: _____

Instructions: Write in member's name and rating in each category.

Group Member	Dependability	Contribution	# of Meetings Attended
1.			
2.			
3.			
4.			
5.			
6.			

Comments: _____

_____

_____

_____

_____

_____

    For each member, provide reasons why you rated as you did by providing concrete descriptive examples. Do not generalize or rely on restatements of above (i.e., "she was cooperative").

PARTICIPANT RATING SCALE: STUDENT EXAMPLES

Objectives

1. To understand how to rate group participants according to preestablished criteria.
2. To analyze the following examples to determine their thoroughness and objectivity.

Explanation

The assignments below were completed by students following the instructions on the "Participant Rating Scale." The students were particularly instructed to provide concrete, descriptive examples (rather than generalizations or evaluative comments) to back up the reasons why they rated each member as they did.

Instructions

Read the two examples below and notice how the second example fulfills the requirements of the assignment entitled "Participant Rating Scale." The second example gives specific examples; the first mainly has generalizations and evaluative comments. Please note that only portions of each example are provided; that is, the ratings of three participants from each example are provided.

Example 1

I rated Sally 2 for dependability. She was present at every group meeting we had. She took notes on our group process for each meeting. She was a very cooperative member of the group and I enjoyed working with her. She always had her share of the work completed both on time and in a thorough manner.

I rated Sally 2 for contribution. She was very helpful in analysis of our problem because she has an eye for detail. She is a relatively quiet person, yet she contributed thoughts in every meeting, never becoming disinterested or silent. She was outspoken in terms of agreement and disagreement on our issue.

I rated John 2 for dependability. He was absent for a few of our meetings but he made up for his absences with his very task-oriented presence at our other meetings. He completed his work on time, had a good attitude toward the project, and helped make the experience enjoyable.

I rated John 2 for contribution. He was very task oriented, which was a needed component in our group. He helped keep us focused and provided many insights to our problem. He also helped a great deal in our problem analysis by making sure we narrowed and defined our problem.

I rated Kathy 3 for dependability. She was present at every group meeting we had. She did all tasks that were requested of her and did them on time. Her attitude toward the group was very impressive, giving it a high priority. She was both easy and extremely enjoyable to work with. I was glad to participate in a group with her.

I rated Kathy 3 for contribution. She provided some excellent ideas to our group's project. She made her biggest contribution, however, with her help in the class presentation. She typed our final outline and made the copies and provided the materials for our visual aids. She also did our daily report of our group meetings. She was an invaluable member of the group not only for these contributions but because of her excellent attitude and commitment level.

Example 2

I rated Sam 1 for dependability because during the sessions he would talk about fraternity subjects. The group met several times outside of class and it was hard to get everyone together at the same time, but on a couple of occasions Sam agreed to be there and didn't show up. He didn't get in touch with us to let us know he wouldn't make it. Sam has such a commanding tone and this made it difficult to be heard because he would talk over you before you finished relating ideas. This showed, to me, that he really wasn't listening to others' ideas.

I rated Sam 2 for contribution because he suggested good ideas for the presentation. For example, he suggested the bell be rung every three minutes to show the frequency of rape. He also suggested the skit to present myths about rape. He conducted an interview with the dean of students.

I rated Mary 2 for dependability because she attended every meeting. When she couldn't be at extra meetings, she always let us know beforehand. Mary listened to everyone's ideas and if she didn't understand something, she would ask questions. An example would be when Tim presented the blind report, Mary asked the purpose of it and how to obtain and fill one out.

I rated Mary 3 for contribution because she was always ready to hear other people's ideas and asked for opinions about her ideas. One example would be the interview questions we asked various people. She was fanatical about forming some universal questions to present to our interviewees. Sam transcribed the statistics, but the males and females didn't match up, so Mary took them home to transcribe them correctly. She suggested the idea of pinning the statistics on the poster board for our presentation to make it easier for the audience to see and follow our comments. Mary interviewed people from the student support center and issued surveys to one of her classes.

I rated Bill 3 for dependability because he attended every meeting. He let us know beforehand if he was unable to attend the extra meetings. He readily listened to others' ideas. An example would be from the very first meeting when we didn't even have a topic. The first question he asked was how I meant to deal with the international topic that I had wanted. Bill had everything he had been assigned to do ready for the meetings. For example, he made copies of the surveys, made the cover for our report, brought statistics from the rape crisis center to class, and put together the report so it was ready to hand out to the class. He was always ready to listen to others' ideas. An example would be when everyone was suggesting ideas for solutions, he would express support and comments like "Great ideas," "Exactly!" and "How can we expand on that?"

I rated Bill 3 for contribution because of all the above; plus, he went to lecture on campus concerning our topic, he typed up our list of interview questions, and interviewed Mr. Davis, which provided great insight to the blind report and criteria for solutions.

THE REFLECTIVE THINKING SEQUENCE

(Based on the work of John Dewey)

I. Identify and analyze the problem.
   What are the present state of affairs, goal(s), obstacles, and causes of the problem?
   A. What exactly are we concerned about?
      1. Is the question or assignment clear to us?
      2. Do we need to define any terms?
      3. What is our area of freedom?
   B. What do we find unsatisfactory about the present situation?
      1. What exactly is wrong?
         a. Who is affected and in what ways?
         b. Under what conditions (when and where)?
      2. How serious do we judge the problem to be?
      3. Is this an old problem?
         a. What actions have been taken previously?
         b. What has been learned from past experiences? From similar situations/ organizations?
      4. What additional information do we need to adequately describe the extent and nature of the problem?
   C. What goal(s) do we hope to achieve?
   D. What are the obstacles to achieving the goal(s)?
      1. What obstacles must be removed in order to achieve the goal(s)?
      2. What are the factors (causes) that contribute to the problem?
   E. How can we summarize the problem, including the present situation, the goal(s), and the obstacles to it?
      1. Do we all agree on this formulation of the problem?
      2. Should we subdivide it into subproblems?
         a. If so, what are they?
         b. In what order shall we take them up?
II. By what criteria shall we judge our ideas and solutions?
   A. What absolute criteria must a solution meet?
   B. What relative standards shall we apply?
III. What are possible solutions?
IV. Which seems to be the best solution according to our criteria?
V. How will we put our solution into effect?

PROBLEM-SOLVING PROJECT

Objectives

1. To work toward cohesiveness in your small group and to produce a quality product.
2. To thoroughly and completely analyze a problem and suggest quality solutions by systematically following the Reflective Thinking Sequence.
3. To become more skilled as a participant observer (to be actively engaged in the problem-solving task while at the same time observing, evaluating, and adapting to the small-group process).
4. To use time efficiently and effectively.

Specific Tasks

1. Attending and participating in all group meetings; making arrangements and compensation with group members if a session must be missed.
2. Analyzing a task (the assignment) according to its component parts, setting deadlines, and dividing the work according to skills and resources of the group.
3. Using the standards of effective small group practice to achieve cohesion and a quality product (consider shared roles, known rules, effective communication interaction, desirable and "do-able" goals, shared leadership, productive conflict management, etc.).
4. Thoroughly analyzing a specific problem.
5. Gathering information about the problem (fact finding).
6. Establishing criteria for selecting a solution.
7. Selecting a solution and making suggestions for implementing the solution.
8. Writing the final report for the class (see below).
9. Presenting the report to the class.
10. Keeping a group journal or record of content (what the group discovers about the problem and solution) to use for writing the final report; *this portion must be done as a group.*
11. Keeping an individual journal of process (what happens in the group's interactions) to use for writing the individual analysis paper; *this portion must be done individually.*

Final Group Written Report and Presentation

Report Format

Three to five pages typed, outline format.
References and/or interview questions attached to report.
Title page with names of group members.

Report Content

In outline form, using The Reflective Thinking Sequence (RTS) handout, specify your problem question and your analysis, solutions, criteria, selected solution, and suggested implementation.

In other words, answer all the relevant questions on the handout in relation to your topic or problem question. Use clear and readable outline format and identify the steps in the RTS that you are addressing (i.e., goal to achieve, obstacles, criteria for solutions, etc.).

Presentation Requirements

Length 50 minutes maximum; includes audience questions.
Date selected from class schedule—see group reports.
All members participate.
Copies of outline for each class member and instructor.
Pages stapled and ready on time.

Presentation Expectations

Outline referred to, not read.
Conversational mode of delivery.
Group focus and concern is on audience's understanding; the purpose is to explain what you discovered about the problem and its solution(s).
Group will field questions effectively and encourage audience participation and questions.

EVALUATION: PROBLEM-SOLVING PROJECT REPORT AND PRESENTATION

Problem-Solving Process

_____Components of problem thoroughly analyzed: goals, obstacles, causes

_____Research and fact finding specified and sufficient

_____Problem summarized and assessed in relation to facts/research

_____Criteria specified and addressed to essential areas

_____Possible solutions considered; solution selected based on criteria and capable of addressing problem as summarized

_____Suggestions (reasonable) made for implementing the solution; overall effectiveness

Presentation and Report

_____Written report used outline format, three to five pages typed, professional: spelling, style, ready

_____Overall understanding created; transitions used, moderator connected ideas

_____Conversational mode of delivery; report referred to, not read

_____Professional presentation: time element considered, group fielded questions effectively and included audience

ANALYSIS PAPER OF PROBLEM-SOLVING PROJECT

Purpose

The purpose of your paper is to demonstrate an understanding of the concepts of group discussion as described in your text and the class handouts. Your grade will be determined by how well you can demonstrate a thorough written analysis and understanding of the concepts in your text and class handouts. Therefore, it is possible for you to not have been an excellent contributor to your group and, if you write a thorough, in-depth analysis, to receive an excellent (A) grade on your paper. You should, however, strive for excellence in group participation and task (as that affects your group grade and your participant rating).

Expectations of Paper

1. Essay form, well written, meeting standards for spelling, usage, organization, and style.
2. Four to six pages, proofed.
3. Two copies of paper; one to be retained and one to be returned with comments.
4. Insightful and thorough analysis that necessarily includes both evaluation and description. You must both evaluate (using small-group concepts) and describe (providing representative examples) what happened during the planning sessions and preparation for the written oral reports. Therefore, this analysis requires you to reflect back on all the sessions—the whole process. Remember, to describe you use examples from sessions, and to evaluate you must apply concepts from text and class handouts.

Task

Recall that your objective in this assignment is to work toward cohesion (effective participation) in your small group and to produce a quality product (thorough problem analysis and solution based on problem and criteria).

Basically, your paper—through description and evaluation—should address:

1. Whether or not that objective happened (why it was a cohesive and quality product).
2. What were your roles or functions in the group and how your participation in the group helped and/or hindered the group task or process.
3. What could you or other members have done to improve the group process or product.

Specifically describe and evaluate:

1. How cohesive was your group and what were your role(s) or functions(s) in the group (consider any, not all, of the following: roles, rules, norms, communication interaction, goals, purposes, leadership functions, conflict, procedures, etc.). Remember that the goal is to go for focus and in-depth analysis.
2. Did your group produce a quality product? How thorough and complete were the problem analysis and solution-selection stages? How did group process and members help or hinder the completion of a quality task/product?
3. Analyze and suggest ways the group process or product (problem analysis) might have been improved and what you learned about group process and problem analysis.

EVALUATION: ANALYSIS PAPER

Content and Purpose

_____Used concepts from text/class handouts relevant to purpose of paper

_____Used descriptive, relevant examples from group experience

_____Conceptually integrated concepts and examples (theory and practice) to demonstrate understanding

_____Demonstrated critical thinking/insightful analysis by the ability to address *why* the group was (or was not) cohesive and roles/functions in the group

_____Demonstrated ability to analyze and evaluate the group product (problem analysis and solution)

_____Demonstrated critical thinking by the ability to suggest ways of improving group process or product

Organization and Format

_____Introduction, complete with purpose and overview of paper

_____Body, focused and centered around identified issues; transitions used to connect ideas

_____Conclusion, summarized and provided value of learning or activity

_____Paper four to six pages, typed and proofed; writing style clear, with acceptable usage; paper received on time; two copies

SAMPLE ANALYSIS PAPER

Following is an analysis of group procedure in regard to both task and interpersonal obstacles in a small group confronted with a problem-solving objective. Our group, at the outset, was primarily faced with the dilemma of providing methods for improvement of the teacher/student learning process.

When our group first got together, there seemed a bit of tension in the air that one could call primary tension, although not in the truest sense. Here, I mean that the tension felt was not of a social nature, because we were comfortable with one another as classmates, but we were extremely ill at ease as to the realm and scope of the task at hand. Due to this lack of a common starting point, we began, in our minds, to escalate the problem into something much larger than it really was. As a result, we each began to feel as though we were getting behind and became anxious. Consequently, our first two meetings were fruitless as to any verifiable task accomplishment. This is not to say that we were not working, but our efforts were not focused and were so broad that no really substantial information came about.

The most beneficial aspect of our group to arise during these first meetings was role emergence. It was clear from the start that Mary was assuming the role of leader while Cathy became more of a secretary by taking roll and recapitulating the previous meetings. Diane was more of an overall notekeeper for the group and, at first, was basically an observer, while Regina and I were more the classic, representative participant observers by switching momentum a lot and accepting responsibility of all the aforementioned roles at various times. I will expound on Regina's and my roles a bit more. Mary's sudden and self-appointed leadership position had stirred some secondary tension within the group. It seemed, for a short time, that this situation was going to get away from us; so Regina and I were placed in the position of performing checks and balances for the first meetings. Through this, we were beginning to see the emergence of our population traits, or the traits of the individual members, and from this arose our internal structure. Internal structure is the interpersonal relations among members of a group. Here, behavioral norms were being formed, leading to an understanding of the degrees of power, influence, and control the group was willing to accept from the various individuals. All in all, our role emergence came about through what is known as intrinsic synergy, or that time and energy spent working out interpersonal relations that lead to group cohesion without contributing directly to task accomplishment.

At about our fourth and fifth meetings, we had narrowed our topic to student/teacher concerns here on campus and had gathered a wealth of information from interviews with both teachers and students and library research. Our roles were well established, with Mary still being the primary leader and the rest of the group beginning to maintain an all-channel network of communication, meaning everyone spoke to anyone freely and without hierarchical concerns. We had now reached a production phase modality whereby we were gaining an increased understanding of our problem and working more cohesively toward the attainment of our goal. Even though things were starting to come together, this is not to say that we were without problems. Although we were working more cohesively, interpersonally we were still somewhat unclear as to our area of freedom and were beginning to improvise our accomplishments. By this I mean we were short of a set structure to follow and had the tendency to pursue unnecessary tangents. At this point, because of our increased solidarity, we began to suffer a particular aspect of groupthink, a collective effort to rationalize our courses of action. We all began agreeing with each others' points a little too readily without truly questioning nonobvious alternatives. This was never actually brought to point because it seemed, in retrospect, to have happened subconsciously. Fortunately, this phase didn't last long and, perhaps due to the realization of our decreasing time factor, we began an earnest and dedicated attempt to perform the reflective thinking sequence step by step. This was the formal structure that we had needed all along; and for some odd reason, as if it had been right under our noses, we had not been following it. Looking back now, I feel we may have fallen victim to another aspect of groupthink, an illusion of invulnerability that created an air of undue optimism. I think maybe we were a little overconfident in our own abilities. With the use of the reflective thinking sequence, our focus and comprehension matured to its highest level, and we began to arrive at some truly tangible production.

Our roles at this juncture had now come full circle. We were all participating equally by now, and everyone was revealing leadership qualities. We each had our own areas of principal interests within the group and each person, more or less, became the leader of their particular area of research. In a subtle way, each of us had sort of an expert authority because we had collectively delegated various areas of study to the individuals and each brought back their findings to the group. Mary was still seen in the collective mind of the group as the main leader, but this was mostly due to carryover of previous interactions. Cathy and Regina furthered their participant observance, as had we all, while Diane and I were both emerging more as serving a group maintenance function. Diane and I rose together as being the nullifiers of tangents by keeping everyone on track and preventing digression. As a sidepoint that was of immeasurable importance in maintaining our momentum and morale, we developed a hearty sense of humor about the project. When things became too acclimated, one of us would just begin to spoof the entire segment, which would chain-react until we were all laughing and having a good time; then we would get back to work. I felt this worth mentioning because it was vital to our cohesion and to maintaining our endurance.

Another factor that prevailed from start to finish in the project and came to be a major influencing factor for the behavior of our group was time. Earlier, I mentioned that in our first meetings we became anxious at not being able to start right away in a productive manner. This was due to the fact that we didn't feel we were going to have enough time to complete our objectives. As we became more focused, we realized that we had maybe too much time in which to do the job. This assumption, unwittingly, led us into a lull, or slack period, which I hinted at earlier. Although we had accomplished a great deal both interpersonally and task-wise, we didn't actually compile our work effectively until the last few meetings. Overall, our primary motivating factor was that of time (or the lack of it) near the end. The anxiety came back upon us as we came to realize the nearing deadline. This anxiety, however, came to be most beneficial for us because it forced our group synergy to peak. Group synergy is the total energy input of the group's members. The nearing of the deadline also molded into our group a syntality, which refers to the phenomenon of a predictable pattern of group behavior. The recognizable behavioral pattern that came about was one of seriousness. We began to move very quickly, being especially cautious of wasted time and energy with a concern for organization. We also started realizing our own individual weak areas in regard to the subject and were actively seeking that information from those whom we knew were better versed in those areas. There was an active attempt to form an information-based collective mind for our upcoming presentation. These were the predictable patterns that arose, and this was certainly our most productive phase.

As a final analysis of our group, we started out not knowing where to begin. We had imagined some enormous problem, so we intimidated ourselves into thinking that it was far beyond our ability to even entertain the thought of coming up with feasible suggestions. Nonetheless, without even realizing what we were doing, we began to talk and share ideas, personal feelings, perceptions, and experiences. I say "without realizing" because what we did to attain a focus was similar to a special discussion technique known as case problem discussion, which is what I have described above. With this manner of explorative discussion as a preliminary to the reflective thinking sequence and a high degree of cohesion, we were able to coalesce into an extremely effective group. There were, however, times when we were somewhat lulled into complacency, but we overcame these shortcomings. We further rose above these pitfalls because, ultimately, we realized that the performance of our group depended primarily on our ability to integrate and organize our individual skills and resources. In the end, having integrated our resources to the best of our ability, I feel we ascertained our solutions with a true assembly effect, meaning that the group's product was superior to what any individual of the group could have accomplished.